THE INTEGRITY
OF LEVITICUS RABBAH

Program in Judaic Studies
Brown University
BROWN JUDAIC STUDIES
Edited by
Jacob Neusner,
Wendell S. Dietrich, Ernest S. Frerichs,
Calvin Goldscheider, Alan Zuckerman

Project Editors (Project)

Number 93

THE INTEGRITY OF LEVITICUS RABBAH
The Problem of the Autonomy of a Rabbinic Document

by
Jacob Neusner

THE INTEGRITY
OF LEVITICUS RABBAH
The Problem of the Autonomy
of a Rabbinic Document

by
Jacob Neusner

Scholars Press
Chico, California

THE INTEGRITY
OF LEVITICUS RABBAH
The Problem of the Autonomy of a Rabbinic Document

by
Jacob Neusner

Library of Congress Cataloging in Publication Data

Neusner, Jacob, 1932-
   The integrity of Leviticus Rabbah.

   (Brown Judaic studies ; 93)
   Includes index.
   1. Midrash rabbah. Leviticus—Criticism, interpretation, etc.
2. Midrash rabbah. Leviticus—Criticism, Redaction. I. Title.
II. Series.
BM517.M67N48 1985   296.1'4   85-10827
ISBN 0-89130-852-0 (alk. paper)
ISBN 0-89130-853-9 (pbk. : alk. paper)

Printed in the United States of America
on acid-free paper

In memory of

Rafi Zaiman

On the fifth Yahrzeit
(1980-1985)

Here in Providence, where
he lived and died, he is
remembered, and his memory
is cherished. His years were
few but his life touched many,
and all of us who knew and shared
in life with him celebrate his
days among us. We shall go
to him, he will not again
come to us.

CONTENTS

PREFACE

This book deals, in a very specific instance, with two problems of broad and general interest, one in literature, the other in the study of religion. The first is what makes a text a text. The second is what makes a group of texts into a canon, a cogent statement all together. While the case at hand is remote from everyday interest, the problem confronts two sizable fields of learning, literature, on the one side, religion, on the other. How so? First, the textuality of a text, the issue of whether a given piece of writing hangs together and is to be read on its own, is a matter of concern beyond the document studied here. Second, the relationship of two or more texts of a single, interrelated literature to the world-view and way of life of a religious tradition viewed whole, the way in which we not only distinguish one document from another but also insist that each be read in dialogue with other writings -- that too confronts a wide audience. In particular, anyone puzzled by how to translate a collection of books into a religion, how to show the relationship of several books to a larger world-view and way of life portrayed, in the aggregate, in them all -- such a one will grasp the problem facing me in this book. The problem of this book is whether or not a rabbinic document stands by itself or forms a scarcely differentiated segment of a larger uniform canon. Since people rarely wonder why a given composition should not be seen by itself, let me spell out the basis for the contrary view.

The reason one might suppose that, in the case of the formative age of Judaism, the document does not exhibit integrity and is not autonomous is simple. The several writings of the rabbinic canon of late antiquity, formed from the Mishnah, ca. A.D. 200, through the Talmud of Babylonia, ca. A.D. 600, with numerous items in between, share materials -- sayings, tales, protracted discussions. Some of these shared materials derive from explicitly-cited documents. For instance, passages of Scripture or of the Mishnah or of the Tosefta, cited verbatim, will find their way into the two Talmuds. But sayings, stories, and sizable compositions not identified with a given, earlier text and exhibiting that text's distinctive traits will float from one document to the next.

That fact has so impressed students of the rabbinic canon as to produce a firm consensus of fifteen hundred years' standing. It is that one cannot legitimately study one document in isolation from others, describing its rhetorical, logical, literary, and conceptual traits and system all by themselves. To the contrary, all documents contribute to a common literature, or, more accurately, religion -- Judaism. In the investigation of matters of rhetoric, logic literature, and conception, whether of law or of theology, all writings join equally to given testimony to the whole. In the Introduction, I address the problem at hand, explain the solution worked out in this work. But to begin with, let me spell out in some detail the theological issues implicit in the literary questions under study here. For if I do not make clear that major theological convictions in Judaism rest on the outcome, readers will not recognize the enormous significance, for the study of the formative history of Judaism, of what appears to be the simple, merely literary question at hand: when is a text a text?

To explain why the issue matters, I point to reviews of my Judaism: The Evidence of the Mishnah (Chicago, 1981: University of Chicago Press). These reviews supply evidence that the issue makes a great impact upon not only Orthodox, but also Reform and Conservative Judaic theologians. Two librarians, one at a Reform seminary in London, the other at a Conservative seminary in New York City, do justice to the weight of the question of whether or not, when we approach the canon of Judaism, we may describe, analyze, and interpret one book at a time. Writing in Midstream, May 1984, and in Conservative Judaism, October 1983, respectively, the two press the single issue of how one can claim to describe the evidence for "Judaism" in a single composition. The issue is expressed in an urgent way by theologians of both Reform and Conservative Judaism; as to the Orthodox position, there can be no reasonable doubt.

So the literary question to which this book is devoted -- the integrity of a document, its autonomy of other writings in the same classification ("canon") -- for many in the community of Judaism bears profound theological meaning. Why should people find so troubling a book that asks about the system of one composition among a larger set of compositions within the same classification, that is, of one species within an encompassing genus? Surely it is reasonable to insist that each species come under description and analysis, while of course recognizing that all species form part of a common genus. The contrary view, that all documents speak always to common issues and never to their distinctive points of insistence, is the puzzling one. Only when the reason this other view presses finds its answer will the importance of the issue of this book so impress readers as to persuade them to work their way through the solution to that problem I have worked out here.

In point of fact, when we take up a single book or document in the canon of Judaism and propose to describe, analyze, and interpret that book in particular, we violate the lines of order and system that have characterized all earlier studies of these same documents. Until now, people have tended to treat all of the canonical texts as testimonies to a single system and structure, that is, to Judaism. What sort of testimonies texts provide varies according to the interest of the scholars, students, and saints who study them. Scholars look for meanings of words and phrases, better versions of a text. For them all canonical documents equally serve as a treasury of philological facts and variant readings. Students also look for the sense of words and phrases and follow a given phrase hither and yon, as their teachers direct them on their treasure hunt. Saints study all texts equally, looking for God's will and finding testimonies to God in each component of the Torah of Moses our Rabbi.

Among none of these circles will the discrete description, analysis, and interpretation of a single text make sense. Why not? Because all texts ordinarily are taken to form a common statement, "Torah" in the mythic setting, "Judaism" in the theological one.

To the contrary, however, scholars in the biblical fields of Old and New Testament, Israel in ancient times and earliest Christianity understand that the work of the hour does not demand more harmonies of the Gospels. They rigorously debate issues of orthodoxy and heterodoxy in earliest Christianity and whether and where, among the diverse Christianities, they may find patterns of Christian truth. In the nineteenth century they abandoned any notion of using all of the (canonical) texts equally and for a single purpose. In the twentieth, such giants as H.E.W. Turner and Walter Bauer ended for all time the simple notions that you can open a book, thumb the pages and pull out a Christianity.

Why the difference for the classical literature of Judaism? We begin with theology and move to texts. For the hermeneutical issue defines the result of description, analysis, and interpretation. From the classical perspective of the theology of Judaisms the entire canon of Judaism ("the one whole Torah of Moses, our rabbi") equally and at every point testifies to the entirety of Judaism. Why so? Because all documents in the end form components of a single system. Each makes its contribution to the whole. If, therefore, we wish to know what "Judaism" or, more accurately, "the Torah," teaches on any subject, we are able to draw freely on sayings relevant to that subject wherever they occur in the entire canon of Judaism. Guided only by the taste and judgment of the great sages of the Torah, as they have addressed the question at hand, we thereby describe "Judaism."

Composites of sayings drawn from diverse books in no way violate the frontiers and boundaries that distinguish one part of the canon from some other part of the same canon. Why not? It is a theological conviction that defines the hermeneutic. Viewed as serving the Torah, which is a single and continuous revelation, all frontiers, all boundaries stand only at the outer limits of the whole. Within, as the saying has it, "There is neither earlier nor later," that is to say, temporal considerations do not apply. But if temporal distinctions make no difference, no others do either.

Accordingly, as Judaism comes to informed expression in the Judaic pulpit, in the Judaic classroom, above all in the lives and hearts and minds of Jews loyal to Judaism, all parts of the canon of Judaism speak equally authoritatively. All parts, all together, present us with one harmonious world-view and homogeneous way of life, one Torah ("Judaism") for all Israel. That view of "the Torah," that is to say, of the canon of Judaism, characterizes every organized movement within Judaism as we now know it, whether Reform or Orthodox, whether Reconstructionist or Conservative, whether in the "Exile" (diaspora) or in the State of Israel. How so? Among circles of Judaism indifferent to considerations of time and place, anachronism and context, every document, whenever brought to closure, testifies equally to that single system. For those circles Judaism emerges at a single moment ("Sinai"), but comes to expression in diverse times and places, so that any composition that falls into the category of Torah serves, without further differentiation, to tell us about the substance of Judaism, its theology and law. That is why asking about the integrity of a given composition, a merely literary question, threatens the faith of Judaism.

An important qualification, however, has now to make its mark. Among those circles of Judaism to whom historical facts do make a difference, for example, Orthodoxy in the West, Reconstructionist, Conservative and Reform Judaism and the like, considerations of what was completed earlier as against what came to closure only later on, for instance, in the second century as against the eighteenth century, do make some difference. Earlier documents provide more compelling and authoritative evidence than later ones. But even in the view of this other sector of Judaism, all documents, if not everywhere equally authoritative, still form part of a continuous whole, Judaism. The distinction between the two positions makes no material difference. Why not? Because both circles hold as self-evident that the numerous components of the canon of Judaism form a continuity, beginning, middle, and end. That is why considerations of priority and of closure, should these considerations find their way into discourse at all, change little and affect nothing. Torah is Torah, early, middle, and late. And so it is -- except from the perspective of one outside the magic circle of the faith. Here we ask exactly how various documents became "Torah," what each document added to the whole, in which ways do the several documents relate to one another and to the larger system, and so, in all, reverting to mythic language, what makes Torah Torah.

For a person engaged in such an inquiry into the formation of Judaism studied through the analysis of the literary evidence of the canon, documents stand in three relationships to one another and to the system of which they form part, that is, to Judaism, as a whole. The specification of these relationships constitutes the principal premise of this book.

Each document, as a matter of theory, is to be seen all by itself, that is, as autonomous of all others. This is the main perspective of the present book, in Part One.

Each document, again as a matter of theory, is to be examined for its relationships with other documents universally regarded as falling into the same classification, as Torah. This is the issue of Part Two, namely, points of intersection between Leviticus Rabbah and other documents.

And, finally, each document is to be allowed to take its place as part of the undifferentiated aggregation of documents that, all together, constitute the canon of Judaism, that is to say, "Torah."

Simple logic makes self-evident the proposition that, if a document comes down to us within its own framework, as a complete book with a beginning, middle, and end, in preserving that book, the canon presents us with a document on its own and not solely as part of a larger composition or construct. So we too see the document as it reaches us, that is, as autonomous. But in Part One I prove that very proposition.

If, second, a document contains materials shared verbatim or in substantial content with other documents of its classification, or if one document refers to the contents of other documents, then the several documents that clearly wish to engage in conversation with one another have to address one another. That is to say, we have to seek for the marks of connectedness, asking for the meaning of those connections. In Parts Two and Three I deal with these facts and their meaning.

Finally, since, as I said at the outset, the community of the faithful of Judaism, in all of the contemporary expressions of Judaism, concur that documents held to be authoritative constitute one whole, seamless "Torah," that is, a complete and exhaustive statement of God's will for Israel and humanity, we take as our further task the description of the whole out of the undifferentiated testimony of all of its parts. These components in the theological context are viewed, as is clear, as equally authoritative for the composition of the whole: one, continuous system. In taking up such a question, we address a problem not of theology alone, though it is a correct theological conviction, but one of description, analysis, and interpretation of an entirely historical order.

In this way, in future work, we may hope to trace the literary evidence -- which is the only evidence we have -- for the formation of Judaism, what it is, how it works. By seeing the several components of the canon of Judaism in sequence, first, one by one, then, one after the other, and finally, all together all at once, we may trace the literary side of the history of Judaism. We may see how a document came into being on its own, in its context (so far as we may posit the character of that context). We interpret the document at its site. As a matter of fact, moreover, all documents of the rabbinic canon except for the Hebrew Scriptures relate to prior ones, on the one side, and all, especially the Scriptures, stand before those to follow, on the other. The Mishnah normally is understood to rest upon the written Torah, and, later in its history in Judaism, came to be called the oral Torah. So even the Mishnah stands not distinct and autonomous, but contingent and dependent. The two Talmuds rest upon the Mishnah, and the several compilations of exegeses of Scripture, called "midrashim," rest upon Scripture. So, in all, like the bones of the body, each book is connected to others (with Scripture and the Mishnah the backbone). All together they form a whole, a frame that transcends the parts and imparts proportion, meaning, and harmony to them.

The bones of the body develop more or less in shared stages, however, while the documents of the Torah, the canon of Judaism, developed in a sequence. The order, if not so linear as it seems on the surface, is mostly clear. First came Scripture, then the Mishnah, then the Talmud of the Land of Israel and earlier compilations of biblical exegeses, then the Talmud of Babylonia and the later compilations of biblical exegeses. In that sequence of the important texts we shall find whatever evidence of growth, development, and change, as we shall ever have available to tell us the history of Judaism. To complete the matter, what do we hope to learn as we relate growth, development, and change in the history of Judaism, traced through the formation and character of its canon, to the growth, development, and change in the history of the Jewish people? It is not only to describe and analyze, but also to explain, the history of the formation of Judaism. That is to say, we may frame theories not only on the formative history of the world-view and way of life we call Judaism, but on the reasons that the history went the route it took, rather than some other route. How so? We may ask why people thought what they thought and did what they did, rather than thinking other thoughts and doing other things. When we can relate the ideas people held and the way they lived their life to the context in which they found themselves, we shall have reached that level of interpretation at which present and past come together in the setting of shared human existence: the meeting of text and context. But we stand at a distance from that elusive goal.

What I have said in general makes sense in particular of Judaism: The Evidence of the Mishnah and Judaism in Society: The Evidence of the Yerushalmi. I mention two other titles, Judaism and Scripture: The Evidence of Leviticus Rabbah and Judaism in Conclusion: The Evidence of the Bavli. These four works yield yet a final one, The Oral Torah: An Introduction. What each item proposes is two exercises which are one. First, I wish to describe a single document. Second, I also want to address to a given document one important question. These two exercises really complement one another. My premise is that a document ordinarily is about something. Except for anthologies of information, people write books to make points, to answer questions, to say something important. In the ancient world people copied and preserved books at great expense, so books had to matter. The premise, then, that a given document tells us something important to those who wrote it and their successors, seems to me self-evident.

It follows that we have to find out what polemic, what point of insistence, what aspect of self-evidence a given text reveals. As I have stressed in every work of mine, we begin the search with the smallest details, we then ask what the details of the text repeatedly stress. This commonly emerges not from what the text says, but from how it says what it says. In the main beams of rhetoric, in the repeated details, ubiquitous, implicit, self-evident, and therefore definitive, I claim to find that principal message that speaks for the work as a whole. The deepest structures of syntax may convey the principles of order. The techniques of rhetoric, broadly construed, properly understood, may speak also to us. They accordingly may deliver a text's substantive message through the forms of proportion and of intelligible, therefore logical, speech.

About what main point do the texts at hand then speak? I see the Mishnah as a complete statement of an entire system. I see the documents of succession, typified by the Yerushalmi, as large-scale efforts to translate the Mishnah's philosophical system into social order. I see counterpart documents of Scripture-exegesis, which treat Scripture as the two Talmuds treat the Mishnah, as exercises in the construction of dialogue between Scripture and the Mishnah. And I see the final document of the canon, the Bavli, as a synthetic work of restatement and completion. The Bavli joins the two main lines of order and systemic structure, the Mishnah and Scripture, and makes them the basis for its proportions and the foundations of its social order.

In my view the various documents of the canon of Judaism produced in late antiquity demand a different hermeneutic altogether from the one of homogenization and harmonization, the ahistorical and anti-contextual one I have outlined. It is one that does not harmonize but that differentiates. It is a hermeneutic shaped to teach us how to read the texts at hand one by one and in a particular context, exactly in the way in which we read any other text bearing cultural and social insight. The texts stand not as self-evidently important but only as examples, sources of insight for a quite neutral inquiry. Let me spell out what I think is at issue between the established hermeneutic and the one I propose.

The three key-words of the inherited hermeneutic are continuity, uniqueness, and survival. Scholars who view the texts as continuous with one another seek what is unique in the system formed by the texts as a whole. With the answer to what is unique, they propose to explain the survival of Israel, the Jewish people. Hence: continuity, uniqueness, survival.

The words to encapsulate the hermeneutic I espouse are these: description, analysis, and interpretation. I am trying to learn how to describe the constituents of the canon, viewed individually, each in its distinctive context. I wish to discover appropriate analytical tools, questions to lead me from description of one text to comparison and contrast between two or more texts of the canon. Only at the end do I address the question of interpretation: how do all of the texts of the canon at hand flow together into a single continuous statement, a "Judaism."

Within the inherited hermeneutic of continuity, survival, and uniqueness, the existence of the group defines the principal concern, an inner-facing one, hence the emphasis on uniqueness in quest, in continuities, for the explanation of survival. Within the proposed hermeneutic of description, analysis, and interpretation, by contrast, the continued survival of a "unique" group does not frame the issue. For my purposes, it is taken for granted, for the group is not the main thing at all. The problematic emerges from without. What I want to know is not how and why the group survived so as to help it survive some more. It is how to describe the society and culture contained within, taken as a given, how to interpret an enduring world-view and way of life, expressed by the artifacts in hand. How did, and does, the group work?

So I claimed that the results of the literary inquiry will prove illuminating for the study of society and culture. I have now to explain why I think so. The answer lies in our will and capacity to generalize, out of details, a judgment on a broad issue of culture, as it is exemplified in the small problem at hand. The issue here is secular. True, I too ask how the components of the canon as a whole form a continuity. I wonder why this document in particular survived to speak for the whole. But for me the answers to these questions generate theories, promise insight for the study of other canonical religions. So far as I shall succeed, it will be because I can learn from these other canonical religions. I have tried to learn from, and also to teach something to, those who study the history, the thought, the social reality, of religions that, like Judaism, form enduring monuments to the power of humanity to endure and to prevail so far.

I suppose that, in the end, we who do this work this way also want to see things whole. True, God alone is the one who really sees things whole, complete, in context and appropriate perspective. But to be like God to us can then mean to try, ourselves, to see that entire context. Alas, our vision is only in and through detail. Being mortal, that is what we are given to see: the world in a grain of sand, and God in the detailed likeness, in the detailed image, of humanity, seen one by one and all at once.

J.N.

Providence, Rhode Island

INTRODUCTION
THE PROBLEM AND ITS SOLUTION

I propose to demonstrate in the case of Leviticus Rabbah that a rabbinic document constitutes a text, not merely a scrapbook or a random compilation of episodic materials. A text is a document with a purpose, one that exhibits the traits of the integrity of the parts to the whole and the fundamental autonomy of the whole from other texts. I shall show that the document at hand therefore falls into the classification of a cogent composition, put together with purpose and intended as a whole and in the aggregate to bear a meaning and state a message. I shall therefore disprove the claim, for the case before us, that a rabbinic document serves merely as an anthology or miscellany or is to be compared only to a scrapbook, made up of this and that. In the present, exemplary instance I shall point to the improbability that a document has been brought together merely to join discrete and ready-made bits and pieces of episodic discourse. A document in the canon of Judaism thus does not merely define a context for the aggregation of such already completed and mutually distinct materials. Rather, I claim, a document constitutes a text. So in method at issue then is what makes a text a text, that is, the textuality of a document. At stake is how we may know when a document constitutes a text and when it is merely an anthology or a scrapbook.

A critical component of the issue at hand concerns materials that occur in both the document under study and other compositions of the same canon. These shared materials occur, for the present case, in both Leviticus Rabbah and the Yerushalmi (Talmud of the Land of Israel) or Genesis Rabbah, both writings of the same period as Leviticus Rabbah. In addition, important parashiyyot (chapters) of Leviticus Rabbah occur, also, in Pesiqta deR. Kahana, and the correspondences are protracted and verbatim. So when we claim, as I shall, that Leviticus Rabbah constitutes an autonomous document and one with its own integrity, we forthwith confront the issue of the place, meaning, and importance of the materials held in common between Leviticus Rabbah and other rabbinic writings. In particular, I shall have to unpack the issue to show what is at stake, and what is not at stake, in the fact at hand. The matter has been compared to the relationship among New Testament Gospels, so that, as we shall see in Chapter Five, it is alleged that the relationship between two or more Synoptic Gospels runs parallel to the relationship between two or more rabbinic documents (at issue in that allegation: the Mishnah and the Tosefta). It is even maintained that since rabbinic documents do share some materials in common, they have to be regarded as "synoptic," in the way in which Mark, Luke, and Matthew are synoptic. Consequently, it is held, "Synoptic texts must always be studied synoptically," a somewhat murky allegation that in due course will come under examination. In any event, the fact that a document shares materials with one or more other documents does call into question the claim that the document at hand is autonomous and to be studied on its own. If a fair proportion of the text under study turns out to occur in other writings, then exactly what we mean by a text's integrity will require some reconsideration. Accordingly, integral to the discussion at hand are two issues: (1) the integrity and autonomy of Leviticus Rabbah, and (2) the issue of shared materials, the meaning for the interpretation of the character and definition of Leviticus Rabbah. We cannot settle (1) without attending in detail to (2).

I choose for the test-case Leviticus Rabbah, because I already have made my own translation of it and have also completed certain studies of its rhetoric, modes of argument, and essential message. I could as well have chosen the Mishnah, the Tosefta, Sifra, the Yerushalmi, the Bavli, Genesis Rabbah, or other documents on which I have worked at length. Each of these, as well as every other document of the canon of Judaism completed in late antiquity, demands equivalent inquiry. Leviticus Rabbah forms no more promising, nor less promising, an arena for study than any other. Still, it is more difficult than the Mishnah, which is a far more cogent formal construction. It also appears to be less difficult (so I have the impression) than Genesis Rabbah, on the one side, and the Fathers according to Rabbi Nathan, on the other. As an outsider to those texts, I do have the impression that they fall more readily into the category of scrapbooks or anthologies than cogent compositions. But only further study will tell. A long series of detailed analyses of each rabbinic composition of late antiquity therefore will flow from the present one. So, to conclude, I hope here to inaugurate a useful method of inquiry into a long-standing and much debated, if little-studied, question: whether and how rabbinic documents on their own constitute complete and autonomous statements, addresses exhibiting integrity and those traits of proportion and composition that we associate with well-crafted literature.

Let me spell out the method I shall follow. It is not complicated and rests upon what seem to me self-evident premises. I proceed in four stages.

First, I have to prove that the document at hand rests upon clearcut choices of formal and rhetorical preference, so it is, from the viewpoint of form and mode of expression, cogent. I have to demonstrate that these formal choices prove uniform and paramount. So in Part One I analyze three large parashiyyot to show their recurrent structures. These I categorize. Then, in the same part, I proceed to survey all thirty-seven parashiyyot and find out whether or not every parashah of the entire document finds within a single cogent taxonomic structure suitable classification for its diverse units of discourse. If one taxonomy serves all and encompasses the bulk of the units of discourse at hand, I may fairly claim that Leviticus Rabbah does constitute a cogent formal structure, based upon patterns of rhetoric uniform and characteristic throughout.

Second, in Part Two I isolate those passages in the document at hand that in fact are not unique to it but are shared with one or more other documents of the same larger canon. These passages will not only link one document to the next. As I said, they also will call into question the claim that any document stands essentially on its own, exhibiting an integrity that distinguishes that document from all others. What is shared and not unique by definition challenges any claim to integrity and autonomy. If, therefore, what is not particular proves to form an important component of the whole, or if it bears a substantial part of the burden of the message of the whole, then the document as a whole cannot be characterized as autonomous. It would appear, rather, that the document under study constitutes yet another utensil for containing a message indifferent to its bearers. Then, as I said, one document cannot demand differentiation from others. The claim that a given document bears its own message and viewpoint and constitutes a statement of integrity will have to give way to the opposite one. We should then have to claim that all documents equally bear the message of the whole. Then any one of them indifferently may supply a context for the expression of what is common to them all. Hence, documents will turn out to constitute not texts but merely contexts. So at issue in the analysis of what is shared is the critical claim at hand.

Third, in Part Three I have to return to the materials unique to the document at hand and bring them into relationship with the materials shared among two or more documents. The compositions particular to the document along with shared materials have to be reexamined and described. These now become the criteria: which sort of materials -- unique or common -- bear the main formal components of the formal construction of the whole? Are the unique or are the shared materials episodic?

If materials unique to Leviticus Rabbah, those that conform to its recurrent literary structures, prove to form the principal parts, then we may say that we deal with a document made up by a distinct set of authors. This authorship has agreed on the formal and rhetorical preferences and has executed them consistently, time and again. If, again, the literary structures unique to the document as a whole cohere and present a cogent composition, then we may claim to know what is primary to the document, what expresses its topical and logical message. More than that, on formal grounds of rhetoric and pattern we again may allege that the document does present its own rhetorical and logical program.

In the same Part, I go back to the materials not particular to the document at hand and undertake to describe them. Do they form a large or negligible proportion? Do they cohere in formal or aesthetic or rhetorical ways? Or do they constitute a miscellany?

If they constitute a miscellany, one might wish to ask whether, in some documents other than the one at hand, the several shared items fit more suitably into an established formal and rhetorical setting than they do in the document under study. If it turns out that what is shared between the document under study and some other document exhibits the characteristic literary traits of that other document, on formal and rhetorical grounds one may claim that that other document, and not the one under study, bears the principal burden of the particular unit of discourse at hand. To state matters simply, it will turn out that in the case of shared items the document under study uses what is not native and natural to it. Rather, the document before us has borrowed from some other document, which then demands study on its terms and in its own analytical context.

But I shall not pursue this question. The reason is that it is not relevant to the issue of the integrity of Leviticus Rabbah in particular. That is to say, what I want to know is whether the materials of Leviticus Rabbah exhibit a particular literary structure, and, if they do, whether materials shared between Leviticus Rabbah and other documents conform or do not conform to that literary structure. How these same shared materials serve other documents in which they occur, what testimony about the character of those other documents these materials supply -- these questions will concern us when we turn to the other documents, in sequence. To make this view more concrete, I point once more to the enormous corpus of shared materials -- five complete parashiyyot out of the thirty-seven of Leviticus Rabbah -- that occur nearly verbatim in Pesiqta deR. Kahana. I can and do prove that these materials conform faithfully to the distinctive and definitive literary patterns and structure of Leviticus Rabbah. That proof serves the purpose of this book, which is, as is clear, to show the integrity, therefore also the autonomy, of Leviticus Rabbah. How these same materials fit into the literary patterns particular to and definitive of Pesiqta deR. Kahana is a quite separate question, to be pursued in the setting of the study of that document, its distinctive literary patterns, its integrity, its autonomy.

It will follow, finally, that we can answer the question, for the document under study, of whether or not we deal with a text, exhibiting traits of composition, deliberation, proportion, and so delivering a message on its own.

If we do, then Leviticus Rabbah demands description, analysis, and interpretation first of all on its own, as an autonomous statement. It requires then comparison and contrast with other compositions of its species of the rabbinic genus, that is to say, it demands to be brought into connection with, relationship to, other rabbinic compositions. It further will have to be read in a still larger context, as part of a continuity of all rabbinic writings of the age -- the later fourth and fifth centuries -- and of late antiquity. So if a document proves to constitute a composition and to exhibit integrity, it will stand in three relationships with all other documents of its category: autonomous of them all, connected to some of them, continuous with them all.

But what if we do not deal with a text, but only a scrapbook? Then we shall turn out to affirm the now-broadly-held opinion that all of the documents in the canon of Judaism speak pretty much at random to a single common program. All contribute to Judaism equally and without differentiation. To describe Judaism -- a theological or legal point -- one may equally cite what is found in one document alongside what is located in some other. We then do not have to pay much attention to the locus of a given passage. We may ignore its relationship to what stands fore and aft. We may assume that all things are part of one thing, whether we call it "the one whole Torah of Moses, our rabbi," or merely "Judaism," "the halakhah," or "theology of Judaism" not making much difference. So, in all, the stakes are very high, and the work at hand protracted.

Having framed the question I propose to answer and how I claim to answer it, let me turn to the context in which the work is carried forward. Why should anybody imagine that a document is other than a text (or a "book"), other than a composition, other than a cogent statement on its own? And, to ask the contrary question, why should anybody claim that a document serves only as a statement of something drawn out of a larger and definitive context, so, as I said, a context rather than a text? And to complete the question, why should anyone claim that a given document may be read not in splendid autonomy and as a statement of integrity but only as part of a larger "synoptic" system of documents?

The answer to these questions on the urgency of the task lies in the traits of the canon as a whole. For the canon of Judaism does consist of documents that intersect and form concurrent and overlapping statements. So it is quite reasonable for people to interpret the facts of intersection and concurrence as they have. It is entirely understandable that people insist all documents testify equally and with little differentiation to a single cogent system, but no document on its own constitutes a system. Or, to state matters as they have come to the surface just now (which proves that in this book I do not beat a dead horse), "Synoptic texts must always be studied synoptically, even if one text is 'later' than another" (Cohen, Conservative Judaism, 1983, 3, p. 56). To explain the urgency of the issue at hand, let me start from the beginning.

The several documents that make up the canon of Judaism in late antiquity relate to one another in three important ways. First, all of them refer to the same basic writing, the Hebrew Scriptures. Many of them draw upon the Mishnah and quote it. So the components of the canon join at their foundations. Second, as the documents reached closure in sequence, the later authorship can be shown to have drawn upon earlier, completed documents. So the writings of the rabbis of the talmudic corpus accumulate and build from layer to layer. Third, among two or more documents some completed units of discourse, and many brief, discrete sayings, circulated, for instance, sentences or episodic homilies or fixed apophthegms of various kinds. So in some (indeterminate) measure the several documents draw not only upon one another, as we can show, but also upon a common corpus of materials that might serve diverse editorial and redactional purposes. The extent of this common corpus can never be fully known. We know only what we have, not what we do not have. So we cannot say what has been omitted, or whether sayings that occur in only one document derive from materials available to the editors or compilers of some or all other documents. That is something we never can know. We can describe only what is in our hands and interpret only the data before us. Of indeterminates and endless speculative possibilities we need take no account.

The commonalities of the documents have so impressed some as to lead to the comparison between the relationships among several rabbinic compositions, on the one side, and those among the synoptic Gospels, on the other. As I shall explain in Chapter Five, Morton Smith's justly famous Tannaitic Parallels to the Gospels (Philadelphia, 1951: Society of Biblical Literature Monograph Series) first expressed this idea, a modern counterpart to the harmonies of the Gospels of olden days. He called it "parallels of parallelism." These same commonalities have reenforced the received theory, which even in its scholarly version may be called fundamentalist, that "the one whole Torah or Moses, our rabbi," circulated in some primary form before individual components -- sayings, stories, units of discourse of a still larger dimension -- attracted the attention of the authors, or compositors, of documents. They only later on took what they wanted from an essentially uniform corpus. These redactors then imposed upon what they selected that formal diversity and rhetorical distinctiveness now exhibited by the several components of the (allegedly) once-uniform and unified canon. So modernists have framed a theory of the literature drawing upon the analogy to the Gospels' Q, and traditionalists have repeated in literary terms the theory of the Torah-myth that pretty much everything is the same as everything else anyhow. To state matters more fairly, whatever we have fits together into one whole and homogeneous Torah, a synthesis and a harmony. That is surely a theological fact of Judaism. But it is exceedingly difficult to discern, among the shared materials of the document at hand, either formal traits in common or substantive viewpoints expressed in those shared materials and distinctive to them. There is, in other words, no counterpart to "Q." There is only a heterogeneous mass of shared materials, and that mass turns out, in volume and proportion to the whole of Leviticus Rabbah, negligible in size as much as it is unformed and miscellaneous in character: unformed and void.

This book serves to demonstrate that essentially negative fact, pertinent to the document under study, Leviticus Rabbah in particular.

In my analytical studies of the history of the ideas of Judaism in its formative age, I have asked systematically, document by document, what each composition contributed, and whether and how the materials in a given composition fit together within the formal limits of that composition. In approaching matters in this way, that is, analytically and by documents, rather than synthetically and as a harmonious whole, I have had to put off to one side the self-evident commonalities among documents. Now therefore I turn back to address the entirely fair criticism that, in taking up documents one by one, I obscure their larger context and their many points in common. As I said, these points in common here prove not many and not definitive. What is unique to the text predominates and bears the message of the whole.

To date I have taken up the issue of homogeneity in a limited and mainly formal setting, for the matter of how sayings and stories travel episodically from one document to the next. This preparatory study, The Peripatetic Saying. The Problem of the Thrice-Told Tale in Talmudic Literature (Chico, 1985) sets the stage for the present one. Why so? Let me state with emphasis: The real issue, I maintain, is not the traveling, but the unique, materials: the documents, and not what is shared among them. The variable -- what moves -- is subject to analysis only against the constant: the document itself.

What makes me say so? It is the ultimate question, which is the integrity of the document itself.

Among the three points in common I listed at the outset -- Scripture, citation of earlier documents, and appearance in two or more documents of already completed writings -- of course, the third makes the deepest impression on those who maintain that the documents are secondary to their contents, so that the role of editors or compositors was limited, scarcely invasive. The fact that completed materials go from one composition to the next supplies a very strong argument that the compositors' labor required making choices among a large body of available material, but did not require making up sizable proportions of the material to be used in a given document. How so? What if two or more documents could be shown to draw upon the same prior, shared source of materials ("Q")? Then the viewpoints of the contingent documents -- the works of the people down the line who made choices -- demand less attention than the perspectives of the original authors of the shared materials ("Q"). The definitive locus of authorship -- original conception and composition of formative ideas -- then will lie not within the pages of a given book but prior to the formation of that book.

If the shared materials predominate, then the authorship of documents turns out to be collective and unitary. The lines of structure will not differentiate among documents but encompass all of them, because what we find in any one document is simply an expression of what is common to the authorship of all documents all together. So, as I said at the outset, documents will be shown to constitute mere miscellanies, locative for what is utopian in the larger system, anthologies and collections of what derives from the sheltering matrix -- from "the Torah," from "Judaism," from synthesis, homogenization, and harmonization. But for Leviticus Rabbah, as we shall see, the shared materials do not predominate. The authorship of this document is distinct from the authorship of other documents with which this one intersects. The lines of structure do differentiate Leviticus Rabbah from other documents. This writing is not a mere miscellany, does not merely supply a location for what is equally in place -- utopian -- in the larger system. This is, in its context, not an anthology and not a collection of some things that derive from the matrix.

It follows that emphasis upon the viewpoint of a given document is not at all misplaced. A "composition" does not constitute a mere composite. The notion that the Mishnah testifies to its own system is not wrong. All documents all together cannot be assumed to testify to a viewpoint common among the entirety of the authorship of "the tradition" or "the Torah," that is to say, the entire corpus of materials in all the canonical books. That must be shown. Until we show it, we do not know it. Nothing is to be viewed "always" or only synoptically, everything must be seen in isolation from the whole. That is what is at stake in the results of literary analysis at hand.

It would be tempting to invoke the analogy of the Synoptics and of Q. But that is misleading. That is to say, one might wish to suppose that a corpus of sayings, drawn together into some usable and authoritative form, circulated and served the interests of two or more sets of compositors (e.g., Luke and Matthew) but not of another such set (e.g., Mark). That analogy would lead us into an inquiry into a problem for which, as I said just now, we have no clearly defined and finite data. That is to say, we should go off in search of sayings shared in two or more documents but omitted among ten or twelve or fifteen others. If, however, we find a saying used in Leviticus Rabbah and Sifra, but not used in all of the other midrash-collections of late antiquity, or in the Mishnah, Tosefta, the two Sifres, and the two Talmuds, we should draw only one conclusion. The saying was useful where it was used and not useful where it was not used. We should have no evidence that such a saying circulated broadly in a defined collection (e.g., a rabbinic "Q"), all the more so that such a defined and finite collection existed. Without "Q" I see nothing at stake in the synoptic question as it applies to rabbinic compositions.

Without tests of falsification, we should never know when we were right and when we were wrong. Any theory of a rabbinic "Q," therefore, would rest upon an analogy to begin with hopelessly out of phase with the data at hand. To state matters in a way more relevant to the rabbinic literature, a theory that posits the circulation of a vast corpus of sayings prior to, and separate from, the existence (the formation and closure) of specific documents is ultimately beyond all tests of falsification and verification. True, such a vast corpus may have circulated. Pieces of it may have surfaced here and there, more or less at random. But we cannot show that. We cannot describe "Q'"s traits. We cannot analyze its viewpoint. We cannot compare the amorphous mass of sayings to the concrete utilization of some sayings in a given document.

And, as we shall see here, we can show that most of a given document is unique to that document and occurs nowhere else and moreover conforms to and expresses what is characteristic of the document in hand and to no other document. So the facts we do have will now be amassed to demonstrate the proposition at hand: a document really is a text because it conforms to a distinctive rhetorical program and presents mostly unique materials. To repeat: we know only what we have, not what we do not have. We therefore can appeal only to what we know, not to what we do not know. And what we know consists of the several documents, jointly and severally, and what they tell us.

The sole point of entry into the problem therefore is this: does a document serve merely as a convenient utensil for the collection and composition of diverse sayings widely available for use anywhere and for any purpose (Part Two)? Or does a document define its own patterns of expression, thought, and composition (Part One)? The issue as I frame it demands a different analogy from "Q." I draw an analogy from the issue of the relationship between Samuel and Kings, on the one side, and Chronicles on the other. Do the books of Chronicles and those of Samuel and Kings share a common source? Do the books of Chronicles draw upon and rework only the available materials of Samuel and Kings? Framing the issue in terms of a set of rabbinic compositions, we ask whether a given book draws upon sources common to it and to other books, or whether a given composition defines and frames its interests and materials essentially independently of those books with which there admittedly are points of intersection and even concurrence. If I ask about the relationships among things that are known, I may come up with solid answers. About possibilities presently lacking all documentation, I cannot overstress, we had best not trouble to speculate.

So, to conclude, when I frame matters in terms of the problem of the rabbinic document, I ask what defines a document as such, the text-ness, the textuality, of a text. How do we know that a given book in the canon of Judaism is something other than a scrapbook? The choices are clear. One theory is that a document serves solely as a convenient repository of prior sayings and stories, available materials that will have served equally well (or poorly) wherever they took up their final location. The other theory is that a composition exhibits a viewpoint, a purpose of authorship distinctive to its framers or collectors and arrangers. Such a characteristic literary purpose -- by this other theory -- is so powerfully particular to one authorship that nearly everything at hand can be shown to have been (re)shaped for the ultimate purpose of the authorship at hand, that is, collectors and arrangers who demand the title of authors. To resort again to a less than felicitous neologism, I thus ask what signifies or defines the "document-ness" of a document and what makes a book a book. I therefore wonder whether there are specific texts in the canonical context of Judaism or whether all texts are merely contextual.

In framing the question as I have, I of course lay forth the mode of answering it -- but only for one book. We need to define the integrity of texts one by one. We have to confront a single rabbinic composition, and ask about its sources. By "sources" I mean simply passages in a given book that occur, also, in some other rabbinic book. Such sources -- prior to the books in which they appear -- fall into the classification of materials general to two or more compositions and by definition not distinctive and particular to any one of them. The word "source" therefore serves as an analogy to convey the notion that two or more sets of authors have made use of a single, available item. About whether or not the shared item is prior to them both or borrowed by one from the other at this stage we cannot speculate.

To summarize: Once we know what is unique to a document, we can investigate the traits that characterize all the unique and so definitive materials. We ask about whether the materials unique to a document also cohere, or whether they prove merely miscellaneous. If they do cohere, we may conclude that the framers of the document have followed a single plan and a program. That would in my view justify the claim that the framers carried out a labor not only of conglomeration, arrangement and selection, but also of genuine authorship or composition in the narrow and strict sense of the word. The document emerges from authors, not merely arrangers and compositors. We take up and analyze in the same way and for the same purpose the items shared between that document and some other or among several documents. We ask about the traits of those items, one by one and all in the aggregate. In these stages we may solve for the case at hand the problem of the rabbinic document: do we deal with a scrapbook or a cogent composition? A text or merely a literary expression, random and essentially promiscuous, of a larger theological context? That is the choice at hand.

I present a sizable segment of Leviticus Rabbah in translation. All translations in this book are my own. Margulies' text, which I have translated, vastly improves upon the standard printed text. We now have a text based on careful study of all manuscript evidents and parallel passages. Providing a translation of that text seems to me self-evidently necessarily. Not only do I translate the superb text of Mordecai Margulies, Midrash Wayyikra Rabbah. A critical edition based on manuscripts and Genizah fragments with variants and notes (Jerusalem, 1953-60) I-V. For the sense of each passage, I also have framed matters in line with Margulies' interpretation, imposing my own view only rarely. So this translation is shaped to render available in English Margulies' superior text and his main points about its meaning. The former now replaces the "standard printed text" translated by J. Israelstam and Judah J. Slotki, Midrash Rabbah Leviticus. Translated into English with notes, glossary, and indices, under the editorship of H. Freedman and Maurice Simon (London, 1939). But the excellent translation of Israelstam and Slotki remains the standard and model for all to follow, and I found much assistance in their work.

Margulies' text diverges from the standard printed one on nearly every page. Since he has assembled the pertinent manuscript evidence and evaluated it all, the text he has framed for us must now take the place of the conventional one. He also has provided a complete commentary. He has identified, for each passage, the parallel appearances. He has explained the meaning of words and phrases in an up-to-date way and in constant dialogue, in particular, with the lexicographical erudition of the age represented by Saul Lieberman. In all, he has provided those textual and philological foundations required for a responsible translation of the original. Those things I find much less within my capacities than the analytical-critical study, in particular, of problems of redaction and (to the minor extent that they are relevant here) form. My own contribution to the study of the document, beyond the translation of the new and excellent text of Margulies, consists in the systematic analysis of the redactional structure of each item, the differentiation between and among materials presently presented as all one and the same, and the explanation of what I believe to be the layers or levels of the composite in hand. I do not mean to exaggerate the value of these areas of inquiry, but I do believe that all further historical and religious study of the document must begin in the literary and analytical issues I systematically introduce. That is why I have found it worth my while to retranslate the text and to undertake my particular sorts of studies of its literary character.

I have had to develop a way of differentiating the several units beyond the received one. The established mode differentiates between one parashah, or chapter, and the next, and, within the parashah, or chapter, between one sizable unit and the next. Hence 1:1 conventionally signifies the first parashah and the first sizable subdivision thereof. As soon as I began my translation, I realized that the subdivision itself consisted of several distinct units of discourse, each with its marks of particularity. In order to show what I believe to be the components of which each subunit of a parashah is made up -- for these, I show, were framed before inclusion in the subunit -- I have preserved what we have and then added further marks of differentiation. The established markings are converted into Roman numerals. Thus I:I stands for the first parashah, or chapter, then the first subunit as signified in the standard printed texts. Then the Arabic letter signifies my further differentiation within the subdivision, thus I:I.1.A signifies the first sentence (A) of the first complete unit of thought (1) of the first subdivision (I) of the first parashah (I) and so on. I cannot claim that all of the instances in which I differentiate a "complete unit of thought" are equally self-evident. In many instances I may have missed further marks of differentiation, and a more critical eye than mine will have to discern them. But I am fairly sure that I have not divided, so differentiated, a complete unit of thought into subdivisions but have consistently preserved the clear recognition of where the full exposition of a theme, topic, or idea begins, attains full exposition, and reaches a conclusion.

Part One

RECURRENT LITERARY STRUCTURES OF LEVITICUS RABBAH

Chapter One

RECURRENT LITERARY STRUCTURES OF LEVITICUS RABBAH

i. Introduction

A literary structure is a composition that adheres to conventions of expression, organization, or proportion, extrinsic to the message of the author. Such a structure conforms to rules that impose upon the individual writer a limited set of choices about how he will convey whatever message he has in mind. Or it will limit an editor or redactor to an equally circumscribed set of alternatives about how to arrange received materials. We obviously cannot allege on the basis of what merely appears to us to be patterned or needlessly formal that we have a structure in hand. Nor shall we benefit from bringing to the text at hand structures shown in other texts to define conventions for communicating ideas in those other texts. A text has to define its own structures for us. This its authors do simply by repeatedly resorting to a given set of literary conventions. It follows that the adjective "recurrent" constitutes a redundancy when joined to the noun "structure." That is to say, we cannot know that we have a structure if the text under analysis does not repeatedly resort to the presentation of its message through that disciplined structure.

Leviticus Rabbah comprises large-scale literary structures. How do we know that fact? It is because, when we divide up the undifferentiated columns of words and sentences and point to the boundaries that separate one completed unit of thought or discourse from the next such completed composition, we produce rather sizable statements conforming to a single set of patterns. While in the Mishnah, for example, we can distinguish a few sentences as a paragraph, and a few paragraphs as a concluded statement, a completed unit of discourse, in Leviticus Rabbah we cannot. Rather, our divisions encompass many more sentences, a great many more words, than is the case in the Mishnah. On the other hand, in comparing the dimensions of completed units of discourse in Leviticus Rabbah to those in the Yerushalmi or the Bavli, we find in the former less sustained, less protracted discourse than in the latter. That is to say, a unit of thought or analysis in one of the two Talmuds in the average will be made up of a great many more subunits or components. On the other hand, these components of large-scale analytical units of discourse will appear autonomous of the larger composition in which they occur. They will not prove cogent within that composition. By contrast, units of discourse in Leviticus Rabbah tend not to run on as do those of the two Talmuds, but the components do prove more cogent with the larger discourse which they serve. In all, what I mean when I claim that Leviticus Rabbah is made up of large-scale literary structures is simple. When we divide a given _parashah,_ or chapter, of Leviticus Rabbah into its sub-divisions, we find these sub-divisions sustained and on occasion protracted, but also stylistically cogent and well-composed.

What these facts mean is that, in Leviticus Rabbah, the repeated patterns follow protracted orbits, covering a sizable volume of material. The patterns are large in scale. We deal not with small-scale syntactic formalization, such as the Mishnah's authors use to good effect, for example three or five sentences made up of parts of the speech arranged in exactly the same way. But we do deal with a stylized mode of discourse, unlike the Tosefta's rather miscellaneous style in conveying its authors' ideas. Were we to be guided by either the Yerushalmi's or the Bavli's writers, further, we should look for rigid but abbreviated rhetorical patterns, signals conveyed by little more than parts of speech so set forth as to convey the purpose and sense of sizable discussion. We should be disappointed were we to ask the authors at hand in Leviticus Rabbah to demonstrate their equivalent skill at the use of rhetoric to lend structure and impart sense to otherwise unformed sentences. Where those authors excel, it is at holding in the balance a rather substantial composite of materials, systematically and patiently working their way from point to seemingly miscellaneous observation, and only at the end drawing the whole to an elegant and satisfying conclusion. So we look for large-scale patterns and point to such unusually sizable compositions as characteristic because they recur and define discourse, parashah by parashah. Indeed, as we shall now see, a given parashah is made up of a large-scale literary structure, which I shall define in a moment, followed by somewhat further, somewhat smaller, fairly formalized constructions.

How shall we proceed to identify the structures that define the document before us? It seems to me we had best move first to the analysis of a single parashah. We seek, within that parashah, to identify what holds the whole together. The second step then is to see whether we have identified something exemplary, or what is no example but in fact a phenomenon that occurs in fact only once or at random. For the first exercise, we take up Parashah Five, and for the second, numbers Sixteen and Twenty-five. As we proceed, of course, we shall then examine all thirty-seven of the parashiyyot and see the extent to which the patterns exhibited in one parashah, then in two others, in fact characterize the entire lot.

ii. Leviticus Rabbah Parashah 5

Let us begin with the parashah as a whole and then proceed to the work of classifying its units of discourse and explaining the order in which units of each classification are presented.

PARASHAH FIVE

V:I

I.   A.   "If it is the anointed priest who sins, [thus bringing guilt on the people, then let him offer to the Lord for the sin which he has committed a young bull without blemish]" (Lev. 4:3).

       B.   "When he is quiet, who can condemn? When he hides his face, who can set him right [RSV: behold him] [whether it be a nation or a man? that a godless man should not reign, that he should not ensnare the people]" (Job 34:29-30).

C. R. Meir interpreted [the matter] [Gen. R. 36:1], "'When he is quiet' -- in his world, 'when he hides his face' -- in his world.

D. "The matter may be compared to the case of a judge who draws a veil inside and so does not see what goes on outside.

E. "So the people of the generation of the flood thought: 'The thick clouds cover him, so he will not see [what we do]' (Job 22:14)."

F. They said to him, "That's enough from you, Meir."

2. A. Another interpretation: "When he is quiet, who can condemn? When he hides his face, who can set him right?" (Job 34:29)

B. When he gave tranquility to the generation of the flood, who could come and condemn them?

C. What sort of tranquility did he give them? "Their children are established in their presence, and their offspring before their eyes. [Their houses are safe from fear, and no rod of God is upon them]" (Job 21:8).

D. R. Levi and rabbis:

E. R. Levi said, "A woman would get pregnant and give birth in three days. [How do we know it?] Here, the word, 'established,' is used, and elsewhere: 'Be establshed in three days' (Ex. 19:15). Just as the word, 'established,' used there involves a span of three days, so the word, 'established,' used here means three days."

F. Rabbis say, "In a single day a woman would get pregnant and give birth.

G. "Here, the word, 'established,' is used, and elsewhere: 'And be established in the morning' (Ex. 34:2). Just as the word 'established' stated there involves a single day, so the word 'established' used here involves a single day."

3. A. "And their offspring before their eyes" -- for they saw children and grandchildren.

B. "They send forth their little ones like a flock, [and their children dance]" (Job 21:11).

C. [The word for "children" means] "their young."

D. Said R. Levi, "In Arabia for children they use the word 'the young.'"

4. A. "And their children dance" (Job 21:11) --

B. ["they dance"] like devils.

C. That is in line with the following verse of Scripture: "And satyrs will dance there" (Is. 13:21).

5. A. They say: When one of them would give birth by day, she would say to her son, "Go and bring me a flint, so I can cut your umbilical cord."

B.   If she gave birth by night, she would say to her son, "Go and light a lamp for me, so I can cut your umbilical cord."

C.   M^{C}SH B: A woman gave birth by night and said to her son, "Go and light a lamp for me, so I can cut your umbilical cord."

D.   [In Aramaic:] When he went out to fetch it, a devil, Ashmadon [Asmodeus], head of the spirits, met him. While the two were wrestling with one another, the cock crowed. [Ashmadon] said to him, "Go, boast to your mother that my time has run out, for if my time had not run out, I could have killed you."

E.   He said to him, "Go, boast to your mother's mother that my mother had not cut my umbilical cord, for if my mother had cut my umbilical cord, I would have beaten you."

F.   This illustrates that which is said: "Their houses are safe from fear" (Job 21:9) -- from destroying spirits.

6.   A.   "And no rod of God is upon them" -- [for their houses are free from suffering.

B.   [And this further] illustrates that which is said: "When he is quiet, who can condemn,] when he hides his face, who can put him right" (Job 34:30).

C.   When [God] hides his face from them, who can come and say to him, "You have not done right."

D.   And how, indeed, did he hide his face from them? When he brought the flood on them.

E.   That is in line with the following verse of Scripture: "And he blotted out every living substance which was upon the face of the earth" (Gen. 7:23).

7.   A.   "Whether it be to a nation [or a man together]" (Job 34:29) -- this refers to the generation of the flood.

B.   "Or to a man" -- this refers to Noah.

C.   "Together" -- he had to rebuild his world from one man, he had to rebuild his world from one nation.

On the surface, the sole point of contact between the base-verse and the intersecting verse, Lev. 4:3 and Job 34:29-30, is in the uncited part of the passage of Job, "that he should not ensnare the people." The anointed priest has sinned and in so doing has brought guilt on the entire people. If, however, that is why the entire assembly of exegeses of Job has been inserted here, that theme plays no rule in making the collection of materials on Job. For at no point in the present unit (or in the next one) does the important segment of the passage of Job come under discussion. The interpretation of Job 34:29 in light of the story of the flood predominates here. No. 1 has Meir's view that the entire passage refers to God's failure to intervene, with special reference to the flood. No. 2 pursues the same line of thought. No. 3 illustrates the notion that their children "are established in their presence," and Nos. 3-4 continue to spell out the phrase-by-phrase exegesis of the same verse. No. 5 pursues the same line of thought. No. 6 shifts the ground of interpretation. Now God is "quiet," but later, in "hiding his face," he brings punishment on them. No. 7 completes the exegesis of the cited passage of Job in line with the view that Job was a contemporary of Noah and spoke of his ties. Noah might then serve as the counterpart and opposite of the priest who brings guilt on the people. But that is by no means the clear intent of the passage at hand.

V:II

1. A. Another interpretation: "When he is quiet, who can condemn" (Job 34:29).

   B. When he gave tranquility to the Sodomites, who could come and condemn them?

   C. What sort of tranquility did he give them?

   D. "As for the earth, out of it comes bread, but underneath it is turned up as by fire. Its stones are the place of sapphires, and it has dust of gold" (Job 28:5-6).

2. A. "That path no bird of prey knows, and the falcon's eye has not seen it" (Job 28:7).

   B. R. Levi in the name of R. Yohanan bar Shahina: "The falcon [bar hadayya-bird] spots its prey at a distance of eighteen mils."

   C. And how much is its portion [of food]?

   D. R. Meir said, "[A mere] two handbreadths."

   E. R. Judah said, "One handbreadth."

   F. R. Yose said, "Two or three fingerbreadths."

   G. [In Aramaic:] And when it stood on the trees of Sodom, it could not see the ground because of the density of [the foliage of] the trees.

3. A. "When he hides his face, who can put him right?" --

   B. When he hid his face from them, who comes to say to him, "You did not do rightly"?

   C. And when did he hide his face from them?

   D. When he made brimstone and fire rain down on them.

   E. That is in line with the following verse of Scripture: "Then the Lord made brimstone and fire rain on Sodom and Gomorrah" (Gen. 19:24).

The second unit simply carries forward the exercise of reading Job 28:5ff., now in line with the story of Sodom and Gomorrah, rather than the Generation of the Flood.

V:III

1. A. Another interpretation of "When he is quiet, who can condemn? When he hides his face, who can set him right?" (Job 34:29).

B. When he gave tranquility to the ten tribes, who could come and condemn them?

C. What sort of tranquility did he give them? "Woe to those who are at ease in Zion, and to those who feel secure on the mountain of Samaria, the notable men of the first of the nations, to whom the house of Israel to come" (Amos 6:1).

2. A. "Woe to those who are at ease in Zion" refers to the tribe of Judah and Benjamin.

B. "Those who feel secure on the mountain of Samaria" refers to the ten tribes.

C. "The notable men of the first of the nations" who derive from the two noteworthy names, Shem and Eber.

D. When the nations of the world eat and drink, they pass the time in nonsense-talk, saying, "Who is a sage, like Balaam! Who is a hero, like Goliath! Who is rich, like Haman!"

E. And the Israelites come after them and say to them, "Was not Ahitophel a sage, Samson a hero, Korah rich?"

3. A. "Pass over to Calneh and see, [and thence go to Hamath the great, then go down to Gath of the Philistines. Are they better than these kingdoms? Or is their territory greater than your territory?]" (Amos 6:2).

B. [Calneh] refers to Ctesiphon.

C. "Hamath the great" refers to Hamath of Antioch.

D. "And go down to Gath of the Philistines" refers to the mounds of the Philistines.

E. "Are they better than these kingdoms? Or is their territory greater than your territory?"

F. "O you who put far away the evil day" (Amos 6:3) [refers to] the day on which they would go into exile.

4. A. "And bring near the seat of violence?" (Amos 6:3). This refers to Esau.

B. "Did you bring yourselves near to sit next to violence" -- this refers to Esau.

C. That is in line with the following verse of Scripture: "For the violence done to your brother Jacob, [shame shall cover you]" (Obad. 1:40).

5. A. "[Woe to] those who lie upon beds of ivory" (Amos 6:4) -- on beds made of the elephant's tusk.

B. "And stink on their couches" (Amos 6:4) -- who do stinking transgressions on their beds.

C. "Who eat lambs from the flock [and calves from the midst of the stall]" (Amos 6:4).

D. They say: When one of them wanted to eat a kid of the flock, he would have the whole flock brought before him, and he would stand over it and slaughter it.

E. When he wanted to eat a calf, he would bring the entire herd of calves before him and stand over it and slaughter it.

6. A. "Who sing idle songs to the sound of the harp [and like David invent for themselves instruments of music]" (Amos 6:5).

B. [They would say that] David provided them with musical instruments.

7. A. "Who drink wine in bowls" (Amos 6:6).

B. Rab, R. Yohanan, and rabbis:

C. Rab said, "It is a very large bowl" [using the Greek].

D. R. Yohanan said, "It was in small cups."

E. Rabbis say, "It was in cups with saucers attached."

F. Whence did the wine they drink come?

G. R. Aibu in the name of R. Hanina said, "It was wine from Pelugta, for the wine would entice (PTH) the body."

H. And rabbis in the name of R. Hanina said, "It was from Pelugta' [separation], since, because of their wine-drinking, the ten tribes were enticed [from God] and consequently sent into exile."

8. A. "And anoint themselves with the finest oils" (Amos 6:6).

B. R. Judah b. R. Ezekial said, "This refers to oil of unripe olives, which removes hair and smooths the body."

C. R. Haninah said, "This refers to oil of myrrh and cinnamon."

9. A. And [in spite of] all this glory: "They are not grieved over the ruin of Joseph" (Amos 6:6).

B. "Therefore they shall now be the first of those to go into exile, [and the revelry of those who stretch themselves shall pass away]" (Amos 6:7).

C. What is the meaning of "the revelry of those who stretch themselves"?

D. Said R. Aibu, "They had thirteen public baths, one for each of the tribes, and one additional one for all of them together.

E. "And all of them were destroyed, and only this one [that had served all of them] survived.

F. "This shows how much lewdness was done with them."

10. A. "When he hides his face, who can set him right?" (Job 34:29).

B. When he hid his face from them, who then could come and say to him, "You did not do right"?

C. How did he hide his face from them? By bringing against them Sennacherib, the king of Assyria.

D. That is in line with the following verse of Scripture: "In the
fourteenth year of King Hezekiah, Sennacherib, king of Assyria,
came up [against all the fortified cities of Judah and took them]"
(Is. 36:1).

11. A. What is the meaning of, "and took them"?

B. Said R. Abba b. R. Kahana, "Three divine decrees were sealed on
that day.

C. "The decree against the ten tribes was sealed, for them to fall into
the hand of Sennacherib; the decree against Sennacherib was
sealed, for him to fall into the hand of Hezekiah; and the decree of
Shebna was sealed, to be smitten with leprosy.

12. A. "Whether it be a nation [or a man]" (Job 34:29) -- this refers to
Sennacherib, as it is said, "For a nation has come up upon my land"
(Joel 1:6).

B. "...or a man" (Job 34:29) -- this refers to Israel: "For you, my
sheep, the sheep of my pasture, are a man" (Ez. 34:31).

C. "Together" (Job 34:29) -- this refers to King Uzziah, who was
smitten with leprosy.

D. That is in line with the following verse of Scripture: "And Uzziah
the King was a leper until the day he died" (2 Chr. 26:21).

13. A. [Margulies: What follows treats "...whether it be a nation or a man
together" (Job 34:29):] Now the justice of the Holy One, blessed be
he, is not like man's justice.

B. A mortal judge may show favor to a community, but he will never
show favor to an individual.

C. But the Holy One, blessed be he, is not so. Rather: "If it is the
anointed priest who sins, [thus bringing guilt on the people,] then
let him offer [for the sin which he has committed] a young bull
[without blemish to the Lord as a sin-offering]" (Lev. 4:3-4).

D. "[If the whole congregation of Israel commits a sin unwittingly, and
the thing is hidden from the eyes of the assembly, and they do any
one of the things which the Lord has commanded not to be done
and are guilty, when the sin which they have committed becomes
know,] the assembly shall offer a young bull for a sin-offering"
(Lev. 4:13-14). [God exacts the same penalty from an individual
and from the community and does not distinguish the one from the
other. The anointed priest and the community both become subject
to liability for the same offering, a young bull.]

Finally, at No. 13, we come to the verse with which we began. And we find a clear
point of contact between the base-verse and the intersecting one, Job 34:29, as Margulies
explains. Still, there is no clear reason for including a sustained exegesis of Amos 6:3ff.

No. 1 completes the original exegesis by applying the cited verse to the ten tribes, first tranquil, then punished, as at V:I, II. 1.C then links Amos 6:1 to the present context. Once Amos 6:1 makes its appearance, we work through the elements of Amos 6:1-7. That massive interpolation encompasses Nos. 2-9. No. 10 resumes where No. 1 left off. No. 11 is tacked on to 10.D, and then Nos. 12, 13 continue the exegesis in terms of Israelite history of Job 34:29. Then, as I said, No. 13 stands completely separate from all that has gone before in V:I-III.12.

What then is the primary intent of the exegete? It is to emphasize the equality of anointed priest and ordinary Israelites. The expiation demanded of the one is no greater than that of the other. Considering the importance of the anointed priest, the ceremony by which he attains office, the sanctity attached to his labor, we cannot miss the polemic. What the anointed priest does unwittingly will usually involve some aspect of the cult. When the community commits a sin unwittingly, it will not involve the cult but some aspect of the collective life of the people. The one is no more consequential than the other; the same penalty pertains to both. So the people and the priest stand on the same plane before God. And the further meaning of the verse of Job then cannot be missed. When God hides his face, in consequence of which the people suffer, it is for just cause. No one can complain; he is long-suffering but in the end exacts his penalties. And these will cover not unwitting sin, such as Scripture Leviticus knows, but deliberate sin, as with the Generation of the Flood, Sodom, and the Ten Tribes. There would then appear to be several layers of meaning in the exegetical construction, which we must regard as a sustained and unified one, a truly amazing achievement.

V:IV

1.   A.   Said R. Abbahu, "It is written, 'Take heed that you do not forsake the Levite [as long as you live in your land] (Deut. 12:19). What follows thereafter? 'When the Lord your God enlarges your territory [as he has promised you] (Deut. 12:20).

    B.   "What has one thing got to do with the other?

    C.   "Said the Holy One, blessed be he, 'In accord with your gifts will they enlarge your [place].'"

    D.   R. Huna in the name of R. Aha, "If a slave brings as his offering a young bull, while his master brings a lamb, the slave takes precedence over his master.

    E.   "This is in accord with what we have learned in the Mishnah: 'If the young bull of the anointed priest and the young bull of the community are waiting [sacrifice], the young bull of the anointed priest takes precedence over the young bull of the community in all aspects of the sacrificial rite' (M. Hor. 3:6)."

2.   A.   "A man's gift makes room for him and brings him before great men" (Prov. 18:16).

    B.   M^{C}SH B: R. Eliezer, R. Joshua, and R. Aqiba went to the harborside of Antioch to collect funds for the support of sages.

C.   [In Aramaic:] A certain Abba Yudan lived there.

D.   He would carry out his religious duty [of philanthropy] in a liberal spirit, but had lost his money. When he saw our masters, he went home with a sad face. His wife said to him, "What's wrong with you, that you look so sad?"

E.   He repeated the tale to her: "Our masters are here, and I don't know what I shall be able to do for them."

F.   His wife, who was a truly philanthropic woman -- what did she say to him? "You only have one field left. Go, sell half of it and give them the proceeds."

G.   He went and did just that. When he was giving them the money, they said to him, "May the Omnipresent make up all your losses."

H.   Our masters went their way.

I.   He went out to plough. While he was ploughing the half of the field that he had left, the Holy One, blessed be he, opened his eyes. The earth broke open before him, and his cow fell in and broke her leg. He went down to raise her up, and found a treasure beneath her. He said, "It was for my gain that my cow broke her leg."

J.   When our masters came back, [in Aramaic:] they asked about a certain Abba Yudan and how he was doing. They said, "Who can gaze on the face of Abba Yudan [which glows with prosperity] -- Abba Yudan, the owner of flocks of goats, Abba Yudan, the owner of herds of asses, Abba Yudan, the owner of herds of camels."

K.   He came to them and said to them, "Your prayer in my favor has produced returns and returns on the returns."

L.   They said to him, "Even though someone else gave more than you did, we wrote your name at the head of the list."

M.   Then they took him and sat him next to themselves and recited in his regard the following verse of Scripture: "A man's gift makes room for him and brings him before great men" (Prov. 18:16).

3.   A.   R. Hiyya bar Abba called for charity contributions in support of a school in Tiberias. A member of the household of Siloni got up and pledged a litra of gold.

     B.   R. Hiyya bar Abba took him and sat him next to himself and recited in his regard the following verse of Scripture: "A man's gift makes room for him and brings him before great men" (Prov. 18:16).

4.   A.   [In Aramaic:] R. Simeon b. Laqish went to Bosrah. A certain Abba [Lieberman deletes: Yudan], "the Deceiver," lived there. It was not -- Heaven forfend -- that he really was a deceiver. Rather, he would practice [holy] deception in doing the religious duty [of philanthropy].

B. [In Aramaic:] He would see what the rest of the community would pledge, and he would then pledge to take upon himself [a gift equivalent to that of the rest of the] community.

C. R. Simeon b. Laqish took him and sat him next to himself and recited in his regard the following verse of Scripture: "A man's gift makes room for him and brings him before great men" (Prov. 18:16).

We find neither a base-verse nor an intersecting one. Rather, what will be the secondary verse -- Prov. 18:16 -- comes in the distant wake of a problem presented by the information of Lev. 4. Specifically, we find reference to the sacrifice of the young bulls of the high priest, of the community, and of the ruler. The issue then naturally arises, which one comes first? The Mishnah answers that question, at M. Hor. 3:6. Reflection upon that answer generates the observation that the anointed priest comes first, as in Scripture's order, in particular when the offerings are of the same value. But if one offering is more valuable than the other, the more valuable offering takes precedence. Then comes secondary reflection on the fact that a person's gift establishes his rank even if it is on other grounds lower than what he otherwise would attain. No. 1 does not pursue that secondary reflection, but invites it at 1.C. The invocation of Prov. 18:16 then is not on account of Lev. 4 at all. It must follow that Nos. 2-4 would better serve a compilation of materials on Deut. 12:19-20 than the present passage. What follows No. 1 serves a purpose in no way closely connected either to the sense or to the syntax of our passage. The entire complex, Nos. 2-4, occurs at Y. Hor. 3:4. It is lifted whole, attached because of the obvious relevance to No. 1. We find no pretense, then, that these stories relate in any way to Lev. 4.

For the story teller at No. 2, the climax comes at L-M, the sages' recognition that their placing of Abba Yudan at the head of the list had made possible the serendipitous accident. Nos. 3 and 4 omit the miraculous aspect entirely.

V:V

1. A. Reverting to the base-text (GWPH): "If it is the anointed priest who sins" (Lev. 4:3).

B. This refers to Shebna.

2. A. "[Thus says the Lord, God of hosts,] 'Come, go to this steward (SKN), to Shebna, who is over the household, [and say to him, 'What have you to do here and whom have you here, that you have hewn here a tomb for yourself, you who hew a tomb on the height and carve a habitation for yourself in the rock? Behold, the Lord will hurl you away violently, O you strong young man! He will seize firm hold on you, and whirl you round and round and throw you like a ball into a wide land; there you shall die, and there shall be your splendid chariots, you shame of your master's house. I will thrust

you from your office and you will be cast down from your station]" (Is. 22:15-19).

B.   R. Eliezer said, "He was a high priest."

C.   R. Judah b. Rabbi said, "He was steward."

D.   In the view of R. Eliezer, who said he was a high priest, [we may bring evidence from Scripture,] for it is written, "And I will clothe him with your robe [and will bind your girdle on him and will commit your authority into his hand]" (Is. 22:21).

E.   In the view of R. Judah b. Rabbi, who said he was steward, [we may bring evidence from Scripture,] for it is written, "And I will commit your authority to his hand" (Is. 22:21).

F.   R. Berekiah said, "What is a 'steward' (SWKN)? It is one who comes from Sikhni.

3.   A.   And he went up and was appointed komes opsarion [the Greek for chief cook] in Jerusalem.

B.   That is in line with the prophet's condemnation, saying to him, "What have you to do here, and whom have you here" (Is. 22:16).

C.   "You exile, son of an exile! What wall have you built here, what pillar have you put up here, and what nail have you hammered in here?!"

D.   R. Eleazar said, "A person has to have a nail or a peg firmly set in a synagogue so as to have the right to be buried in that place [in which he is living]."

E.   "And have you hewn here a tomb for yourself?" (Is. 22:16). He made himself a kind of a dovecot and put his tomb on top of it.

F.   "You who hew a tomb on the height" (Is. 22:16) --

G.   R. Ishmael in the name of Mar Uqba, "On the height the decree was hewn out concerning him, indicating that he should not have a burial place in the land of Israel."

H.   "You who carve a habitation for yourself in the rock" (Is. 22:16) -- a stone coffin.

I.   "Behold, the Lord will hurl you away violently" (Is. 22:17) -- one rejection after another.

J.   "...hurl away violently (GBR)" -- [since the word GBR also means cock:] said R. Samuel b. R. Nahman, "[In Aramaic:], it may be compared to a cock which is driven and goes from place to place."

K.   "He will seize a firm hold on you" (Is. 22:17), [since the words for "firm hold" may also be translated, "wrap around," thus: "And he will wrap you around"] the meaning is that he was smitten with sara^{c}at, in line with that which you find in Scripture, "And he will wrap his lip around" (Lev. 13:45).

L.   "And whirl you round and round [and throw you like a ball]" (Is. 22:18) -- exile after exile.

M. "Like a ball" -- just as a ball is caught from hand to hand and does not fall to the ground, so [will it be for him].

N. "Into a wide land" -- this means Casiphia (Ezra 8:17).

O. "There you shall die and there shall be your splendid chariots" (Is. 22:18) --

4. A. In accord with the position of R. Eliezer, who said that Shebna had been a high priest, [the reference to the splendid chariots implies] that he had been deriving personal benefit from the offerings.

B. In accord with the view of R. Judah b. Rabbi, who said that he had been steward, [the reference to the splendid chariots implies] that he had derived personal benefit from things that had been consecrated for use in the upkeep of the sanctuary.

C. "You shame of your master's house" (Is. 22:18).

D. In accord with the position of R. Eliezer, who said that Shebna had been a high priest, [the shame was] that he had treated the offerings in a disgraceful way.

E. In accord with the view of R. Judah b. Rabbi, who said that he had been steward, [the shame was] that he had treated both of his masters disgracefully, that is Hezekiah, on the one side, Isaiah on the other.

5. A. R. Berekhiah in the name of R. Abba b. R. Kahana: "What did Shebna and Joahaz [2 Kngs. 18:18] do? They wrote a message and attached it to an arrow and shot it to Sennacherib through the window. In the message was written the following: "We and everyone in Jerusalem want you, but Hezekiah and Isaiah don't want you."

B. Now this is just what David had said [would happen]: "For lo, the wicked bend the bow, they have fitted their arrow to the string" (Ps. 11:2).

C. "For lo, the wicked bend the bow" -- this refers to Shebna and Joahaz.

D. "They have fitted their arrow to the string" -- on the bowstring.

E. "To shoot in the dark at the upright in heart" (Ps. 11:2) -- at two upright in heart, Hezekiah and Isaiah.

What the exegete contributes to the explanation of Lev. 4:3 is simply the example of how an anointed priest may sin. The rest of the passage is a systematic exposition of the verses about Shebna. But the entire matter of Shebna belongs here only within Eliezer's opinion that he was a high priest. That is a rather remote connection to the present passage of Leviticus. So because of the allegation that Shebna was high priest, the entire passage -- fully worked out on its own -- was inserted here. The redactor then appeals to theme, not to content, in drawing together the cited verses of Leviticus and Isaiah. Nos.

2, 4 are continuous with one another. No. 3 inserts a systematic, phrase by phrase exegesis of Is. 22:15ff. No. 5 then complements the foregoing with yet further relevant material. So the construction, apart from No. 1, is cogent and well-conceived. Only linkage to Lev. 4:3 is farfetched.

V:VI

1. A. "If it is the anointed priest who sins" (Lev. 4:3).

   B. [What follows occurs at T. Hor. 2:4, explaining M. Hor. 3:4, cited above at V:IV.1.E:] [If] the anointed high priest must atone [for a sin] and the community [SBWR for SRYK] must be atoned for [in line with Lev. 4:13], it is better that the one who [has the power to] make atonement take precedence over the one for whom atonement is made,

   C. as it is written, "And he will atone for himself and for his house" (Lev. 16:17).

   D. ["His house"] refers to his wife.

2. A. "If it is the anointed priest who sins" (Lev. 4:3) --

   B. Will an anointed priest commit a sin!

   C. Said R. Levi, "Pity the town whose physician has gout [and cannot walk to visit the sick], whose governor has one eye, and whose public defender plays the prosecutor in capital cases."

3. A. "[If it is the anointed priest who sins,] thus bringing guilt (L'SMT) [on the people, then let him offer for the sin which he has committed a young bull...]" (Lev. 4:3).

   B. Said R. Isaac, "It is a case of death (MWT) by burning ('S) [inflicted on one who commits sacrilege by consuming offerings from the altar]"

   C. "The matter may be compared to the keeper of a bear, who ate up the rations of the bear. The king said, 'Since he went and ate up the bear's rations, let the bear eat him.'

   D. "So does the Holy One, blessed be he, say, 'Since Shebna enjoyed benefit from things that had been consecrated to the altar [for burning], let fire consume him.'"

4. A. Said R. Aibu [Y. Ter. 8:3, A.Z. 2:3], "M^{C}SH B: Once there was a butcher in Sepphoris, who fed Israelites carrion and torn-meat. On the eve of the Day of Atonement he went out drinking and got drunk. He climbed up to the roof of his house and fell off and died. The dogs began to lick him.

   B. "[In Aramaic:] They came and asked R. Hanina the law about moving his corpse away from the dogs [on the Day of Atonement].

   C. "He said to him, "'You will be holy people to me, therefore you shall not eat any meat that is torn of beasts in the field, you shall cast it to the dogs" (Ex. 22:30).

D.   "'This man robbed from the dogs and fed carrion and torn-meat to
     Israelites. Leave him to them. They are eating what belongs to
     them.'"

5.   A.   "He shall bring the bull to the door of the tent of meeting before
          the Lord, [and lay his hand on the head of the bull and kill the bull
          before the Lord]" (Lev. 4:4).

     B.   Said R. Isaac, "The matter may be compared to the case of a king,
          one of whose admirers paid him honor by giving him a handsome
          gift and by offering him lovely words of praise. The king then said,
          'Set this gift at the gate of the palace, so that everyone who comes
          and goes may see [and admire] it,'

     C.   "as it is said, 'And he shall bring the bull [to the door of the tent of
          meeting]'"

The opening units, Nos. 1-4, form a kind of appendix of miscellanies to what has
gone before. No. 1 reaches back to V:IV, explaining the passage of the Mishnah cited
there. No. 2 is joined to No. 3, which relates to the cited passage to Shebna. So Nos. 2-3
complete the discussion of V:V. It seems to me that No. 4 is attached to No. 3 as an
illustration of the case of a public official who abuses his responsibility.

No. 5 provides a fresh point, moving on to a new verse. There is no intersecting
verse; the exegesis is accomplished solely through a parable.

V:VII

1.   A.   "[If the whole congregation of Israel commits a sin unwittingly and
          the thing is hidden from the eyes of the assembly, and they do any
          one of the things which the Lord has commanded not to be done
          and are guilty, when the sin which they have committed becomes
          known, the assembly shall offer a young bull for a sin-offering and
          bring it before the tent of meeting;] and the elders of the
          congregation shall lay their hands [upon the head of the bull before
          the Lord]" (Lev. 4:13-15).

     B.   [Since, in laying their hands (SMK) on the head of the bull, the
          elders sustain (SMK) the community by adding to it the merit they
          enjoy,] said R. Isaac, "The nations of the world have none to sustain
          them, for it is written, 'And those who sustain Egypt will fall' (Ez.
          30:6).

     C.   "But Israel has those who sustain it, as it is written: 'And the
          elders of the congregation shall lay their hands [and so sustain
          Israel] (Lev. 4:15).'"

2.   A.   Said R. Eleazar, "The nations of the world are called a congre-
          gation, and Israel is called a congregation.

     B.   "The nations of the world are called a congregation: 'For the
          congregation of the godless shall be desolate' (Job 15:34).

C. "And Israel is called a congregation: 'And the elders of the congregation shall lay their hands' (Lev. 4:15).

D. "The nations of the world are called sturdy bulls and Israel is called sturdy bulls.

E. "The nations of the world are called sturdy bulls: 'The congregation of [sturdy] bulls with the calves of the peoples' (Ps. 68:31).

F. "Israel is called sturdy bulls, as it is said, 'Listen to me, you sturdy [bullish] of heart' (Is. 46:13).

G. "The nations of the world are called excellent, and Israel is called excellent.

H. "The nations of the world are called excellent: 'You and the daughters of excellent nations' (Ex. 32:18).

I. "Israel is called excellent: 'They are the excellent, in whom is all my delight' (Ps. 16:4).

J. "The nations of the world are called sages, and Israel is called sages.

K. "The nations of the world are called sages: 'And I shall wipe out sages from Edom' (Ob. 1:8).

L. "And Israel is called sages: 'Sages store up knowledge' (Prov. 10:14).

M. "The nations of the world are called unblemished, and Israel is called unblemished.

N. "The nations of the world are called unblemished: 'Unblemished as are those that go down to the pit' (Prov. 1:12).

O. "And Israel is called unblemished: 'The unblemished will inherit goodness' (Prov. 28:10).

P. "The nations of the world are called men, and Israel is called men.

Q. "The nations of the world are called men: 'And you men who work iniquity' (Ps. 141:4).

R. "And Israel is called men: 'To you who are men I call' (Prov. 8:4).

S. "The nations of the world are called righteous, and Israel is called righteous.

T. "The nations of the world are called righteous: 'And righteous men shall judge them' (Ez. 23:45).

U. "And Israel is called righteous: 'And your people -- all of them are righteous' (Is. 60:21).

V. "The nations of the world are called mighty, and Israel is called mighty.

W. "The nations of the world are called mighty: 'Why do you boast of evil, O mighty man' (Ps. 52:3).

X. "And Israel is called mighty: 'Mighty in power, those who do his word' (Ps. 103:20).

We see two distinct types of exegeses, one to which the base-passage is central, the other to which it is peripheral. Yet the two passages belong together, and we have every reason to suppose that they were made up as a single cogent statement. No. 1 focuses upon the double meaning of the word SMK, one, lay hands, the other, sustain, drawing the contrast stated by Isaac. Once such a contrast is drawn, a catalogue of eight further contrasts will be laid out. Since the opening set, 2.A-B, depends upon the passage at hand, we must accept the possibility that Eleazar's statement has been constructed to work its way through the contrast established by Isaac. For both authorities make the same point. Even though the nations of the word are subject to the same language as is applied to Israel, they still do not fall into the same classification. For language is dual. When a word applies to Israel, it serves to praise, and when the same word applies to the nations, it underlines their negative character. Both are called congregation, but the nations' congregation is desolate, and so throughout, as the context of the passage cited concerning the nations repeatedly indicates. The nations' sages are wiped out; the unblemished nations go down to the pit; the nations, called men, only work iniquity. Now that is precisely the contrast drawn in Isaac's saying, so, as I said, the whole should be deemed a masterpiece of unitary composition. Then the two types of exegesis -- direct, peripheral -- turn out to complement one another, each making its own point.

V:VIII

1. A. R. Simeon b. Yohai taught, "How masterful are the Israelites, for they know how to find favor with their creator."

   B. Said R. Yudan, [in Aramaic:] "It is like the case of Samaritan [beggars]. The Samaritan [beggars] are clever at beginning. One of them goes to a housewife, saying to her, 'Do you have an onion? Give it to me.' After she gives it to him, he says to her, 'Is there such a thing as an onion without bread?' After she gives him [bread], he says to her, 'Is there such a thing as food without drink?' So, all in all, he gets to eat and drink."

   C. Said R. Aha [in Aramaic:] "There is a woman who knows how to borrow things, and there is a woman who does not. The one who knows how to borrow goes over to her neighbor. The door is open, but she knocks [anyhow]. Then she says to her neighbor, 'Greetings, good neighbor. How're you doing? How's your husband doing? How're your kids doing? Can I come in? [By the way], would you have such-and-such a utensil? Would you lend it to me? [The neighboring housewife] says to her, 'Yes, of course.'

   D. "But the one who does not know how to borrow goes over to her neighbor. The door is closed, so she just opens it. She says [to the neighboring housewife], 'Do you have such-and-such a utensil? Would you lend it to me?' [The neighboring housewife] says to her, 'No.'"

E. Said R. Hunia [in Aramaic:], "There is a tenant-farmer who knows
how to borrow things, and there is a tenant-farmer who does not
know how to borrow. The one who knows how to borrow combs his
hair, brushes off his clothes, puts on a good face, and then goes
over to the overseer of his work to borrow from him. [The
overseer] says to him, 'How's the land doing?' He says to him,
'May you have the merit of being fully satisfied with its [wonder-
ful] produce.' 'How are the oxen doing?' He says to him, 'May you
have the merit of being fully satisfied with their fat.' 'How are
the goats doing?' 'May you have the merit of being fully satisfied
with their young.' 'And what would you like?' Then he says, 'Now
if you might have an extra ten _denars_, would you give them to
me?' The overseer replies, 'If you want, take twenty.'

F. "But the one who does not know how to borrow leaves his hair a
mess, his clothes filthy, his face gloomy. He too goes over to the
overseer to borrow from him. The overseer says to him, 'How's the
land doing?' He replies, 'I hope it will produce at least what [in
seed] we put into it.' 'How are the oxen doing?' 'They're
scrawny.' 'How are the goats doing?' 'They're scrawny too.' 'And
what do you want?' 'Now if you might have an extra ten _denars_,
would you give them to me?' The overseer replies, 'Go, pay me
back what you already owe me!'"

G. Said R. Hunia, "David was one of the good tenant-farmers. To
begin with, he starts a psalm with praise [of God], saying, 'The
heavens declare the glory of God, and the firmament shows his
handiwork' (Ps. 19:2). The Heaven says to him, 'Perhaps you need
something?' 'The firmament shows his handiwork.' The firmament
says to him, 'Perhaps you need something?'

H. "And so he would continue to sing: 'Day unto day utters speech,
and night to night reveals knowledge' (Ps. 19:3).

I. "Said to him the Holy One, blessed be he, 'What do you want?'

J. "He said before him, 'Who can discern errors?' (Ps. 19:13).

K. "'What sort of unwitting sin have I done before you!'

L. "[God] said to him, 'Lo, this one is remitted, and that one is
forgiven you.'

M. "'And cleanse me of hidden sins' (Ps. 19:13). '...from the secret
sins that I have done before you.'

N. "He said to him, 'Lo, this one is remitted, and that one is forgiven
to you.'

O. "'Keep back your servant also from deliberate ones.' This refers to
transgressions done in full knowledge.

P.   "'That they may not have dominion over me. Then I shall be faultless' (Ps. 19:14). This refers to the most powerful of transgressions.

Q.   "'And I shall be clear of great transgression' (Ps. 19:14)."

R.   Said R. Levi, "David said before the Holy One, blessed be he, 'Lord of the age[s], you are a great God, and, as for me, my sins are great too. It will take a great God to remit and forgive great sins: "For your name's sake, O Lord, pardon my sin, for [your name] is great" (Ps. 25:11).'"

Once more the construction appears from beginning to end to aim at a single goal. The opening statement, 1.A, makes the point, and the closing construction, Gff., illustrates it. In the middle come three apt narratives serving as similes, all told in Aramaic, and all following exactly the same pattern. Then the systematic account of a passage of Scripture is provided to make exactly the same point. I cannot state the exact sense of the passage on the heaven and the firmament, G, but from that point, the discourse is pellucid. Q-R should be separated from G-P, since what Levi's statement does is simply augment the primary passage. The unity of theme and conception accounts for the drawing together of the entire lot. To be sure, B-F can serve other purposes. But since Hunia's statement, E-F, introduces his exegesis of Ps. 19, the greater likelihood is that a single hand has produced the entire matter (possibly excluding Q-R) to make a single point. Why has the redactor thought the passage appropriate here? The offering for unwitting sin of Lev. 4, to which K makes reference in the progression through the types of sins, from minor to major, for which David seeks forgiveness, certainly accounts for the inclusion of the whole. Then whoever made up the passage did not find the stimulus in Lev. 4. For the rather general observation of 1.A states the framer's message. That message pertains to diverse contexts, as the exposition of Ps. 19 makes clear; nothing would compel someone to make up a passage of this sort to serve Lev. 4 in particular.

Let us now turn to the classification of the units of discourse of which the parashah is composed. What we want to know is the structure of the parashah as a whole, where its largest subunits of thought begin and end and how they relate to one another. How shall we recognize a complete unit of thought? It will be marked off by the satisfactory resolution of a tension or problem introduced at the outset. A complete unit of thought may be made up of a number of subdivisions, many of them entirely spelled out on their own. But the composition of a complete unit of thought always will strike us as cogent, the work of a single conception on how a whole thought should be constructed and expressed. While that unitary conception drew upon already available materials, the main point is made by the composition as a whole, and not by any of its (ready-made) parts.

In the first classification we take up the single most striking recurrent literary structure of Leviticus Rabbah. It is what we may call the base-verse/intersecting-verse construction. In such a construction, a base-verse, drawn from the book of Leviticus, is juxtaposed to an intersecting-verse, drawn from any book other than a pentateuchal one. Then this intersecting-verse is subjected to systematic exegesis. On the surface the exegesis is out of all relationship with the base-verse. But in a stunning climax, all of the exegeses of the intersecting-verse are shown to relate to the main point the exegete wishes to make about the base-verse. What that means is that the composition as a whole is so conceived as to impose meaning and order on all of the parts, original or ready-made parts, of which the author of the whole has made use. For the one example in Parashah 5, the base-verse is Lev. 4:3 and the intersecting-verse Job 34:29-30. Here is the outline of the first three subdivisions of the parashah.

V:I.1.C-F	Lev. 4:3, Job 34:29-30 and the generation of the flood
V:I.2.A-C	Lev. 4:3, Job 34:29-30 and the generation of the flood
V:I.2.E-G	Lev. 4:3, Job 34:29-30 and the generation of the flood
V:I.3.A	Lev. 4:3, Job 34:29-30 and the generation of the flood
V:I.3.B-D	Job 21:11
V:I.4	Job 21:11
V:I.5.A-B	Generation of the flood
V:I.5.C-F	Ma^{c}aseh
V:I.6.A-E	Job 34:29-30, Gen. 7:23. Relevance: Reference to God's hiding his face.
V:I.7.A-C	Job 34:29. Refers to Noah.
V:II.1	Job 34:29. Refers to Sodomites. First comes tranquility, then punishment. Job 28:7
V:II.2	Further exegesis of Job 28:7.
V:II.3	God hid his face from Sodomites (Job 34:29) and then punished them (Gen. 19:24).
V:III.1	Job 34:29. Refers to Ten Tribes, first tranquility, then punishment. Amos 6:1.
V:III.2	Further comment on Amos 6:1
V:III.3	Further comment on Amos 6:2
V:III.4	Amos 6:3
V:III.5	Amos 6:4
V:III.6	Amos 6:5
V:III.7	Amos 6:6
V:III.8	Amos 6:6
V:III.9	Amos 6:6, 7. All of the units on Amos simply comment on clauses of verses.
V.III.10	Job 34:29. How God hid his face from the Ten Tribes. Isaiah 36:1.
V:III.11	Isaiah 36:1

V:III.12   Job 34:29. Refers to Sennacherib (Joel 6) and Israel (Ez. 34:31).
V:III.13   Job 34:29 linked to Lev. 4:3-4. God exacts the same penalty
                from an individual or a community, so Job 34:29 and also Lev.
                4:13-14.

As we saw when we followed the text in detail, the composition moves with striking
cogency over its chosen examples: the Generation of the Flood, the Ten Tribes,
Sennacherib and Israel. So three large-scale illustrations of Job 34:29-30 are laid out, and
then the entire composition reverts to Lev. 4:3ff. to make a single point about all that has
gone before.

Another form of the base-verse/intersecting-verse construction is secondary in size
and in exegetical complexity to the one just now surveyed. In this simple version of the
same construction, the base-verse is given a simple exemplification, and then, just as in
the first type, the exegete will assemble passages on that exemplificatory entry. We have
two instances. The first example is V:V. Since Lev. 4:3 refers to the sin of an anointed
priest, the exegete wishes to show us how an anointed priest may sin and so he invokes the
name of Shebna. The rest follows.

V:V.1   Lev. 4:3. Refers to Shebna.
V:V.2   Shebna (Is. 22:15-19)
V:V.3   Shebna (Is. 22:16-18)
V:V.4   Shebna and Joahaz

The second example is somewhat more subtle. Here we have a play on a word used in the
base-verse. Then a whole series of verses will be adduced to make a point based on that
play on words. These proof-texts cannot be called intersecting-verses in the way in
which, in the earlier classification and in the first example of the present one, the cited
verses intersect with, but take over discourse from, the base-verse. Quite to the
contrary, the base-verse generates a point, which then is richly expanded by the cited
verses. Nonetheless, I should regard the present example as a variation on the foregoing.
The reason is that, in a strictly formal sense, the pattern remains what we have seen to
this point: the base-verse, then a set of illustrative verses that make the main point the
exegete wishes to associate with or about the base-verse. But the alternative viewpoint,
that would distinguish the present example and declare it a classification by itself, surely
has merit.

V:VII.1-2   Lev. 4:13-15. Exegesis of the verse, with special attention to a
                word-play. The upshot is that Israel is distinguished from the
                nations. Then a long catalogue of such distinctions is appended.

A third classification derives from the clause-by-clause or exegesis of the
base-verse, with slight interest in intersecting-verses or in illustrative materials deriving
from other books of the Scripture. The base-verse in this classification defines the entire
frame of discourse, either because of its word-choices or because of its main point.

Where verses of other passages are quoted, they serve not as the focus of discourse but only as proof-texts or illustrative-texts. They therefore function in a different way from the verses adduced in discourse in the first two classifications, for, in those former cases, the intersecting-verses form the center of interest. As we see at V:VI, we deal with the subject-matter of Lev. 4:3-4, on the one side, and we also explain the derivation of words used in the cited verse, on the other. These are distinct modes of exegesis -- ideational, philological -- but the difference is slight in determining the classification at hand. It is simply exegesis of verses of Leviticus, item by item. Here are examples of the exegetical type of unit of discourse.

V:VI.1   Lev. 4:3. Precedence in atonement rite.

V:VI.2   Lev. 4:3. How can an anointed priest sin?

V:VI.3   Lev. 4:3. Explanation of a word used in the cited verse and Shebna.

V:VI.4   Lev. 4:3 Illustration.

V:VI.5   Lev. 4:4. Why bring the bull to the tent of meeting as Lev. 4:4 specifies.

The category of miscellanies and how they are joined now demands attention. By a "miscellany," I mean a construction that does not relate to any base-verse in Leviticus 4 or to the cited intersecting-verses; that does not address any theme or principle pertinent to the base-verse or to its larger context; and that appears to have been formed for purposes entirely distinct from the explanation or amplification of a passage of the book of Leviticus. One such example is at V:IV.1-4, at which, as we see, the general theme of Lev. 4:3 -- the sacrifices of several officials, in order -- triggers the inquiry into which offering comes first. But at issue is the principle that whoever sacrifices proportionately more in terms of his means is the one who gets the more credit. That notion is unrelated to Lev. 4:3. The passage is cogent. Here is the outline, which, as we see, deals with Prov. 18:16 and provides anthology of rather coherent materials for that verse.

V:IV.1   God recognizes the value of a gift to the cult, e.g., in accord with the donor's sacrifice. Deut. 12:19, 20; M. Hor. 3:6.

V:IV.2   "A man's gift makes room for him" (Prov. 18:16) and long illustrative story.

V:IV.3   Prov. 18:16

V:IV.4   Prov. 18:16

A second example, drawn from Parashah 5, serves Ps. 19:2-3, 13-14, and the reason for its inclusion with reference to Lev. 4 is not entirely clear.

V:VIII.1   Israel knows how to placate God. The point is joined to Ps. 19:23, 13-14. This construction does not belong to Lev. 4.

We therefore discern three categories of units of discourse, illustrated by generally rather sizable subunits. These are, first, the complex base-verse/intersecting-verse construction; second, the simple base-verse/intersecting-verse construction; and, third, the clause-by-clause exegetical construction. We note, finally, the category of mis-cellanies, always marked by the simple trait of irrelevance to the passage at hand.

Can we discern an order followed by the several types of units of discourse?

1. Complex base-verse/intersecting-verse construction:

    V:I-III

2. Simple base-verse/intersecting-verse construction:

    V:V

    V:VII

3. Clause-by-clause exegetical construction:

    V:VI

4. Miscellanies

    X:IV, VIII

The obvious problem is at V:V-VII. Can we account for the insertion of V:VI between V:V and V:VII? We certainly can. V:VI. 1-4 form an appendix to V:V -- pure and simple. The organizer of the whole had no choice but to insert his appendix behind the materials supplemented by his appendix. The same sort of reasoning then accounts for the insertion of miscellanies, e.g., V:IV after V:I-III. What V:IV does is simply carry forward the problem of which beast comes first when a number of beasts are awaiting offering for the purposes of atonement for various officials. That issue is very important to the author of V:III. So the first of the two cases in which we have miscellanies turns out to exemplify a rather careful mode of arranging materials. Where a major point carries in its wake exemplificatory materials, these will be inserted before the parashah moves on to new matters. There is no difficulty in explaining why the arranger of the whole has placed V:VIII at the end; what we do not know is why, to begin with, he selected that unit of discourse. But that issue need not detain us.

We emerge with two hypotheses, one firm, the other less so.

The first is the hypothesis that the units of discourse are framed in accord with conventions that define and distinguish three recurrent literary structures: (1) complex base-verse/intersecting-verse construction; (2) simple base-verse/intersecting-verse construction; (3) clause-by-clause exegetical construction (invoking a broad range of intersecting-verses only for narrowly-illustrative purposes). We noted, in addition, a category we called "miscellaneous."

The second hypothesis is that the categories of units of discourse also explain the order of arrangement of types of units of discourse. First will come the complex base-verse/intersecting-verse construction; then will come the simple base-verse/in-tersecting-verse construction; finally we shall have clause-by-clause exegetical con-structions. If we were to assign cardinal numbers to these types of constructions I, II, and III, we should also be able to use ordinal numbers, first, second, third. Why? Because in accord with the stated hypothesis, type I will come first, type II second, and type III third.

Readers will find these results parallel to these in my Talmud of the Land of Israel. 35. Introduction. Taxonomy, pp. 1-42.

iii. Leviticus Rabbah Parashiyyot 16 and 25

Having developed two hypotheses out of Parashah 5, let us now proceed to test them through the detailed analysis of two further parashiyyot, reviewed line by line. If the point of entry proves correct, we should be able to show that further parashiyyot divide into exactly the same taxonomic scheme that serves the original one. That fact having been shown for 8% of the whole read line by line (5, 16, 25), we may proceed directly to the classification of the entire composition, the thirty-seven parashiyyot of Leviticus Rabbah. At the same time we may pursue the further inquiry into whether the original hypothesis on the ordering of types of units of discourse -- first, complex base-verse/intersecting-verse construction, second, simple base-verse/intersecting-verse construction, third, sequential exegeses of verses of Leviticus, then miscellanies -- in some substantial measure proves valid.

PARASHAH SIXTEEN

XVI:I

1. A. "This shall be the law of the leper [for the day of his cleansing]" (Lev. 14:2).

    B. "There are six things which the Lord hates, and seven which are an abomination to him: [haughty eyes, a lying tongue, hands that shed innocent blood, a heart that devises wicked plans, feet that make haste to run to do evil, a false witness who breathes out lies, and a man who sows discord among brothers]' (Prov. 6:16-19).

    C. R. Meir and rabbis:

    D. R. Meir said, "Six and seven add up to thirteen."

    E. And rabbis say, "Seven [is the number of abominations]."

    F. How do rabbis interpret the use of "And" ["And seven" (Prov. 6:16)]?

    G. This refers to the seventh on the list [gossiping], which is the worst of the lot.

    H. And which one is it? It is "he who sows discord among brothers."

    I. And what are the others? "Haughty eyes, a lying tongue, hands that shed innocent blood, a heart that devises wicked plans, feet that make haste to run to do evil, a false witness who breathes out lies, and a man who sows discord among brothers" (Prov. 6:17-19).

2. A. Said R. Yohanan, "And all of those who do such things are smitten with leprosy.

    B. "'Haughty eyes' [is shown] by the case of the daughters of Zion, 'Because the daughters of Zion are haughty, and [walk with outstretched necks, glancing wantonly with their eyes, mincing along as they go, tinkling with their feet, the Lord will smite with a scab the heads of the daughters of Zion, and the Lord will lay bare their secret parts]' (Is. 3:16-17)."

C.   "Because the daughters of Zion are haughty" -- because they carry themselves [stiffly as] spears and walk arrogantly.

D.   "And walk with outstretched necks" -- for one of them would put on her jewelry and would stretch her neck forward to show her jewelry.

E.   "Glancing wantonly with their eyes" --

F.   R. Nissi of Caesarea said, "For they would paint their eyes with red paint."

G.   R. Simeon b. Laqish said, "With red collyrium."

H.   "Mincing along as they go" -- When one of them was tall, she would bring two short ones, one to walk on either side of her, so that she would appear to float above them. But if one of them was short, she would wear thick sandals, so that she would look taller.

I.   "Tinkling with their feet" --

J.   R. Abba bar Kahana said, "For she would make the figure of a dragon [with bells] on her slippers."

K.   And rabbis say, "She would bring a chicken bladder and fill it with balsam and put it under the heal of her sandal. When she would see a bunch of boys, she would stamp on it [and would pop], and the odor would go through them like the poison of a snake."

L.   Now the Holy One, blessed be he, said to Jeremiah, "What are such people as these doing here? Let them get up and go into exile from here."

M.   And Jeremiah so would say to them, "Repent, before the enemy comes."

N.   They said to him, "If the enemy comes against us, what can they do to us, who say, 'Let him make haste, let him speed his work, that we may see it; [let the purpose of the Holy One of Israel draw near, and let it come, that we may know it]' (Is. 5:19). A general will see me and take me, a hyparch will see me and take me, a commander will see me and take me and seat me on a chariot.

O.   "'So let the purpose of the Holy One of Israel draw near, and let it come, that we may know it' (Is. 5:19) --

P.   "so that we may know whose [opinion] will be brought to reality, ours or his!"

Q.   Once their sins had proved sufficient cause, and the enemy came, they made themselves up and came out before them like whores.

R.   A general saw one and took her, a hyparch saw one and took her, a commander saw one and took her and seated her on a chariot.

S.   Said the Holy One, blessed be he, "Let their opinion not come true."

T.   What did he do? "The Lord smote (SPH) with a scab the crown of the head of the daughters of Zion" (Is. 3:17).

3. A. R. Eleazar and R. Yose b. R. Haninah.

   B. R. Eleazar said, "He smote them with leprosy.

   C. "That is in line with the following verse of Scripture: 'For a swelling, an eruption (SPHT) or a spot' (Lev. 14:56)."

   D. And R. Yose b. R. Haninah said, "He brought up swarms of lice onto their heads."

   E. R. Hiyya b. R. Abba said, "He made them into slave-women [NSHIM MKUDNOT].

   F. What does MKUDNOT mean? Enslaved women [Aramaii].

4. A. R. Berekhiah and Hilpai b. R. Zebed in the name of R. Isi: "What is the meaning of the word sippah [SPH -- smote with a scab]? To flow, so as to preserve the holy seed, so that the holy seed should not be diluted among the peoples of the earth [cf. Ezra 9:2]."

5. A. Said the Holy One, blessed be he, I know that the nations of the world will not keep away from those who suffer from leprosy."

   B. What did he do?

   C. "The Lord will lay bare their secret parts" (Is. 3:17).

   D. The Holy One, blessed be he, made a gesture at her source, and it produced blood until it filled up the chariot.

   E. And the conqueror speared the woman with his spear and laid her before his chariot, and the chariot rolled over her and split her.

   F. That is what Jeremiah referred to in saying, "Get out! Unclean! Men cried to them, Get out, Get out, Do not touch!" (Lam. 4:15).

   G. R. Reuben said, "The Hebrew word for 'get out,' 'suru,' is the Greek word for sweep, 'siron'" [prob. meaning].

6. A. "A lying tongue" (Prov. 6:17).

   B. The proof [that one who lies is smitten by leprosy derives] from Miriam.

   C. "And Miriam and Aaron spoke against Moses" (Num. 12:1).

   D. And how do we know that she was smitten with leprosy?

   E. As it is said, "And the cloud departed from on the tent" (Num. 12:10).

7. A. "And hands that shed blood" (Prov. 6:17).

   B. [We learn that God hates such a person] from Joab.

   C. For it is said, "And the Lord will return his blood upon his [Joab's] own head" (1 Kgs. 2:32).

   D. And how do we know that he was smitten with leprosy?

   E. "May it fall upon the head of Joab, [and upon all his father's house, and may the house of Joab never be without one who has a discharge or who is leprous or who holds a spindle or who is slain by the sword or who lacks bread]" (2 Sam. 3:29).

8. A. "A heart that devises wicked plans" (Prov. 6:18).

B.   [We know that God hates such a one] from the case of Uzziah, who planned to humiliate the high priesthood.

C.   And how do we know that he was smitten with leprosy?

D.   As it is said, "And the Lord smote the king, and he became a leper" (2 Kgs. 15:5).

9.   A.   "Feet that make haste to run to do evil" (Prov. 6:17).

B.   [We learn that this is one God despises] from the case of Gehazi, for it is said, "Gehazi, the servant of Elisha the man of God, said, 'See, my master has spared this Naaman the Syrian, in not accepting [from his hand what he brought. As the Lord lives, I will run after him and get something from him'" (2 Kgs. 5:20).

C.   And how do we know that he was smitten with leprosy?

D.   "Therefore the leprosy of Naaman shall cleave to you [and to your descendants forever. So he went out from his presence a leper, as white as snow]' (2 Kgs. 5:27).

10. A.   "A false witness who breathes out lies" (Prov. 6:19).

B.   [We know that God hates this from the case] of Israel, who gave false testimony by saying to the calf, "This is your God, O Israel" (Ex. 32:4).

C.   And how do we know that they were smitten with leprosy?

D.   As it is said, "And Moses saw the people, that it had broken out, for Aaron had made it break out" (Ex. 32:25).

E.   What is the meaning of "breaking out"?

F.   R. Yohanan said, "This teaches that an epidemic of leprosy and discharge broke out among them.

G.   "That is in line with the following verse of Scripture [referring to the leper]: 'And his head will be broken out' (Lev. 13:45)."

11. A.   "And a man who sows discord among brothers" (Prov. 6:19).

B.   [The precedent derives] from Pharoah, who brought discord between Abraham and Sarah.

C.   How do we know that he was smitten with leprosy?

D.   As it is said, "And the Lord smote Pharoah with great leprosy-signs, as well as his house" (Gen. 12:17).

12. A.   Said Rabban Simeon b. Gamaliel, "Once I was walking from Tiberias to Sepphoris. An old man came my way and said to me, 'My lord, there are twenty-four different kinds of skin disease, and only for ratan [a kind of leprosy] is sexual relations bad.'"

B.   Said R. Pedat, "And that was what hit the wicked Pharoah."

13. A.   Therefore Moses warned Israel and said to them, "'This is the law of the leper (mesora)' -- the law of the gossip (mosi ra)" (Lev. 14:2).

The theme of leprosy, rather than the specific formulations of the base-text, defines the organizing principle and explains -- right up front -- the selection of the intersecting verse. It would be difficult to point to a tighter or more carefully composed construction, since Yohanan, 2.A, tells us the purpose of the exegesis and how it will work. With his guidance, we see the outlines of the basic formulation, readily picking out materials added for amplification or clarification. (Would that we could so simply account for the choice of every intersecting verse!) Since the "sowing of discord among brothers" involves gossip, moreover, the selection is not only for formal and external reasons. The intersecting verse itself contains indications of its pertinence to the theme at hand. The absence, then, of a base-verse in the formal sense in no way impedes the substantive or aesthetic success of the whole.

It seems to me that 1.C-H are secondary and needless. Then we move from the intersecting verse directly to No. 2, that is, Yohanan's explicit linking of the interesecting verse to the base-theme. But, as we soon see, the theme, leprosy, merges with the language of the base-verse, for _mesora_, leper, is linked to _mosi ra_. Then the bulk of the exemplificatory materials deal with people who sin by things that they say. Whether or not we assign 2.B to Yohanan, the rest of No. 2 cannot be his. So the explication of the whole is the work of the compositor, who has collected or made up the clause-by-clause amplifications of the intersecting verse. When we reach the end of No. 2, we find inserted materials on Is. 3:17, Nos. 3, 4. No. 5 then completes the matter. Nos. 6-11 (the last supplemented by No. 12) then systematically work through the remainder of the intersecting verse, following a very well disciplined pattern. No. 13 signs off with a formulaic exegesis, essentially ignoring all that has gone before.

XVI:II

1. A.   "Who is the man who desires life [and covets many days, that he may enjoy good? Keep your tongue from evil and your lips from speaking deceit]" (Prov. 34:12-13).

    B.   There was the case of a peddlar who was making his rounds in the villages near Sepphoris, proclaiming, "Who wants to buy the elixir of life! Come and buy."

    C.   He came into the village of Akhbara, near the home of R. Yannai, who was in session, studying in his chamber. [Yannai] heard him shouting, "Who wants to buy the elixir of life? Come and buy!"

    D.   R. Yannai looked out at him and said, "Come up here and sell to me."

    E.   He said to him, "You don't need it, neither you nor people like you."

    F.   [Yannai] urged him nonetheless and he came up to him. [The peddlar] took out a scroll of the Psalms and showed him the verse, "'Who is the man who desires life, and covets many days that he may enjoy good?'

G. "What is written after that verse? 'Keep your tongue from evil and your lips from speaking deceit. Depart from evil and do good, seek peace and pursue it' (Ps. 34:13-14)."

H. Said R. Yannai to him, "For my whole life I have been reading this verse of Scripture, but I did not know how to explain it, until this peddlar came and told me."

2. A. "Who is the man who wants life?" (Ps. 34:12).

B. Said R. Haggai, "So too did Solomon announce: 'Who keeps his mouth and his tongue keeps his soul from troubles (MSRWT)' (Prov. 21:23). [That is,] he keeps his soul from leprosy (MSR^{C}T)."

3. A. Therefore Moses admonished Israel, saying to them, "This is the law of the leper" (Lev. 14:2) -- the law of the gossip."

The relevance of the verse, No. 1, once more proves thematic, rather than linguistic. The tale works out the relevance of the intersecting verse, which is then underlined at No. 3. No. 2 provides a still better intersecting verse than No. 1, since now there is a clear point of intersection of language, not only theme.

XVI:III

1. A. "Though his height mount up to the heavens [and his head reach to the clouds, he will perish forever like his own dung; those who have seen him will say, Where is he?]" (Job 20:6-7).

B. "Though his height mount up to the heavens" -- the word for "height" means "on high."

C. "And his head reach to the cloud" -- to the cloud [in Aramaic].

D. "He will perish forever like his own dung" --

E. Just as shit stinks, so he stinks.

F. "Those who have seen him will say, 'Where is he?'" --

G. They will see him but not recognize him.

H. For so it is written in regard to the friends of Job: "They raised their eyes up at a distance but they did not recognize him" (Job 2:12).

2. A. R. Yohanan and R. Simeon b. Laqish:

B. R. Yohanan said, "It is forbidden to walk to the east side of a mesora closer than four cubits."

C. And R. Simeon said, "Closer than a hundred cubits."

D. But they do not really differ.

E. The one who has said that one may come no closer than four cubits speaks of a time at which the wind is not blowing.

F. And the one who has said that one may come no closer than a hundred cubits speaks of a time at which the wind is blowing.

         G.   Even at a distance of a hundred cubits [under such conditions] it is forbidden to go.

3.   A.   R. Meir would not eat an egg from the lepers' alley.

         B.   R. Ammi and R. Assi would not go into the lepers' alley.

         C.   R. Simeon b. Laqish, when he saw one of them in the town, would throw stones at him, saying to him, "Go home. Don't dirty up the other people."

         D.   R. Hiyya taught: "'He will dwell by himself' (Lev. 13:46). He will dwell alone."

         E.   R. Eleazar b. R. Simon, when he would see one of them, would hide himself from him, on account of what is written concerning him.

4.   A.   "This is the law of the leper" (Lev. 14:2) -- the law of the gossip.

My best guess on why the intersecting verse is taken to speak of a leper derives from Job 20:12, "Though wickedness is sweet in his mouth and though he hides it under his tongue..." Perhaps that statement made the exegetes see the entire passage as referring to the person who gossips, hence the leper. The systematic exegesis of the verse explains its components and assumes that each refers to the leper. Nos. 2, 3 then amplify the idea that the leper is to be avoided, disappears, and is no more seen. No. 4 then adds the expected formal link.

XVI:IV

1.   A.   "But to the wicked God says, 'What right have you to recite my statutes [or take my covenant on your lips? For you hate discipline and you cast my words behind you. If you see a thief, you are a friend of his, and you keep company with adulterers]" (Ps. 50:16-18).

         B.   Ben Azzai was in session and expounding, and the fire licked round about him.

         C.   They came and told R. Aqiba, "Ben Azzai is in session and expounding, and the fire is licking round about him."

         D.   He came to him and said, "Are you dealing with the innermost chambers of the Chariot-vision?"

         E.   He said to him, "No. I am only stringing together a chain of verses of the Torah to those of the Prophets, and teachings of the prophets to those of the Writings, and on that account, the teachings of the Torah are rejoicing as on the very day on which they were given from Sinai.

         F.   "For was not the very essence of the giving of the words of Torah from Sinai done through fire?

         G.   "That is in line with the verse: 'And the mount was burning with fire, up to the very heart of heaven' (Deut. 4:11)."

2. A. Said R. Levi, "We find in the Torah, the Prophets, and the Writings, that the Holy One, blessed be he, takes no delight whatsoever in praise coming from a wicked person.

    B. "Whence that proof in the Torah? 'And the leper... shall cover his upper lip [and shall cry, Unclean, unclean]' (Lev. 13:45).

    C. "Whence that proof in the Prophets? '[Now the king was talking with Gehazi, the servant of the man of God, saying, Tell me all the great things that Elisha has done. (But Gehazi, who was wicked, did not get to speak of God's miracle, done through Elisha, for)] while he was telling the king how Elisha had restored the dead to life, [behold, the woman whose son he had restored to life appealed to the king for her house and her land. And Gehazi said, My lord, O King, here is the woman, and here is her son whom Elisha restored to life]' (2 Kgs. 8:4-5)."

    D. Now is it possible that she was standing behind the door?

    E. Rabbis said, "Even if she had been located at the other end of the world, the Holy One, blessed be he, would have flown her and brought her so that that wicked man would not get the chance to report the wonders done by the Holy One, blessed be he."

    F. [Levi continues:] "In the case of the Writings, whence?

    G. "'But to the wicked, God says, What right have you to recite my statutes' (Ps. 50:16)."

3. A. R. Eleazar in the name of R. Yose b. Zimra: "A human body has two hundred forty-eight limbs, some of them bent, some of them standing up.

    B. "The tongue is located between the two cheeks, and a watercourse is located underneath it, arranged in any number of folds.

    C. "Come and see how many fires it has caused!

    D. "Now if it were upright and standing, how much the more so!"

4. A. Therefore Moses admonished Israel, saying to them, "This is the law of the leper" (Lev. 14:2) -- the law of the gossip.

So far as I can see, the point of the introductory tale, about Ben Azzai, is simply that a particularly exemplary mode, now illustrated, of exegesis is to string together verses of Torah, Prophets, and Writings that say the same thing or illustrate the same point. No. 2 then makes its own point, 2.A. For that purpose, Lev. 13:45 and Ps. 50:16 serve as part of a construction with its own interests. Accordingly, we do not have a composition based upon an intersecting and base-verse (or even theme). No. 3 is thematically relevant to the present topic. No. 4 is merely conventional.

XVI:V

1. A. "Let not your mouth lead your flesh into sin" (Qoh. 5:5).

B.   R. Joshua b. Levi applied the verse to speak of those who promise in public to give charity and then fail to do so:

C.   "Let not your mouth lead your flesh into sin" -- Do not give the power to one of your limbs to lead all of your limbs into sin. "Your mouth will lead your entire body into sin."

D.   "'And do not say before the messenger [that it was a mistake; why should God be angry at your voice and destroy the work of your hands?]' (Qoh. 5:5).

E.   "The messenger is the leader of the community [who collects charity funds].

F.   "'That it was an error.' 'I made a pledge but I did not make a pledge.'

G.   "'Why should God be angry at your voice' -- at that very voice that made a pledge but did not pay it up.

H.   "'And destroy the work of your hands.' Even the little property that you have, you will bring into disarray."

2.   A.   R. Benjamin interpreted the verse to speak of those who misinterpret the Torah:

B.   "'Let your mouth not lead your flesh into sin' --

C.   "Do not give the power to one of your limbs to lead all of your limbs into sin. Your mouth will lead your entire body into sin.

D.   "'Do not say before the messenger' -- this [refers to] the master.

E.   "'That it was a mistake.' He pretended that he had studied Scripture, but he had never studied; [he pretended he] had repeated Mishnah-traditions but had never repeated them.

F.   "'Why should God be angry at your voice?'

G.   "At that very voice that misinterpreted the words of Torah [by pretending to know things that the person really did not know].

H.   "'And destroy the work of your hands' -- Even the few tractates that you actually do know, you bring into disarray."

3.   A.   R. Hananiah interpreted the verse to speak of those who gossip.

B.   "'Do not let your mouth lead your flesh into sin' -- Do not give the power to one of your limbs to lead all of your limbs into sin. Your mouth will lead your entire body into sin.

C.   "'Do not say before the messenger' -- this [refers to] the messenger who oversees the body.

D.   "'That it was a mistake.' 'I gossiped and yet I did not gossip.'

E.   "'Why should God be angry at your voice?'

F.   "At that very voice that expressed gossip.

G.   "'And destroy the work of your hands' -- even the few limbs that you have in your body you will bring into disarray [through leprosy]."

4. A. R. Mani interpreted the verse to speak of vowing:

B. "'Do not let your mouth lead your flesh into sin' -- Do not give the power to one of your limbs to lead all of your limbs into sin. Your mouth will lead your entire body into sin.

C. "'Do not say before the messenger' -- this [refers to] the elder [who has the power to examine the vow and release it].

D. "'That was an error.' 'I vowed but I did not vow.'

E. "'Why should God be angry at your voice?' -- at that very voice that took a vow but did not pay it.

F. "'And destroy the work of your hands' -- even those few religious duties that you have to your credit you bring into disarray."

5. A. Rabbis for their part interpret the verse to speak of Miriam:

B. "'Let not your mouth lead your flesh into sin' --

C. "Do not give the power to one of your limbs to lead all of your limbs into sin. Your mouth will lead your entire body into sin.

D. "'Do not say before the messenger' -- [this refers] to Moses.

E. ("That is in line with the following verse of Scripture: 'And he sent forth a messenger and took us out of Egypt' (Num. 20:16).)

F. "'That it was an error.' 'For we have done foolishly and we have sinned' (Num. 12:11).

G. "'Why should God be angry at your voice?' At that voice: 'And the Lord was angry at them and he departed' (Num. 12:9).

H. "'And destroy the work of your hands.'"

I. Said R. Yohanan, "Miriam sinned with her mouth, but all the rest of her limbs [also] were smitten.

J. "That is in line with the following verse of Scripture: 'And when the cloud removed from over the tent, behold, Miriam was leprous, as white as snow' (Num. 12:10)."

6. A. Said R. Joshua b. Levi, "A word is worth a penny, but silence is worth two."

B. For we have learned [in M. Abot 1:17]: Simeon, his son, says, "All my days I have grown up among the sages, and I have found no virtue for the body better than silence. Not interpretation is the main thing, but deed, and whoever talks too much brings sin."

The intersecting verse is thoroughly explained in terms of five different theories, Nos. 1-5, about which sorts of people sin by speaking in some way or another. These are, first, promising to give charity and failing to do so; pretending to know the Torah but not knowing it; gossiping; vowing; Miriam in particular. No. 6 tacks on some miscellanies about not talking too much. The pattern imposed on the several exegeses is blatant. The relevance to the larger context of <u>Parashah</u> Sixteen is self-evident at Nos. 3 and 5. The construction has been organized to allow for a climax at one relevant point, the figure of

Miriam. It would have been better had the framer put gossiping at No. 4. The formal character of the exegeses is shown in the repeated formulas, e.g., for "Let not your mouth lead your flesh into sin." The formative work lay in selecting pertinent themes for the exemplification of the intersecting verse. What was said about those themes was essentially a matter of repeating a convention.

XVI:VI

1. A. Said R. Joshua b. Levi, "The word 'torah' [law] occurs with regard to the leper on five different occasions:

    B. "'This is the Torah governing a spot of leprosy' (Lev. 13:59).

    C. "'This is the Torah governing him on whom is a spot of leprosy' (Lev. 14:32).

    D. "'This is the Torah governing every spot of leprosy and itch' (Lev. 14:54).

    E. "'This is the Torah governing leprosy' (Lev. 14:57).

    F. "And the encompassing reference: 'This will be the Torah governing the leper' (Lev. 14:2) -- the Torah governing the common gossip.

    G. "This teaches you that whoever repeats gossip violates all five scrolls of the Torah."

2. A. Therefore Moses admonished the Israelites, saying to them, "This will be the Torah governing the leper (mesora)" (Lev. 14:2) -- the Torah governing the gossip.

No. 1 systematically surveys the pertinent verses to make its point. No. 2 repeats the conventional conclusion, as out of place here as in all its other points of appearance.

XVI:VII

1. A. "The priest shall command them to take for him who is to be cleansed two living clean birds [and cedarwood and scarlet stuff and hyssop]" (Lev. 14:4).

    B. Said R. Judah b. R. Simon, "Birds chirp a lot. This one who [symbolizes] speaks gossip [who chirps a lot].

    C. "Said the Holy One, blessed be he, 'Let the one with a voice [the bird] come and effect atonement for what the voice [of the gossip has done]'"

2. A. And R. Joshua b. Levi said, "The birds must be free-ranging, [not raised in captivity], [but which nonetheless] have eaten the bread [of the penitent] and drunk of his water.

    B. "Now is there not an argument a fortiori: If birds, who eat of a man's bread and drink of his water, effect atonement for him, a priest, who derives from Israel the benefit of the twenty-four priestly gifts, all the more so [should have the power to effect atonement for Israel]."

C.   In a proverb people say, "He who eats of the heart of the palm will be flogged with the frond of a palm."

No. 1 makes a relevant point. No. 2 is aimed at the validation of the priests' power to effect atonement for Israelites and has no bearing on the present context.

XVI: VIII

1. A.   Said R. Aha, "A person is responsible that ailments should not come upon him."

    B.   This view of R. Aha derives from what R. Aha said [about the following verse of Scripture:] "'And the Lord will remove on your account every ailment' (Deut. 7:15).

    C.   "It is on your account that ailments (not) come upon you."

2. A.   R. Honia and R. Jacob Ephrata in the name of R. Eliasa: "'And the Lord will remove from you every ailment' (Deut. 7:15). This refers to burning."

    B.   R. Jacob b. R. Aha in the name of R. Yohanan: "'And the Lord will remove from you every ailment' (Deut. 7:15) This refers to depressing thoughts."

    C.   And R. Abin said, "This refers to the evil impulse. For in the beginning it is sweet but at the end it is bitter."

    D.   R. Tanhuma in the name of R. Eleazar, and R. Menahama in the name of Rab: "'And the Lord will remove from you every ailment' This refers to bile."

    E.   This is in line with the view of R. Eleazar: "Ninety-nine die of bile and one by the hands of Heaven."

    F.   Rab and R. Hiyya the Elder both say, "Ninety-nine die of the evil eye and one at the hands of Heaven."

    G.   R. Haninah and R. Nathan both say, "Ninety-nine die of cold, and one at the hands of Heaven."

    H.   Rab is consistent with his setting, and R. Haninah likewise is consistent with his setting.

    I.   Rab is consistent, for Rab lived in Babylonia, where the evil eye was commonplace.

    J.   R. Haninah is consistent, because he lived in Sepphoris, where it was very cold.

3. A.   Antoninus said to Our Holy Rabbi [Judah the Patriarch], "Pray for me."

    B.   He said to him, "May you be saved from cold."

    C.   He said to him, "That's no prayer. With one extra cover, the cold goes its way."

D.   He said to him, "May you be saved from heat."

E.   He said to him, "Lo, that is the prayer that you should say for me.

F.   "For it is said, 'There is no hiding from his heat' (Ps. 19:7)."

4.   A.   R. Samuel b. R. Nahman in the name of R. Nathan, "Ninety-nine die of heat, and one at the hands of Heaven."

B.   And rabbis say, "Ninety-nine die of transgression, and one at the hands of Heaven."

I take it that the main point is Aha's observation that since gossips bring leprosy on themselves, people in general are responsible for whatever ailments they suffer. The bulk of the rest, serving Deut. 7:15, is at Y. Shab. 14:3, with very minor changes and re-arrangements. Inclusion here in no way serves the exegesis of the passage at hand.

XVI:I X

1.   A.   "And the priest shall command them to kill one of the birds [in an earthen vessel over running water]' (Lev. 14:5).

B.   Why does the priest kill one bird and leave the other?

C.   It is to tell you that just as it is impossible for the slain bird to return to life, so it is impossible for the leprosy-marks to return.

D.   At that moment the Holy One, blessed be he, calls to his legions and tells them, "See that it was not for nothing that I smote this man."

2.   A.   But: "Because of the iniquity of his covetousness I was angry, I smote him, I hid my face and was angry. But he went on back-sliding in the way of his own heart" (Is. 57:17).

B.   R. Abba b. R. Kahana said, "The one who vomits returns to his vomit.

C.   "That is in line with the following verse of Scripture: 'As a dog returns to his vomit, [so is a fool who repeats his folly]' (Prov. 26:11)."

D.   R. Joshua b. Levi said, "[He went on backsliding in the way of his own heart' (Is. 57:17)] means, 'The fool returns to the way of his folly.'

E.   "That is in line with the following verse of Scripture: 'A fool repeats his folly' (Prov. 26:11)."

3.   A.   "I have seen his ways, but I will heal him; [I will lead him and requite him with comfort, creating for his mourners the fruit of the lips" (Is. 57:18). The opening phrase in Aramaic means, "I will heal him]."

B.   "I will lead him" (Is. 57:18) -- I will guide him.

C.   "I will requite him in comfort, creating for his mourners ('BYLYW)" -- this refers to his limbs ('YBRYM), which are in mourning for him.

4. A. "Creating [for his mourners] the fruit of the lips" (Is. 57:18).

    B. R. Joshua b. Levi said, "If the lips of a man are fluent in prayer, he may be confident that his prayer is heard.

    C. "What is the text that indicates it?

    D. "'You will strengthen their heart, you will incline your ear' (Ps. 10:17)."

5. A. "Peace, peace [to the far and to the near, says the Lord, and I will heal him]" (Is. 57:19).

    B. If he is "near," he is already at peace in and of himself.

    C. But if it is to "the one who is far" --

    D. R. Huna and R. Yudan in the name of R. Aha, "This refers to the leper, who was put away at a distance but then brought near."

6. A. "Says the Lord, I will heal him" (Is. 57:19). "I will heal him in himself."

    B. "Heal me, O Lord, and I shall be healed, save me, and I shall be saved, for you are my praise" (Jer. 17:14).

The opening allegation, that the leper will not return to his folly, No. 1, is what accounts for the long exegesis of Is. 57:17. The passage goes over the notion that God heals the sinner. This is then a secondary expansion of the introductory and important point. While the leper was smitten on account of the sin of gossip, once he is purified, he is not likely to return to his sin. The work on Is. 57:17-19 then flows fairly smoothly, with a number of translations into Aramaic of the Hebrew words. Nos. 2, 3, 4, and 5 systematically work through the elements of the cited verse. No. 6 then concludes with an intersecting verse of Jeremiah, also referring to God's healing. The unit makes for a strong conclusion to a picture of the sins of the leper.

PARASHAH TWENTY-FIVE

XXV:I

1. A. "When you come into the land and plant [all kinds of trees for food, then you shall count their fruit as forbidden; three years it shall be forbidden to you, it must not be eaten. And in the fourth year all their fruit shall be holy, an offering of praise to the Lord. But in the fifth year you may eat of their fruit, that they may yield more richly for you: I am the Lord your God]" (Lev. 19:23-25).

    B. "She [= wisdom, Torah] is a tree of life to those who lay hold of her; [and those who hold her fast are called happy]" (Prov. 3:18).

    C. R. Huna in the name of R. Aha: "[The meaning is] that the words of Torah should not appear in your sight like the case of a man who had a daughter of marriageable age, whom he wanted to attach to anyone [he could find].

D.   "Rather: 'My son, if you receive my words and treasure up my commandments with you [then you will understand the fear of the Lord and find the knowledge of God]' (Prov. 2:1 [5]).

E.   "If you have merit, you will receive my words."

F.   R. Hunia in the name of R. Benjamin b. Levi: "[The matter may be compared] to the case of a king who said to his son, 'Go out and take up trading.'

G.   "He said to him, 'Father, I am afraid, by land of thugs, and by sea of pirates.'

H.   "What did his father do for him? He took a staff and hollowed it out and put an amulet in it and handed it over to his son, saying to him, 'Let this staff be in your hand, and you will not have to be afraid of anybody.'

I.   "So said the Holy One, blessed be he, to Israel, 'My children, keep yourselves busy in the Torah, and you will not have to be afraid of anybody.'"

2.   A.   [With reference to "She is a tree of life to those that lay hold of her," including those who support the ones who actually study Torah, and now speaking of the following verse: "Cursed be he who does not confirm the words of this law by doing them" (Deut. 27:26)], had the cited verse stated, "Cursed be he who does not study [the words of this Torah]," there would be no enduring [for Israel, since most of the Jews do not study the Torah].

B.   But [it says], "Cursed be he who does not confirm...," [and the Jews do carry out the teachings of the Torah].

C.   If it had said, "She is a tree of life to those that labor in her," there would be no enduring.

D.   But [it says], "She is a tree of life to those that lay hold of her," [by supporting and following the ones who do study the Torah].

3.   A.   R. Huna said, "If a person stumbles into a transgression so that he becomes liable to death at the hands of Heaven, what should he do so that he may live?

B.   "If he was trained to recite a single page of Scripture, let him recite two, if he was trained to repeat one chapter of Mishnah, let him repeat two.

C.   "And if he was not trained either to recite Scripture or to repeat Mishnah, what should he do so as to live?

D.   "Let him go and take up the responsibility of communal leader or charity-collector, and he will live.

E.   "For if it had said 'Cursed be he who does not study...,' there would be no enduring. But [it says], 'Cursed be he who does not confirm.'

F. "If it had said, 'It is a tree of life to those that labor in it,' there would be no enduring, but [it says], 'It is a tree of life to those that lay hold of it.'"

4. A. "For wisdom is a defense as money is a defense" (Qoh. 7:12).

B. R. Aha in the name of R. Tanhum b. R. Hiyya: "If one had learned Torah and taught it, kept and done [its teachings], but had the power to protest [wrongdoing] and did not protest, or to support [disciples of sages] and did not support them, lo, this one falls into the category of cursed.

C. "That is in line with the following verse of Scripture: '[Cursed be he] who does not confirm...' (Deut. 27:26)."

D. R. Jeremiah in the name of R. Hiyya: "If one did not study [Torah] and did not carry out [its teachings], did not keep them and did not teach them to others, and did not have the power to support [disciples of sages] but [nonetheless] he did so, [or] did not have the power to protest [wrongdoing] but nonetheless he did so, lo, this one falls into the category of blessed."

The exposition of the base-verse rests upon its reference to a "tree," and as we see in the intersecting verse, that is understood to invoke the theme of the Torah, "the tree of life." Accordingly, here we have the case of an intersecting verse which, to the rabbinical exegetes in general, makes explicit reference to the theme of the base-verse. The sense of No. 1 is not entirely articulated at C-E. The point is that the Torah should be regarded as a desirable bride, and not as the leftover. How that links to F-I, I cannot say. The point now is that the Torah protects Israel. Perhaps that reinforces the notion that the Torah is very valuable and not to be viewed as something forced upon Israel. Nos. 2, 3, and 4 go over the notion that people who do not study the Torah should at least support those who do. This rather general notion does not carry forward the proposition of No. 1, only the theme.

XXV:II

1. A. R. Huna and R. Jeremiah in the name of R. Hiyya b. R. Abba: "The Holy One, blessed be he, is going to provide shade and canopies in the Garden of Eden for those who carry out religious duties alongside those who study Torah.

B. "And there are three verses of Scripture [that so indicate].

C. "'For wisdom is a defense as money is a defense' (Qoh. 7:12). [Money given to support disciples of sages serves as wisdom, that is, study of Torah.]

D. "'Happy is the man who does this, [and the son of man that supports it]' (Is. 56:2) [that is, supports study of Torah, as much as studies it].

E. "'And the verse at hand: 'It is a tree of life [even to those that support it]' (Prov. 3:18).

2. A. Simeon, the brother of Azariah, said in his name --

  B. Now was not Simeon greater [in learning] than Azariah?

  C. But because Azariah went into trade and provided for Simeon, therefore the law was taught in his [Azariah's] name.

  D. Along these same lines: "And of Zebulun he said, 'Rejoice, Zebulun, [in your going out, and Issachar in your tents'" (Deut. 33:18).

  E. Now was Issachar not greater than Zebulun? But because Zebulun went voyaging on the sea in trade and came home and provided for Issachar, his reward was given to him for his labor. Therefore the verse was cited in his name.

3. A. "Rejoice, Zebulun, in your going out, and Issachar in your tents" (Deut. 33:18).

  B. Said R. Tanhuma, "Whoever goes forth en route [to war] and does not have his heart set on war in the end will fall in war. But that is not the case for the tribe of Zebulun. Whether or not they set their heart [on war], when they go forth to war, they conquer.

  C. "That is in line with the following verse of Scripture: 'Of Zebulun fifty thousand seasoned troops, equipped for battle with all the weapons of war, to help David not with a double heart [i.e. with singleness of purpose]' (1 Chr. 12:33).

  D. "What is the meaning of 'not with a double heart'?

  E. "Whether they had set their heart [on war] or did not set their heart [on war], they went out to war and conquered."

4. A. R. Judah b. Pedaiah gave the following exposition: "Who will remove the dirt from your eyes, O first Man, for you were unable to stand firm on what you had been commanded [concerning the forbidden fruit] for a single moment, while lo, your children have to wait three years for the unready fruit."

  B. Said R. Huna, "When Bar Qappara heard this, he said, 'Judah, son of my sister, has given a fine exposition."

  C. "When you come into the land, you will plant all kinds of trees for food..." (Lev. 19:23).

Nos. 1-3 carry forward the antecedent discussion about the worth of supporting those who study the Torah as much as those who actually study it. No. 1 reads the cited verses along these lines. No. 2 then introduces a separate example of the same proposition. The proof-text of No. 2, Deut. 33:18, is then given its own exegesis in No. 3. No. 4 presents a genuinely fresh idea, relevant to the base-verse but not to the intersecting one.

XXV:III

1. A. R. Judah b. R. Simon opened [discourse by citing the following verse]: "After the Lord your God will you walk" (Deut. 13:5).

   B. Said R. Judah b. R. Simon, "Now is it possible for a mortal man to walk after the Holy One, blessed be he,

   C. "him concerning whom it is written, 'In the sea is your way, and your path is in the mighty water' (Ps. 77:20)?

   D. "And yet you say, 'After the Lord your God will you walk!'

   E. "Now it is further said, 'And to him will you cleave' (Deut. 13:5).

   F. "And is it possible for a mortal to go up to heaven and to cleave to fire,

   G. "him concerning whom it is written, 'For the Lord your God is consuming fire' (Deut. 4:24).

   H. "'His throne was of fiery flames... a river of fire' (Dan. 7:9-10)?

   I. "And yet you say, 'To him will you cleave!'

   J. "But from the very beginning of the creation of the world, [the Holy One] was occupied first of all only in the planting of trees in line with the following verse of Scripture: 'And the Lord God planted the Garden of Eden' (Gen. 2:8).

   K. "So you too, when you enter the Land of Israel, you should first of all be occupied in the planting of trees."

   L. "'When you come into the land, you will plant [all kinds of trees for food]' (Lev. 19:23)."

The fresh reading of the base-verse generates the ironic exegesis of the cited verse. People cannot be "like God" except by planting orchards, as God did in creating the world. Lev. 19:23 is read as imperative. The intersecting verses, Deut. 13:5, then serves as a pretext for the principal exposition, rather than forming the focus of exegesis on its own.

XXV:IV

1. A. R. Joshua of Sikhnin in the name of R. Levi opened [discourse by citing the following verse]: "'I made great works; I built houses [and planted vineyards] for myself; [I made myself gardens and parks and planted in them all kinds of fruit trees]' (Qoh. 2:24).

   B. "'I made great works:' Said the Holy one, blessed be he, to Moses, "Go and say to the original patriarchs, 'I made great works. I have done great things for your children, in line with everything to which I stipulated with you.'

   C. "'I built houses:' 'Houses filled with every good thing' (Deut. 6:11).

   D. "'I planted vineyards for myself:' 'Vineyards and olive trees that you did not plant' (Deut. 6:11).

E. "'I made myself pools [from which to water the forest of growing
    trees]' (Qoh. 2:6): 'And fully dug wells, which you did not dig'
    (Deut. 6:11).

F. "'Fountains and depths' (Qoh. 8:7), 'from which to water the forest
    of growing trees' (Qoh. 2:6).

G. (Said R. Levi, "Not even reeds for arrows did the Land of Israel
    lack.")

H. "'I made myself gardens and parks:' 'A land of wheat and barley'
    (Deut.8:8).

I. "'I planted in them all kinds of fruit trees:' 'When you come into
    the land, you will plant [all kinds of trees for food]' (Lev. 19:23)."

Lev. 19:23 is now made to serve the exposition of the intersecting verse, which is
read as God speaking to the patriarchs, with the message that he had done what he had
promised. The exposition runs smoothly, beginning to end.

XXV:V

1. A. "Who has put wisdom in the inward parts of the clouds" (Job 38:36)

    B. What is the meaning of "inward parts?" In the private places.

    C. "Or who has given understanding to the cock" (Job 38:36).

    D. What is the meaning of "cock?" Rooster.

    E. Said R. Levi, "In Arabia, they call a chicken a hen."

    F. When a hen's young are little, it collects them, puts them under its
        wings, warms them, and grubs for them. But when they are big, if
        one of them wants to get near her, she pecks at his head and says
        to him, "Go, grub in your own dunghill."

    G. So when the Israelites were in the wilderness for forty years, the
        manna came down, the well spurted up, the quail was always at
        hand for them, the clouds of glory encompassed them, and the
        pillar of cloud journeyed before them. When they entered the Land
        of Israel, Moses said to them, "Each one of you must now take his
        spade and go out and plant trees.

    H. "'When you come into the land, you will plant...' (Lev. 19:23)."

2. A. Hadrian (may his bones be ground up) was walking through the
        paths of Tiberias. He saw an old man standing and digging holes to
        plant trees. He said to him, "Old man, old man, if you got up early
        [to do the work, when you were young], you would not have stayed
        late [to plant in your old age]."

    B. He said to him, "I got up early [and worked in my youth] and I
        stayed late [working in my old age], and whatever pleases the
        Master of heaven, let him do."

    C. He said to him, "By your life, old man! How old are you today?"

D. He said to him, "I am a hundred years old."

E. He said to him, "Now you are a hundred years old, and you are standing and digging holes to plant trees! Do you honestly think that you're going to eat the fruit of those trees?"

F. He said to him, "If I have the merit, I shall eat it. But if not, well, just as my forefathers labored for me, so I labor for my children."

G. He said to him, "By your life! If you have the merit of eating of the fruit of these trees, be sure to let me know about it."

H. After some time the trees produced figs. The man said, "Lo, the time has come to tell the king."

I. What did he do? He filled a basket with figs and went up and stood at the gate of the palace.

J. [The guards] said to him, "What is your business here?"

K. He said, "To come before the king."

L. When he had gone in, he said to him, "What are you doing here?"

M. He said to him, "I am the old man you met. I was the one who was digging holes to plant trees, and you said to me, 'If you have the merit of eating the fruit of those trees, be sure to let me know.' Now I in fact did have the merit, and I ate of their fruit, and these figs here are the fruit of those trees."

N. Then said Hadrian, "I order you to bring a chair of gold for him to sit on.

O. "I order you to empty this basket of his and fill it with golden denars."

P. His servants said to him, "Are you going to pay so much respect to that old Jew?"

Q. He said to him, "His Creator honors him, and should I not honor him?"

R. The wife of the neighbor [of that man] was wicked. She said to her husband, "Son of darkness, see how the king loves figs and trades them for golden denars."

S. What did [the man] do? He filled a sack with figs and went and stood before the palace.

T. They said to him, "What is your business here?"

U. He said to them, "I heard that the king loves figs and trades them for golden denars."

V. They went and told the king, "There is an old man standing at the gate of the palace carrying a sackful of figs. When we asked him, 'What are you doing here, ' he told us, 'I heard that the king loves figs and trades them for golden denars.'"

W. [The king] said, "I order you to set him up before the gate of the palace. Whoever goes in and out is to throw [a fig] in his face."

X.   Toward evening they freed him and he went home. He said to his wife, "For all the honor [that I got], I owe you!"

Y.   She said, "Go and boast to your mother that they were figs and not etrogs, that they were soft and not hard!"

The intersecting verse serves only to allow the exegete to speak of the conduct of the hen with its offspring, so as to make the point that when the Israelites were in the wilderness and weak, God provided for them, but when they reached the land, they were to plant trees to provide for themselves. I see no important connection between No. 2 and the base-verse, except for the shared theme of tree-planting.

XXV:VI

1.   A.   R. Huna in the name of Bar Qappara said, "Abraham, our father, sat and constructed an argument a fortiori [as follows]:

     B.   "The matter of uncircumcision is stated with regard to a tree [Lev. 19:23] and the matter of uncircumcision is stated with regard to a man.

     C.   "Just as the matter of uncircumcision stated with regard to a tree applies to the place at which it produces fruit,

     D.   "so the uncircumcision stated with regard to a man applies to the place in which he produces progeny."

     E.   Said R. Hanan b. R. Pazzi, "And did Abraham, our father, actually know anything about constructing arguments a fortiori or arguments based on analogy?

     F.   "But he found an intimation of the matter in the following verse of Scripture: 'And I will set my covenant between me and you, [and I will make you multiply very much]' (Gen. 17:2).

     G.   "[The mark of the covenant is to be] in the place at which a man is fruitful and multiplies."

2.   A.   R. Ishmael taught, "The Holy One, blessed be he, wanted to take the priesthood away from Shem [as its progenitor], as it is said, 'And Melchizedek, king of Salem, brought out bread and wine; he was priest of God Most High. [And he blessed [Abraham] and said, "Blessed be Abram by God Most High, maker of heaven and earth, and blessed be God Most high who has delivered your enemies into your hand"]' (Gen. 14:18-19).

     B.   "Since he placed the blessing of Abraham before the blessing of the Omnipresent, Abraham said to him, 'Now does one place the blessing of the servant before the blessing of his master?'

     C.   "The Omnipresent removed [the priesthood] from Shem and handed it over to Abraham, as it is said, 'The Lord says to my lord, [Sit at my right hand.]' (Ps. 110:1). And after that statement it is written,

'The Lord has sworn and will not change his mind, You are a priest forever after the matter of Melchizedek' (Ps. 110:4). It is on account of the matter of Melchizedek.

D. "That is in line with the following verse of Scripture: 'He was priest of God Most High' (Gen. 14:18)."

3. A. R. Ishmael and R. Aqiba:

B. R. Ishmael said, "Abraham was high priest, as it is said, 'The Lord has sworn and will not change his mind. [You are a priest forever]' (Ps. 110:4).

C. "And it is written, 'And you will circumcise the flesh of your foreskin' (Gen. 17:11).

D. "Now where was he to make the mark of circumcision [since as we now see, it could apply to the ear, mouth, heart, and body equally, so far as biblical usage is concerned]?

E. "If he were to circumcise his ear, he would then not be fit to make an offering.

F. "If he were to circumcise his mouth, he would not be fit to make an offering.

G. "If he were to circumcise his heart, he would not be fit to make an offering.

H. "At what point, then, could he make the mark of circumcision and yet be [unblemished and thus] fit to make an offering? It could only be circumcision of the body [at the penis]."

I. R. Aqiba says, "There are four sorts of uncircumcision.

J. "'Uncircumcision' is stated with regard to the ear: 'And lo, their ears are uncircumcised' (Jer. 6:10).

K. "'Uncircumcision' is stated with regard to the mouth: 'And I am of uncircumcised lips' (Ex. 6:30).

L. "'Uncircumcision' is stated with regard to the heart: 'And all of the house of Israel are of uncircumcised heart' (Jer. 9:25).

M. "Yet it is written, 'Walk before me and be perfect [and un-blemished] (Gen. 17:1).

N. "Whence then could he be circumcised? If he should be circumcised at the ear, he would not be perfect.

O. "If he should be circumcised at the mouth, he should not be perfect.

P. "If he should be circumcised at the heart, he should not be perfect.

Q. "Where then could he be circumcised and be perfect?

R. "One must say, 'This refers to the circumcision of the body.'"

S. Nagra said, "It is written, '[Circumcise] at eight days of age' (Gen. 17:12).

T. "Where then should one place the mark of circumcision?

U. "If one circumcises at the ear, he will be unable to hear.

V.   "If he did so at the mouth, he will be unable to speak.

W.   "If he did so at the heart, he will be unable to think.

X.   "Where should he be circumcised and remain able to hear, speak, and think?

Y.   "It must follow that this refers to circumcision of the body."

Z.   Said R. Tanhuma, "What Nagra says is most reasonable."

4.   A.   "And the uncircumcised male who is not circumcised" (Gen. 17:14).

B.   R. Yudan in the name of R. Isaac and, R. Berekhiah in the name of R. Isaac, and there is one who teaches it in the name of R. Yose b. Halapta, "'And the uncircumcised male...' (Gen. 17:14).

C.   "Now is there such a thing as an uncircumcised female?

D.   "But the point is that at the place which people examine to know whether one is male or female, there they make the mark of circumcision [on the male]."

The reference of the base-verse to "uncircumcision" with regard to the trees, Lev. 19:23, accounts for the introduction of the theme of circumcision. But is is only at No. 1 that the base-verse makes its impact, and then only by an allusion to Lev. 19:23, which is not explicitly cited. From that point onward, the passage pursues its own interests. No. 2 is necessary to set the stage for No. 3. No. 4 then proves the same proposition as No. 3.

XXV:VII

1.   A.   R. Levi bar Sisi gave the following exposition: "'And you were a whore with the sons of Egypt, your neighbors, large of flesh' (Ez. 16:26). What does 'large of flesh' mean?

B.   "Now did one have one leg and another three?"

C.   "Rabbi said, 'They had large penises.'"

2.   A.   R. Berekhiah and R. Simon in the name of R. Samuel bar Nehemiah, "It is written, 'And [Joshua] circumcised the children of Israel at the Hill of Foreskins' (Josh. 5:3).

B.   "What is the meaning of 'Hill of Foreskins?' That it was in the shape of a mountain made of foreskins."

The theme of circumcision continues. The base-verse is not in view.

XXV:VIII

1.   A.   "His legs are alabaster columns, [set upon bases of fine gold]" (Song of Songs 5:15).

B.   "His legs" refer to the world.

C.   "Alabaster columns (SS):" For [the world] rests on the six (SST) days of creation, for it is written, "For in six days did God create the world" (Ex. 20:11).

D. "Set upon bases of fine gold:" This refers to words of Torah, "which are more to be desired than fine gold" (Ps. 19:11).

2. A. Another interpretation: "Set upon bases of fine gold" refers to the sections of the Torah which are interpreted both in light of what precedes them and also in light of what follows them.

B. To what may they be compared?

C. R. Huna in the name of Bar Qappara said, "To a column that has a base on the bottom and a capitol on the top.

D. "So too are the sections of the Torah to be interpreted both in light of what precedes them and also in light of what follows them." [This proposition is now illustrated.]

3. A. "When you come into the land and plant all kinds of trees for food" (Lev. 19:23).

B. And it is written [in the immediately preceding verses], "If a man lies carnally with a woman [who is a slave].." (Lev. 19:20-22).

C. Now what has one matter got to do with the other?

D. But [it is to teach] that one who weeds [and farms] with his fellow gradually becomes part of the household. Since he comes and goes in his house, he becomes suspect [of having sexual relations] with his slave girl.

E. He says, "Is it not a sin-offering that I now owe, is it not a guilt-offering? I'll bring a sin-offering, I'll bring a guilt-offering."

F. For R. Yudan in the name of R. Levi said, "Those who in this world treat slave-girls as though they are [sexually] permitted are destined to hang by the scalp of their head in the world to come.

G. "That is in line with the following verse of Scripture: 'But God will shatter the heads of his enemies, the hair crown of him who walks in his guilty ways' (Ps. 68:21)."

H. What is the meaning of "walks in his guilty ways"?

I. Everybody says, "Let that man go in his guilt, let that man go in his guilt."

4. A. Passages of the Torah also may be interpreted in light of what follows them.

B. For it is said, "For three years it shall be [as though] uncircumcised for you" (Lev. 19:23).

C. And it is written, "You shall not eat any flesh with the blood in it" (Lev. 19:26).

D. What has one thing got to do with the other?

E. Said the Holy One, blessed be he, to Israel, "You are prepared to wait for the uncircumcised fruit tree for three years; and for your wife do you not wait, while she observes the period of her menstruation?

F.   "For your uncircumcised tree you are prepared to wait for three years; and for [meat of] your beast are you not prepared to wait until the blood is fully drained from it?"

5.   A.   And who observed the religious duty governing the blood?

B.   It was Saul, for it is said, "Then they told Saul, Behold the people are sinning against the Lord [by eating with the blood. And he said, You have dealt treacherously; roll a great stone to me here.] And Saul said, Disperse yourselves among the people [and say to them, Let every man bring his ox or his sheep] and slay them here; [and eat, but do not sin against the Lord by eating with the blood]" (1 Sam. 14:33-34).

C.   What is the meaning of "here (BZH)?" Rabbis say, "A knife fourteen fingers long did he show them, B stands for two, Z for seven, H for five, so he said to them, 'In this manner will you slaughter and eat meat [with a knife of proper length].'"

D.   How did the Holy One, blessed be he, reward him?

E.   One has to say, it was on the day of battle.

F.   That is in line with the following verse of Scripture: "So on the day of the battle there was neither [sword nor spear] found [in the hand of any of the people with Saul and Jonathan; but with Saul and Jonathan his son [weaponry] was found. And the garrison of the Philistines went out to the pass of Mickmash]" (1 Sam. 13:22).

G.   First it says, "was not found," and then it says, "But... was found!" Who provided it to him?

H.   R. Haggai in the name of R. Isaac said, "An angel provided him [with the needed weapons]."

I.   And rabbis say, "The Holy One, blessed be he, provided him with the needed weapons."

6.   A.   It is written, "And Saul built an altar to the Lord; it was the first altar built to the Lord" (1 Sam. 14:35).

B.   How many altars had the earlier ancients already built -- Noah, Abraham, Isaac, Jacob, Moses, Joshua -- and yet you say, "It was the first [altar]!"

C.   Rabbis say, "That one was the first built by kings."

D.   Said R. Yudan, "Because he was ready to give his life for this matter, Scripture treated it in his behalf as if he were the first one who built an altar to the Lord."

7.   A.   Said R. Simeon b. Yosi b. Laqoniah, "Now in this world, a person builds a building, and someone else uses it.

B.   "A person may plant a tree, and someone else eats its fruit.

C.   "But in the age to come: 'They shall not build and another inhabit, [they shall not plant and another eat].... They shall not work in vain' (Is 65:22-23).

D.   "'And their seed shall be known among the nations' (Is. 61:9)."

Now we reach a fine exposition of the context of the base-verse, Lev. 19:23, in relationship to related verses. No. 1 sets the stage by introducing the exegetical basis. No. 2 then makes the main point, which applies, specifically, at Nos. 3 and 4 to Lev. 19:23. Nos. 5-6 then spin out exegeses of the verses cited in the preceding, and No. 7 ends the discussion of Lev. 19:23 with an eschatological promise. So the construction is tight at Nos. 2-4, 7, and bears the conventional amplification at Nos. 5-6.

The first four tables differentiate among the units of discourse of the parashiyyot in accord with the classifications yielded by Parashah 5. The fifth then examines the order in which the several types of units of discourse make their appearance.

1. Complex base-verse/intersecting-verse constructions

XVI:I. 1-3	Lev. 14:2 and Prov. 6:16-19. Exegesis of Prov. 6:16-19 leads to the climax that leprosy is caused by gossip.
XVI:II. 1-3	Lev. 14:2 and Prov. 34:12-13. As above.
XVI:III. 1-4	Job 20:6-7 and Lev. 14:2. As above.
XXV:I. 1-3	Lev. 19:23-25 and Prov. 3:18. Torah is the tree of life.
XXV:I.4	Qoh. 7:12. Wisdom is a defense. That Torah protects Israel is the unifying proposition.
XXV:III	Deut. 13:5 and Lev. 19:23. People are like God when they plant trees.

2. Simple base-verse/intersecting-verse constructions

XXV:IV	Qoh. 2:24. Read in light of Lev. 19:23.
[XXV:VIII.7	This brief finis may fall into the classification at hand.]

3. Exegesis of successive verses of Leviticus

XVI:VI. 1	The word Torah occurs with respect to the leper.
XVI:VII. 1-2	Lev. 14:4. Birds linked to gossips.
XVI:IX. 1-6	Lev. 14:5. Leper does not repeat his sin. Is. 57:17 tacked on and fully explained, no backsliding.
XXV:V. 1	Lev. 19:23 placed into narrative context.
XXV:VI. 1	Uncircumcision of tree, man.
XXV:VIII. 1-7	The principle that passages of the Torah are interpreted by reference to the juxtaposed passages is illustrated by Lev.

19:23 and Lev. 19:20-22. The point of No. 2 is applied to Lev.
19:23 at Nos. 3-4, which are then complemented at Nos. 5-6.
No. 7 then completes the exegesis of Lev. 19:23 by reference
to Is. 65:22-23.

4. Miscellanies

XVI:IV.1-4
Ps. 50:16-18, Lev. 13:45. God takes no delight in the praise
of the wicked. Tacked on because of Lev. 13:45, part of
repertoire of proof-texts.

XVI:V.1-6
Qoh. 5:5 is thoroughly exemplified. Tacked on because some
examples relate to leprosy.

XVI:VIII.1-4
People are responsible for their ailments. Leprosy not
mentioned but the point as it pertains to leprosy is in the
preceding unit [XVI:VII].

XXV:II
Torah-study, includes reference to proof-text of XXV:I.
Those who support Torah-study gain merit. Same general
point as XXV:I.

XXV:V.2
Story on planting trees.

XXV:VI.2-4
Sayings on circumcision.

XXV:VII.1
Sayings on circumcision.

5. The order of types of units of discourse in
Parashiyyot 16 and 25

I   = Complex base/intersecting
II   = Simple base/intersecting
III   = Standard exegeses
IV   = Miscellany

XVI:I	I
XVI:II	I
XVI:III	I
[XVI:IV	IV. Supplements opening units.]
[XVI:V	IV. Supplements opening units.]
XVI:VI	III
[XVI:VIII	IV. Complements preceding unit's point.]
XVI:IX	III

All of the classified units follow the expected order, type I, then type III. The
inserted units, of a miscellaneous or unclassified nature, are attached to expand the
classified ones, as indicated.

XXV:I	I
[XXV:II	IV. Goes over same points as XXV:I, but not within the disciplined pattern of XXV:I.]
XXV:III	I
XXV:IV	II
XXV:V.1	III
[XXV:V.2	IV. Story on planting trees, carries forward XXV:V.1's theme.]
XXV:VI.1	III
[XXV:VI.2-4	IV. Sayings on circumcision, theme of XXV:VI.1.]
[XXV:VII	IV. Sayings on circumcision, theme of XXV:VI.1.]
XXV:VIII	III

The order is types I, II, III, with type IV interspersed for the reasons given.

iv. The Recurrent Literary Structures: Types of Units of Discourse and their Consistent Order

The upshot may now be stated very briefly. First, we are able to classify within the taxa yielded by Parashah 5 all completed units of discourse of parashiyyot 16 and 25. (Usually entire constructions, marked with a Roman numeral, are treated whole, where these prove to be unitary in redaction, but sometimes only parts of constructions, those marked with Arabic numerals are classified.) That fact imparts credibility to the original taxonomy. Indeed, the only puzzling fact is that we find so few exempla for the taxon II, simple base-verse/intersecting-verse constructions. I should have expected a clearer indication that that classification, applied objectively, indeed encompasses a broad range of units of discourse. The classification, miscellanies (IV), does not encompass a considerable proportion of the whole, but it also is not negligible. If we count up the units covered by Arabic numerals -- that is, the subdivisions of the major divisions of the parashah at hand, those marked by Roman numerals, what is the result? We find that 43 out of 65 individual units fall into the classifications I-III, and 22 out of 65 prove to be miscellaneous, that is, roughly two-thirds to one-third.

Clearly, the classification of "miscellany" demands treatment on its own. I could break it down into its subdivisions. But I prefer to treat it as a counterpart to the other classifications, and this I do by simply asking about where the redactors have inserted units of discourse I call miscellaneous and why they have done so. When I answer that question, I show that what is miscellaneous also and invariably proves to be extraneous to the established patterns of large-scale construction of units of discourse. So differentiation among miscellaneous units is pointless, since all such units bear in common a single trait: irrelevance. All serve a single purpose: supplement to what is relevant.

Can we then account for the location of all units that do not fall into the classification-scheme at hand? In each case we indeed are able to do so. The fact that the framers of the three parashiyyot we have examined ordered the types of units of discourse in a consistent way -- base-verse/intersecting-verse constructions, then ordinary exegesis-constructions -- establishes the plan of the whole. Then the insertion of miscellanies is readily explained. These sizable compositions meant to complement these definitive constructions are systematically added with a generous, but not lavish, hand. The authors of Leviticus Rabbah at some stage determined to complement their fundamental construction -- their composition of the three differentiated types of units of discourse, given in fixed order. This they did by adding materials not integral to their basic composition, and by doing so without regard to the fixed order of types of units of discourse integral to the basic composition. To state matters simply, it is as if the Mishnah were presented to us along with large selections of the Tosefta or other materials of the same provenance ("Tannaitic") all in one document -- that is, much as the Yerushalmi and the Bavli present the Mishnah.

What we now have to do is survey the remainder of the thirty-seven parashiyyot of Leviticus Rabbah. We have to see whether the proposed taxonomy indeed encompasses the entirety of the document. We further must ask whether the theory of the ordinal relationship of types of units of discourse to one another likewise finds substantiation in the rest of Leviticus Rabbah. Only when we can account for the inclusion and positioning of the miscellaneous materials, those falling outside the three taxa bearing clearcut definitions, can we make certain that we understand the recurrent literary structures of Leviticus Rabbah. If, then, the taxonomy remains stable, on the one side, and the order of the types of units of discourse proves consistent, on the other, we may claim to define the recurrent literary structures of Leviticus Rabbah.

Chapter Two

THE LITERARY STRUCTURE AND ORGANIZATION OF LEVITICUS RABBAH

i. Sorting Out the Major Units of Discourse

Leviticus Rabbah is made up of thirty-seven parashiyyot, and each parashah is comprised of from as few as five to as many as fifteen subdivisions. In my translation and explanation of the text, I was able to show that these subdivisions in the main formed cogent statements. In these diverse smaller units of discourse, sayings, stories, exegeses of verses of Scripture, protracted proofs of a single proposition, and the like, ordinarily served a purpose cogent to the whole subdivision of a parashah. Any analysis of the overall structure and organization of the document as a whole, therefore, must begin with the principal divisions, the thirty-seven parashiyyot, specifically to analyze the character of the subdivisions. What we wish to know is whether a given parashah will be composed of materials that derive from a limited repertoire of patterns of expression. Do the authors of the several parashiyyot organize in a cogent way the repertoire of materials that they choose to use? So we are concerned to demonstrate two things. First we wish to see whether the primary constituents of discourse, the subdivisions of the parashiyyot, fall into a limited taxonomic framework. Second, we have to find out whether or not the types of units of discourse -- the subdivisions of the parashiyyot -- are arranged in a consistent order.

So the suggestive results of Chapter One now demand systematic reconsideration, so that the entirety of the data will be subjected to examination. Only then shall we see that Leviticus Rabbah follows a disciplined literary plan throughout. In light of that fact, we take up the issue of materials shared by Leviticus Rabbah with some other contemporary compilation or composition, asking about the relationships between what is shared and the fixed literary patterns of Leviticus Rabbah, on the one side, and what is unique and those same fixed literary patterns, on the other. That is the route that will bring us to the issue of whether or not we deal, in the case of Leviticus Rabbah and documents with which it intersects, with a synoptic problem, and, if we do, what that synoptic problem is. So the work of characterizing the disciplined literary patterns of Leviticus Rabbah, those definitive of the document as a whole, has now to reach fruition. The question is: does Leviticus Rabbah reveal a literary structure, or, from a formal and rhetorical viewpoint, is it a mere miscellany?

ii. Taxonomy of Units of Discourse

The types of units of discourse outlined in Chapter One in the main find definition in formal, therefore objective traits. I have tried to avoid any subjective judgment. That is to say, if I call a recurrent mode of organization the base-verse/intersecting-verse construction, all I mean to say is that, in the sort of passage under discussion, (1) a verse of the book of Leviticus will be followed by (2) a verse from some other book of the Hebrew Scriptures. The latter (2) will then be subjected to extensive discussion. But in the end the exposition of the intersecting-verse will shed some light, in some way, upon (1) the base-verse, cited at the outset. If I call a recurrent pattern one of exegesis of a verse, all I mean is that, in this type of discourse, a verse of the book of Leviticus will be subjected to sustained analysis and amplification, but not with reference to some other intersecting-verse but now, commonly with regard to numerous proof-texts, or to no proof-texts at all.,

Where in Chapter One a measure of subjectivity found its way into my discussion, it had to do with the distinction between the complex and the simple base-verse/intersecting-verse constructions. Who is to decide what is always simple or invariably complex? To remove that element of subjectivity, let me offer a different criterion from that of complexity or simplicity. It is merely the location of the base-verse and intersecting-verse. In what I called "the complex version," the base-verse always comes first, the intersecting-verse follows. That is a logical arrangement, since the focus of analysis will be upon the intersecting-verse. In what I called "the simple version," by contrast, the intersecting-verse will always come first, and the base-verse will follow, either at the beginning, or, far more commonly, at the very end. That is because the discussion of the intersecting-verse will be completed when the introduction of the base-verse is accomplished. What is the upshot? The sole difference between the one type and the other is the positioning of the base- and intersecting-verses. In the catalogues that follow, we retain the taxonomy of Chapter One, with the difference in definition just now explained.

1. Base-verse/intersecting-verse constructions
[base-verse cited first]

I:I	Lev. 1:1 and Ps. 103:20
I:V	Lev 1:1 and Prov. 25:7
I:VI	Lev 1:1 and Prov. 20:15
II:I-II	Lev. 1:2 and Jer. 31:20
III:I	Lev. 2:1-2 and Qoh. 4:6
IV:I	Lev. 4:1-2 and Qoh. 3:16
V:I-III	Lev. 4:3 and Job 34:29-30
VI:I	Lev. 5:1 and Prov. 24:28
VI:II	Lev. 5:1 and Prov. 29:24
VII:I	Lev. 6:2 and Prov. 10:12
VIII:I	Lev. 6:13 and Ps. 75:6
IX:I-III	Lev. 7:11-12 and Ps. 50:23
X:I-III	Lev. 8:1-3 and Ps. 45:7
XI:I-IV	Lev. 9:1 and Prov. 9:1-6
XII:I	Lev. 10:9 and Prov. 23:31-2

XIV:I	Lev. 12:1-2 and Ps. 139:5
XV:I-II	Lev. 13:1-3 and Job 28:25-27
XVI:I	Lev. 14:2 and Prov. 6:16-19
XVII:I	Lev. 14:33-34 and Prov. 73:1-5
XVIII:I	Lev. 15:1-2 and Qoh. 12:1-7
XIX:I-III	Lev. 15:25 and Song 5:11
XX:I	Lev. 16:1 and Qoh. 9:2
XXI:I-IV	Lev. 16:3 and Ps. 27:1
XXII:I-IV	Lev. 17:3-5 and Qoh. 5:8
XXIII:I-VII	Lev. 18:1-3 and Song 2:2
XXIV:I	Lev. 19:2 and Is. 5:16
XXV:I-II	Lev. 19:23-25 and Prov. 3:18
XXVI:I-III	Lev. 21:1 and Ps. 12:7
XXVII:I	Lev. 22:27 and Ps. 36:6
XXVIII:I-III	Lev. 23:10 and Qoh. 1:3
	[not an ideal example of the form]
XXIX:I	Lev. 23:24 and Ps. 119:89
XXX:I	Lev. 23:39-40 and Prov. 8:10
XXXI:I	Lev. 24:1-2 and Ps. 71:19
XXXII:III	Lev. 24:10 and 1 Sam. 17:4
XXXV:IV	Lev. 26:3 and Jer. 33:25
XXXVI:I	Qoh. 5:5 and Lev. 27:2
XXXVII:II	Job 34:11 and Lev. 27:1-5

2. Intersecting-verse/base-verse constructions
[base-verse comes only at the end]

II:II	Ps. 22:23-4 and Lev. 2:1
III:III	Is. 55:7 and Lev. 2:1
[III:VI.3	Lev. 2:3 and Ps. 17:15]
IV:II	Qoh. 6:7 and Lev. 4:2
IV:III	Prov. 19:2 and Lev. 4:2
VI:II	Ps. 51:19-21 and Lev. 6:9
VII:II	Jud. 14:14 and Lev. 6:13
IX:V	Prov. 14:9 and Lev. 7:12
X:IV	Prov. 24:11 and Lev. 8:2
XI:V-V	Ps. 18:26-27 and Lev. 9:1
XII:II	Ps. 19:7-9 and Lev. 10:8-9
XII:I	Prov. 15:31-2 and Lev. 10:16-17
XIII:I	Hab. 3:6 and Lev. 11:1-2
XIII:III	Prov. 30:5 and Lev. 11:1-2

XIV:II	Job 36:3 and Lev. 12:2
XIV:III	Job 10:12 and Lev. 12:2
XIV:IV	Job 38:8-11 and Lev. 12:2
XIV:V	Ps. 51:5 and Lev. 12:2
XIV:VI	Ps. 130:3 and Lev. 12:2
XIV:VII	Qoh. 11:2 and Lev. 12:3
XV:II	Job 38:25 and Lev. 13:2
XVI:I	Prov. 34:12-13 and Lev. 14:2
XVI:III	Job 20:6-7 and Lev. 14:2
XVII:II	Job 20:28-29 and Lev. 14:34
XVIII:II	Hab. 1:7 and Lev. 15:2
XVIII:III	Is. 17:11 and Lev. 15:2
XIX:IV	Qoh. 10:18 and Lev. 15:25
XX:II	Ps. 75:4 and Lev. 16:2
XX:III	Qoh. 2:2 [and Lev. 16:2]
XX:IV	Job 38:27-29 and Lev. 16:2
XX:V	Job 37:1 and Lev. 16:2
XX:VI	Prov. 17:26 and Lev. 16:2
XXI: V-VI	Prov. 24:6 and Lev. 16:3
XXII:VI.2-3	Prov. 30:7-9 and Lev. 17:3
[XXIII.VII.2	Ez. 23:2 and Lev. 18:1-3]
XXIV:II	Ps. 92:8 and Lev. 19:2
XXIV:III-IV	Ps. 20:2 and Lev. 19:2
XXV:IV	Qoh. 2:24 and Lev. 19:23
XXV:V	Job 38:30 and Lev. 19:23
XXVI:IV-V	Ps. 19:3 and Lev. 21:1
XXVI: VI	Ps. 19:9 and Lev. 21:1
XXVII:II	Job 41:11 and Lev. 22:26
XXVII:III	Ez. 29:16 and Lev. 22:26
XXVII:IV-V	Qoh. 3:15 and Lev. 22:26-27
XXVII:VI	Mic. 6:3 and Lev. 22:26-27
XXVII:VII	Is. 41:24 and Lev. 22:26-27
XXVIII:IV	Job 5:5 and Lev. 23:10
XXIX:II	Jer. 30:10 and Lev. 23:24
XXIX:III	Ps. 47:5 and Lev. 23:24
XXIX:IV	Ps. 89:16 and Lev. 23:24
XXIX:V	Prov. 15:24, 6:23 and Lev. 23:24
XXIX:VI	Ps. 81:4 and Lev. 23:24
XXIX:VII	Is. 48:17 and Lev. 23:24
XXIX:VIII	Ps. 62:9 and Lev. 23:24
XXX:II	Ps. 16:11 and Lev. 23:40

XXX:III	Ps. 102:17-18 and Lev. 23:40
XXX:IV	Ps. 96:12-14 and Lev. 23:40
XXX:V	Ps. 26:6-7 and Lev. 23:40
XXXI:II	Ps. 119:140 and Lev. 24:2
XXXI:III	Job 14:15 and Lev. 24:2
XXXI:IV	Ps. 18:29 and Lev. 24:2
XXXI:V	Prov. 21:22 and Lev. 24:2
XXXI:VI	Job 25:3 and Lev. 24:2
XXXII:I	Ps. 12:8 and Lev. 24:10-13
XXXII:II	Qoh. 10:20 and Lev. 24:14
XXXII:V	Song 4:12 and Lev. 24:11
XXXIII:I	Prov. 18:21 and Lev. 25:14
XXXIII:III	Amos 9:1 and Lev. 25:14
XXXIV:I	Ps. 41:1-2 and Lev. 25:25
XXXIV:II	Prov. 19:17 and Lev. 25:25
XXXIV:III	Prov. 11:17 and Lev. 25:25
XXXIV:IV	Prov. 29:13 (and 22:2) and Lev. 25:25
XXXIV:V	Prov. 7:14 and Lev. 25:25
XXXV:I	Ps. 119:59 and Lev. 26:3
XXXV:II	Prov. 8:32 and Lev. 26:3
XXXVI:I.1,4	Ps. 102:25 and Lev. 26:42

[Reversal of order in Lev. 26:42 is what is noted. But the composition as a whole in no way forms a suitable example of this pattern.]

XXXVI:II	Ps. 80:8-10 and Lev. 26:42
XXXVI:III	Prov. 11:21 and Lev. 26:42
[XXXVI:IV	Is. 43:1 and Lev. 26:42. Base-verse not cited.]

3. Verse-by-verse exegetical constructions

I: VII-VIII.1	Lev. 1:1. Re God's calling Moses.
I:VIII.2-3	Lev. 1:1. Meaning of word "call."
I:IX	As above. Call to Moses in particular.
I:X-XI	Lev. 1:1. Tent of meeting.
II:IV	Lev. 1:2. Speak to Israel in particular.
II:V	Continues II:IV.
II:VI	Lev. 1:2. Why formulated this way.
II:VII	Lev. 1:2. Bringing offerings.
III:IV	Lev. 1:16
III:V	Lev. 1:16-17
III:VI	Lev. 2:1-2
IV:IV-V	Lev. 4:1

V:V–VI	Lev. 4:3
V:VII	Lev. 4:13-15
VI:IV	Lev. 5:1
VI:V	Lev. 5:1
VII:III	Lev. 6:1
VII:IV	Lev. 6:2
VII:V	Lev. 6:2
VIII:IV	Lev. 6:13
IX:IV	Lev. 7:12
X:VIII	Lev. 8:1-2
X:IX.1-2	Lev. 8:2-3
XI:VIII	Lev. 9:1
XIII:IV	Lev. 11:2
XV:V	Lev. 13:2 as juxtaposed to Lev. 12:2.
XV:VI	Lev. 13:2
XV:VIII	Lev. 13:3
XV:IX	Lev. 13:2
XVI:V	
XVI:VI	
XVI:VII	
XVI:IX	
XVII:III	
XVII:V	
XVII:III	
XVIII:IV	
XVIII:V	
XIX:VI	
XX:VIII	
XX:IX	
XX:X	
XX:XI	
XX:XII	
XXI:VII	
XXI:IX	
XXI:XI	
XXI:XII	
XXII:V	
XXII:VII	
XXII:VIII	
XXIII:IX	
XXIV:V	
XXIV:VI	

XXIV:VIII
XXIV:IX
XXV:VI
XXVI:VII.1
XXVI:VIII
XXVII:VIII
XXVII:IX
XXVII:X
XXVII:XI
XXVII:XII
XXVIII:V
XXVIII:VI
XXIX:VIII B
XXIX:IX
XXX:VI
XXX:VII
XXX:VIII
XXX:IX
XXX:X
XXX:XI
XXX:XII
XXX:XIV
XXX:XV
XXX:XVI
XXXI:X
XXXII:IV
XXXII:VII.1
XXXV:VI
XXXV:VII
XXXV:VIII
XXXV:IX
XXXV:X
XXXV:XI
XXXV:XII
XXXVI:V

4. Miscellanies

I:II
I:III
I:IV
I:XII

I:XIII
I:XIV
III:VI.5-8
[IV:IV   Joined to IV:V.]
IV:VI
IV:VII
IV:VIII
V:IV
V:VIII
VI:III
VI:VI
VII:II
VII:VI
VIII:III
IX:VI
IX:VII
IX:VIII
IX:IX
X:V
X:VI-VII
X:IX.3-8
X:VI-VII
X:IX
XI:VI
XI:IX
XII:II
XIII:V
XIV:VIII
XIV:IX
XV:IV
XV:VII
XVI:IV
XVI:VIII
XVII:IV
XIX:V
XX:VII
XXI:VIII
XXI:X
XXII:VI.1
XXII:IX
XXII:X
XXIII:VIII

XXIII:X
XXIII:XI
XXIII:XII
XXIII:XIII
XXIV:VII
XXV:III
XXV:VII
XXV:VIII
XXVI:VIL2-6
XXIX:X
XXIX:XI
XXIX:XII
XXX:XIII
XXI:VII
XXXI:VIII
XXXI:IX
XXXII:VI
XXXII:VII
XXXII:VIII
XXXIII:II
XXXIII:IV
XXXIII:V
XXXIII:VL2
XXXIV:VI
XXXIV:VII
XXXIV:VIII
XXXIV:IX
XXXIV:X
XXXIV:XI
XXXIV:XII
XXXIV:XIII
XXXIV:XIV
XXXIV:XV
XXXIV:XVI
XXXV:III
XXXV:V
XXXVI:I
XXXVI:VI
XXXVII:III
XXXVII:IV

Let us now survey the results as a whole. We have counted, in all, 304 entries on the four catalogues:

I.	38	12.5%
II.	84	27.6%
III.	94	30.9%
IV.	88	28.9%

The three defined taxa thus cover 71% of the whole, a somewhat higher proportion than we noted in Chapter One. The two truly distinctive patterns, types I and II, cover a sizable part of the whole -- 40%. Obviously, in due course, we shall have to pay more attention to the materials catalogued as merely miscellaneous, since they are far from lacking all taxonomic traits. But the criteria for differentiation and classification will not derive from an inductive sorting out of materials in Leviticus Rabbah in particular. As we shall see in Part Two, nearly all of the materials shared by Leviticus Rabbah with other contemporary documents, in particular Genesis Rabbah and the Yerushalmi, fall into the classification of miscellaneous. So when we seek to classify the miscellaneous items, we shall find categories supplied by documents sharing a given item, e.g., Leviticus Rabbah and Genesis Rabbah or Leviticus Rabbah and the Yerushalmi. Another sort of classification, we shall see very soon, will be simply the matter of length: A brief saying or episodic exegesis, consisting of one or two or three stichs, as against a protracted discussion, a sizable story, a systematic and extensive exegesis of a verse of Scripture or a long sequence of exegetical proofs of a proposition. But the definitive trait of the classification of miscellaneous remains the simple fact that all items at hand ignore the literary structure and organization definitive of Leviticus Rabbah. But most of those items can be shown in one way or another to serve the topical or even logical program of those who structured and organized the document. And that is the probative fact for the proposition that Leviticus Rabbah uniformly exhibits integrity and constitutes an autonomous and cogent document, a text. But in so stating, I have gotten ahead of my story.

iii. The Order of Types of Units of Discourse

Having classified the units of discourse of which our thirty-seven parashiyyot are composed, we now go back to ask whether the types of units of discourse follow a single pattern, or whether a given type will appear in any sequence promiscuously, at the beginning, middle, or end of a given parashah. So from the taxonomy of the units of discourse, we proceed to the structure of the thirty-seven parashiyyot as a whole. We ask whether the editors exhibited preferences for a given type of unit of discourse when they faced the task in particular of beginning a parashah or of ending one.

I:I	I
[I:II	IV. The relevance to Moses is via the theme of the righteous proselyte, Pharoah's daughter.]
[I:III	IV. As above. Names of Moses.]
[I:IV	IV. Ps. 89:20 applies to Abraham, David, Moses.]

I:V   I
I:VI   I
I:VII   III
I:VIII   III
I:IX   III
I:X   III
I:XI   III
[I:XII   IV. Supplement on tent of meeting, the theme of I:X-XI.]
[I:XIII   IV. Continues I:XII.]
I:XIV   IV. As above.

II:I-III   I
II:IV-V   III
II:VI   III
II:VII   III

III:I   I
III:II   II
III:III   II
III:IV   III
III:V   III
III:VI   III
III:VI.5-8   IV

IV:I   I
IV:II   II
IV:III   II
IV:IV-V   III
[IV:VI   IV. Collective responsibility. Relevant to Lev. 4:13.]
IV:VII   IV. Soul-sayings.
IV:VIII   IV. As above.

V:I   I
V:II   I
V:III   I
[V:IV   IV. As explained.]
V:V-VI   III
V:VII   III
[V:VIII   IV. As explained.]

VI:I   I
VI:II   I

[VI:III	IV. Theme of VI:I-II, false oath.]
VI:IV	III
VI:V	III
VI:VI	IV. Is. 8:18-20
VII:I	I
VII:II	II
VII:III	III
VII:IV	III
VII:V	III
VII:VI	IV. Relevant in theme, not in detail.
VIII:I	I
VIII:II	II
[VIII:III	IV. Thematically relevant.]
VIII:IV	III
IX:I	I
IX:II	I
IX:III	I
IX:IV	III
IX:V	II
[IX:VI	IV. Thematically relevant.]
[IX:VII	IV. Thematically relevant.]
[IX:VIII	IV. Thematically relevant.]
[IX:IX	IV. Continues theme of peace tangentially introduced in IX:VIII.]
X:I	I
X:II	I
X:III	I
X:IV	II
[X:V	IV. Theme of repentance through prayer. Relevant in a general way.]
[X:VI-VII	IV. Relevant to theme of atonement of sin.]
X:VIII	III
X:IX.1-2	III
X:IX.3-8	IV
XI:I	I
XI:II	I
XI:III	I

XI:IV	I
XI:V-VI	II
[XI:VI	IV. Intersects with the base-verse only incidentally.]
XI:VIII	III
XI:IX	IV
XII:I	I
[XII:II	IV. Theme relevant.]
XII:III	II
[XII:IV	IV. As above.]
[XII:V	IV. As above.]
XIII:I	II
XIII:II	II
XIII:III	II
XIII:IV	III
[XIII:V	IV. Intersects in reference to the theme.]
XIV:I	I
XIV:II	II
XIV:III	II
XIV:IV	II
XIV:V	II
XIV:VI	II
XIV:VII	II
XIV:VIII	IV. Thematically relevant.
XIV:IX	IV
XV:I	I
XV:II	I
XV:III	II
[XV:IV	IV. Intersects with theme.]
XV:V	III
XV:VI	III
[XV:VII	IV. Same exegetical mode as foregoing.]
XV:VIII	III
XV:IX	III
XVI:I	I
XVI:II	II
XVI:III	II
[XVI:IV	IV. Intersects with theme.]

XVI:V	III
XVI:VI	III
XVI:VII	III
[XVI:VIII	IV. Intersects with theme.]
XVI:IX	III
XVII:I	I
XVII:II	II
XVII:III	III
[XVII:IV	IV. Intersects with theme.]
XVII:V	III
XVII:VI	III
XVII:VII	III
XVIII:I	I
XVIII:II	II
XVIII:III	II
XVIII:IV	III
XVIII:V	III
XIX:I	I
XIX:II	I
XIX:III	I
XIX:IV	II
[XIX:V	IV. Shared language: many days.]
XIX:VI	III
XIX:VII	III
XX:I	I
XX:II	II
XX:III	II
XX:IV	II
XX:V	II
XX:VI	II
[XX:VII	IV. Introduces basic theme of XX:VIII.]
XX:VIII	III
XX:IX	III
XX:X	III
XX:XI	III
XX:XII	III
XXI:I	I
XXI:II	I

XXI:III	I
XXI:IV	I
XXI:V	II
XXI:VI	II
XXI:VII	III
[XXI:VIII	IV. Takes up theme of foregoing.]
XXI:IX	III
[XXI:X	IV. Continues foregoing.]
XXI:XI	III
XXI:XII	III
XXII:I	I
XXII:II	I
XXII:III	I
XXII:IV	I
XXII:V	III
XXII:VI.1	IV
XXII:VI.2-3	II
XXII:VII	III
XXII:VIII	III
[XXII:IX	IV. Intersects in theme.]
XXII:X	IV
XXIII:I	I
XXIII:II	I
XXIII:III	I
XXIII:IV	I
XXIII:V	I
XXIII:VI	I
XXIII:VII.1	I
[XXIII:VIII	IV. Defective text.]
XXIII:IX	III
[XXIII:X	IV. Continues foregoing theme.]
[XXIII:XI	IV. Continues foregoing theme.]
[XXIII:XII	IV. Continues foregoing theme.]
[XXIII:XIII	IV. Continues foregoing theme.]
XXIV:I	I
XXIV:II	II
XXIV:III	II
XXIV:IV	II
XXIV:V	III

XXIV:VI	III
[XXIV:VII	IV. Intersects in theme.]
XXIV:VIII	III
XXIV:IX	III

XXV:I	I
XXV:II	I
[XXV:III	IV. Thematic intersection.]
XXV:IV	II
XXV:V	II
XXV:VI	III
[XXV:VII	IV. Continues theme of foregoing.]
[XXV:VIII	IV. Continues theme of foregoing.]

XXVI:I	I
XXVI:II	I
XXVI:III	I
XXVI:IV	II
XXVI:V	II
XXVI:VI	II
XXVI:VII.1	III
[XXVI:VII.2-6	IV. Intersects at the end.]
XXVI:VIII	III

XXVII:I	I
XXVII:II	II
XXVII:III	II
XXVII:IV	II
XXVII:V	II
XXVII:VI	II
XXVII:VII	II
XXVII:VIII	III
XXVII:IX	III
XXVII:X	III
XXVII:XI	III
XXVII:XII	III

XXVIII:I	I
XXVIII:II	I
XXVIII:III	I
XXVIII:IV	II
XXVIII:V	III
XXVIII:VI	III

XXIX:I	I
XXIX:II	II
XXIX:III	II
XXIX:IV	II
XXIX:V	II
XXIX:VI	II
XXIX:VII	II
XXIX:VIII	II
XXIX:VIII B	III
XXIX:IX	III
[XXIX:X	IV. Continues theme of foregoing.]
[XXIX:XI	IV. While Lev. 23:24 is cited, the point is distinctive to the unit of discourse.]
[XXIX:XII	IV. Intersects in theme.]
XXX:I	I
XXX:II	II
XXX:III	II
XXX:IV	II
XXX:V	II
XXX:VI	III
XXX:VII	III
XXX:VIII	III
XXX:IX	III
XXX:X	III
XXX:XI	III
XXX:XII	III
[XXX:XIII	IV. Intersects with base-verse.]
XXX:XIX	III
XXX:XV	III
XXX:XVI	III
XXXI:I	I
XXXI:II	II
XXXI:III	II
XXXI:IV	II
XXXI:V	II
XXXI:VI	II
[XXXI:VII	IV. Thematically relevant.]
[XXXI:VIII	IV. Thematically relevant.]
[XXXI:IX	IV. Thematically relevant.]
XXXI:X	III
XXXI:XI	III

XXXII:I	II
XXXII:II	II
XXXII:III	I
XXXII:IV	III
XXXII:V	II
[XXXII:VI	IV. Intersects in one detail.]
[XXXII:VII	IV. Continues foregoing.]
[XXXII:VIII	IV. Continues foregoing.]
XXXIII:I	II
[XXXIII:II	IV. Interest in exegesis of a word in the base-verse.]
XXXIII:III	II
[XXXIII:IV	IV. As above.]
[XXXIII:V	IV. As above.]
XXXIII:VI.1	III
[XXXIII.VI.2-7	IV. Tacked on because of thematic intersection.]
XXXIV:I	II
XXXIV:II	II
XXXIV:III	II
XXXIV:IV	II
XXXIV:V	II
[XXXIV:VI	IV. Exegesis of word in the base-verse.]
[XXXIV:VII	IV. Thematic intersection.]
[XXXIV:VIII	IV. Thematic intersection.]
[XXXIV:IX	IV. Thematic intersection.]
[XXXIV:X	IV. Thematic intersection.]
[XXXIV:XI	IV. Thematic intersection.]
[XXXIV:XII	IV. Thematic intersection.]
[XXXIV:XIII-XVI	IV. Is. 58:7 -- thematic intersection.]
XXXV:I	II
XXXV:II	II
[XXXV:III	IV. May exemplify theme of base-verse.]
XXXV:IV	I
[XXXV:V	IV. Explains word in base-verse.]
XXXV:VI	III
XXXV:VII	III
XXXV:VIII	III
XXXV:IX	III
XXXV:X	III
XXXV:XI	III
XXXV:XII	III

XXXVI:I	[II] IV
XXXVI:II	II
XXXVI:III	II
XXXVI:IV	II
XXXVI:V	III
[XXXVI:VI	IV. Thematic intersection.]

XXXVII:I	II
XXXVII:II	II
[XXXVII:III	IV. Thematic intersection.]
[XXXVII:IV	IV. Thematic intersection.]

The results may now be stated through the summary that follows:

Type I comes in first position in the following parashiyyot:

I, II, III, IV, V, VI, VII, VIII, IX, X, XI, XII, XIV, XV, XVI, XVII, XVIII, XIX, XX, XXI, XXII, XXIII, XXIV, XXV, XXVI, XXVII, XXVIII.

Type II comes in first position in the following parashiyyot:

XII, XXXII, XXXIII, XXXIV, XXXV

Type III comes in first position in the following parashiyyot: --

Type IV comes in first position in the following parashiyyot:

XXXVI

Type I comes in second position in the following parashiyyot:

V, VI, IX, X, XI, XV, XVII, XXII, XXIII, XXVI, XXVII, XXVIII, XXXVII

Type II comes in second position in the following parashiyyot:

III, IV, VII, VIII, XIII, XIV, XVI, XVII, XVIII, XIX, XX, XXI, XXIV, XXV, XXIX, XXX, XXXI, XXXII, XXXIV, XXXV, XXXVI

Type III comes in second position in the following parashiyyot:

II

Type IV comes in second position in the following parashiyyot:

XII, XXXIII

Type I comes last in the following parashiyyot: --

Type II comes last in the following parashiyyot: --

Type III comes last in the following parashiyyot:

II, VIII, XV, XVI, XVII, XVIII, XIX, XX, XXI, XXIV, XXVI, XXVII, XXVIII,
XXX, XXXI, XXXV

Type IV comes last in the following parashiyyot:

I, III, IV, V, VI, VII, IX, X, XI, XII, XIII, XIV, XXII, XXIII, XXV, XXIX,
XXXII, XXXIII, XXXIV, XXXVI, XXXVII

We may compare the proportions as follows:

Type I comes in first position in	31/37	83.7%
Type II comes in first position in	5/37	13.5%
Type III comes in first position in	0/37	0.0%
Type IV comes in first position in	1/37	2.7%
Type I comes in second position in	13/37	35.1%
Type II comes in second position in	21/37	56.7%
Type III comes in second position in	1/37	2.7%
Type IV comes in second position in	21/37	5.4%
Type I comes in last position in	0/37	0.0%
Type II comes in last position in	0/37	0.0%
Type III comes in last position in	16/37	43.2%
Type IV comes in last position in	21/37	56.7%

I have probably overstated the instances in which type I comes in second position. Many of the entries of type I involve sustained and unitary compositions, in which a single intersecting-verse is worked out over a series of two or three subdivisions of a parashah. Otherwise the proportions conform to the impressions yielded by the catalogues just now presented.

To state the result very simply: the framer of a passage ordinarily began with a base-verse/intersecting-verse construction. He very commonly proceeded with an intersecting-verse/base-verse construction. Then he would provide such exegeses of pertinent verses of Leviticus as he had in hand. He would conclude either with type III or type IV constructions, somewhat more commonly the latter than the former. So the program of the authors is quite simple. They began with types I and II -- 100% of the first and second position entries, proceeded with type III, and concluded with type III or IV.

So Leviticus Rabbah consists of two main types of units of discourse, first in position, expositions of how verses of the book of Leviticus relate to verses of other books of the Hebrew bible, second in position, exposition of verses of the book of Leviticus viewed on their own, and, varying in position but in any event very often concluding a construction, miscellaneous materials.

In more than casual ways we are reminded of the preferences and policies of the Yerushalmi's framers. As I showed in The Talmud of the Land of Israel. 35. Introduction. Taxonomy (Chicago, 1983), the compositors of the Yerushalmi began their discourse with a close reading of a Mishnah-paragraph, very often in reference to its Scriptural basis; they then proceeded to examine the principles of the Mishnah-paragraph and to expound them in their own terms, and finally, they went on to whatever else struck them as relevant in a given context. The exposition of one verse of the Hebrew Scriptures, one in Leviticus, in the light of some other, one in Job or Proverbs or Psalms, for example, served a purpose for Leviticus Rabbah not terribly different from that served in the Yerushalmi by the provision of scriptural proof-texts for Mishnah's sentences. The articulation and expansion of the explanation of a given verse in Leviticus finds its counterpart in the Yerushalmi in exactly the same procedure for the Mishnah. And the rest would find its place in sequence afterward.

It would be bizarre to claim that Leviticus Rabbah's authorship intended to supply a kind of Talmud to the book of Leviticus. But it is not entirely farfetched to recognize points of correspondence. In the Yerushalmi the evocation of a scriptural proof-text for a Mishnaic sentence served to demonstrate the unity of the Mishnah's rules with the Scripture's principles. In Leviticus Rabbah the citation of a verse of Job or Proverbs or Psalms in amplification of a verse (and thus a theme) of Leviticus underlined the deep unity of the several parts of the Torah: Pentateuch and Writings. So the upshot in both documents was to show the cogency and harmony of what later would be called "the one whole Torah of Moses, our rabbi." (This is not the place to ask who denied that cogency and dismissed the possibility of harmony.)

iv. Literary Patterns of Leviticus Rabbah

I have now established several facts.

First, Leviticus Rabbah, viewed whole, does not comprise a mere random selection of diverse types of literary expression. The fact that 70% of the whole falls into three taxonomic categories, of which two may be distinguished only on narrowly formal grounds, proves otherwise. The authors of the document adhered to extremely limited choices of literary conventions, saying whatever they wished to say about the book of Leviticus in essentially two ways only.

Second, it follows that, seeing the composition at the end of its formation as we do, the document had not only compilers, but authors. These authors (whether original writers or editors) took an active role in the formal expression of the points to be made. They produced not a collection but a composition. What in fact did the authors accomplish?

The authors of Leviticus Rabbah undertook a twofold program. They wished to provide both an exegesis and an expansion, into a larger context, of the book of Leviticus. This was along two lines.

First, as I just said, they wished to establish links between statements in the book of Leviticus and statements in other biblical books, among which Proverbs, Psalms, and Job figured prominently. They did this so as to set forth principles or beliefs or ideals or values transcending any one biblical book and (in their mind) expressed in many books. So they in some measure accomplished the demonstration that the Torah speaks everywhere about the same things, a single, cogent and everywhere harmonious revelation. The forms the authors took for making this large, substantive point prove congruent to their theological purpose. A verse from Leviticus juxtaposed with a verse from some other biblical book, standing fore or aft, established a tension to be resolved through the demonstration that the two diverse verses really meant the same thing.

Second, the authors wished to amplify or explain points in individual verses of the book of Leviticus, ordinarily those same verses that, earlier in a composition, stood in tension with verses of some other biblical book. This exercise came second in order. It served the purpose of clarifying details once the main point had been made.

The authors also made ample provision for illustrative materials to hammer home their basic points. These illustrative materials, of a broad and diverse character, in no way conformed in literary patterns to the exegetical program that defined what was primary to the document as a whole. Materials I catalogued as miscellaneous exhibited noteworthy diversity in form, pattern, or structure. But in respect to the main point made by a given saying, story, or composite, each item simply restated the point dominant in a parashah as a whole.

I indicated the connections between miscellanies and classified units of discourse in the preceding catalogue. Ordinarily, where the editors proposed to insert such miscellanies, they would choose one of two positions for them. Either they would place a miscellaneous item either as a supplement to an item bearing the distinctive literary traits of the document as a whole, e.g., in immediate juxtaposition to a Type I or a Type II unit of discourse. Or they would locate such an item at the end of a given parashah, that is, after the repertoire of types I, II, and III had been fully exposed.

We now therefore know that units of discourse that fall into the classifications of types I, II, or III in their fixed order define that literary structure that imparts to Leviticus Rabbah the formal and stylistic unity exhibited by its principal components. So we may indeed speak of literary patterns -- structures of completed discourse -- that recur in Leviticus Rabbah. The recurrent traits prove to be both in formal character (for types I and II) and in conventional sequence (for all four types). Leviticus Rabbah, viewed whole and in its constitutive components, finds definition in a dominant literary structure and a recurrent mode of literary organization.

Part Two

SOURCES SHARED BY LEVITICUS RABBAH WITH
OTHER CANONICAL DOCUMENTS

Chapter Three
BRIEF SAYINGS COMMON TO LEVITICUS RABBAH AND OTHER TEXTS

i. The Problem

Leviticus Rabbah exhibits distinctive literary patterns. These permit us to describe the literary choices of form, order, and proportion made by the authors of the document. But knowing the final shape of the document and identifying the authors' distinctive policies for giving to their ideas a highly patterned literary form leaves open one question. That is, we now ask about components of units of discourse, whether individual sentences of complete paragraphs -- shared by Leviticus Rabbah and other texts. Why so? Since we wish to find out whether Leviticus Rabbah exhibits a fundamental integrity or whether the document constitutes a mere collection of already-available materials, we must turn forthwith from the largest components of the thirty-seven parashiyyot -- the principal units of discourse of which each parashah is made up -- to the smallest.

What is at stake in this shift in interest, from the perspective afforded by seeing matters whole to the angle of vision afforded by close examination of the parts? The question now concerns the extent to which the authors of Leviticus Rabbah have made use of bits and pieces of materials utilized, also, in other canonical documents of the system of Judaism at hand. We shall now identify passages of Leviticus Rabbah that occur in other compositions of the same age. What we want to know is a simple thing. Do these brief sayings that occur in both Leviticus Rabbah and some other document of the times play a large or a small role in Leviticus Rabbah? A clear assessment of the proportion of shared materials, in the form of phrases or sentences or small groups of sentences such as stichs (given in my translation with the mark of a letter) will settle this urgent question: does Leviticus Rabbah intersect with other documents in any appreciable measure, or does Leviticus Rabbah present materials that are mostly unique to its authors or editors? Here through a detailed probe we shall answer these basic questions.

Once we have done so, we shall be able to show the relationships -- the proportions, the comparisons -- between the smaller sets of materials of Leviticus Rabbah that are particular to that document and those of episodic components of Leviticus Rabbah that are held in common between Leviticus Rabbah and some other rabbinic writing, or among several rabbinic documents all together.

At this second stage in the inquiry therefore I have to sort out what in the extant literature is unique to Leviticus Rabbah from what is not, I propose to characterize the latter types of discourse as I said, both large (entire units of discourse) and small (brief components of units of discourse, e.g., sentences, paragraphs).

The simplest approach again is to begin with a thorough examination of a single parashah, chosen more or less at random. Once we have found in one parashah appropriate modes of characterizing the data on materials held in common between Leviticus

Rabbah and other rabbinic writings, we test the proposed method by applying it to two further parashiyyot. In this way our text once more instructs us on how to proceed. The preliminary probes are in this chapter; the survey of a population of data covering the bulk of the document is in Chapter Four.

It goes without saying that at issue are canonical documents generally assumed to have come into being prior to the time of Leviticus Rabbah, that is, in the late fourth or early fifth century, or at approximately the same time. Excluded then are the Talmud of Babylonia and the later compilations of scriptural exegeses ("midrashim"). What is used in later documents need not have come from Leviticus Rabbah, but can have derived from a source common to the editors of our document and many others. Hence, we do not care, in attempting to assess the integrity of Leviticus Rabbah, whether materials here recur, later on, in the Bavli, let alone in medieval compilations of biblical exegeses. What is used in earlier documents likewise can have come from a common source accessible to the authors of Leviticus Rabbah and, e.g., the authors of the Tosefta or Genesis Rabbah or the Yerushalmi. Here we do care. About what? What is important to us is the extent to which our document is made up of materials shared by its authors and the writers of other books of its time or earlier. Included then in general are the Mishnah (including tractate Avot), Tosefta, the Yerushalmi, and Genesis Rabbah. (Of Sifra and the two Sifres we are less certain.) It further is self-evident that at issue are verbatim correspondences between a passage of one document and one of some other. I am not interested in listing instances in which the gist or the main idea, let alone the theme or basic value, of a given passage occurs in numerous other passages across the broad sweep of rabbinic literature of late antiquity (let alone medieval and even early modern times). When people claim that the rabbinic canon is "synoptic" or that vast intersections among documents make it impossible to view each composition by itself, they point not to shared symbols or ideals or laws but to shared languages, entire compositions. On that basis they claim that we must read everything in light of everything else, nothing on its own. So, for our part, we want to know precisely how much of the actual wording of Leviticus Rabbah is shared with other writings prior to, or contemporary with, that document.

What we seek to find out is a simple matter. Do the authors of Leviticus Rabbah draw heavily upon an available corpus of materials that serve, also, the authors of other compositions prior to, or in the time of, their work on Leviticus Rabbah? Or can we demonstrate that the bulk of the document, is particular, in that extant cannon, to Leviticus Rabbah? These are matters of fact that can readily be settled.

ii. A Preliminary Probe: Parashah 7

I present the entire parashah and underline and identify those passages that occur in both Leviticus Rabbah and some other document of the rabbinic canon completed prior to, or in the time of, that document. My source for cross-references is Margulies' footnotes.

VII:I

1.   A.   "[The Lord said to Moses,] 'Command Aaron [and his sons, saying, This is the law of the burnt-offering ']' (Lev. 6:2 [RSV: 6:9]).

B.   "Hatred stirs up strife, but love covers all offenses" (Prov. 10:12).

C.   The hatred that Israel brought between themselves and their father in heaven "stirs up strife" (MDNYM), [that is to say,] provoked judgments (DYNY DYNYM).

D.   Said R. Ishmael b. R. Nehemiah, "For nearly nine hundred years hatred was pent up between Israel and their father in heaven [because of their idolatry in Egypt] from the time that they went forth from Egypt until Ezekiel arose. That is in line with the following verse of Scripture: '[On that day I swore to them that I would bring them out of the land of Egypt into a land that I had searched out for them, a land flowing with milk and honey, and most glorious of all lands,] and I said to them, "Cast away the detestable things your eyes feast on, [every one of you, and do not defile yourselves with the idols of Egypt; I am the Lord your God." But they rebelled against me and would not listen to me; they did not every man cast away the detestable things their eyes feasted on, nor did they forsake the idols of Egypt]' (Ez. 20:8).

E.   "'But I dealt with them for the sake of my great name, that it not be profaned.' That is in line with the following verse of Scripture: 'But I acted for the sake of my name, that it should not be profaned in the sight of the nations among whom they dwelt in whose sight I made myself known to them in bringing them out of the land of Egypt' (Ez. 20:9).

F.   "'But love covers all offenses' (Prov. 10:12).

G.   "It is the love with which the Holy One, blessed be he, loved Israel: 'I have loved you, said the Lord' (Mal. 1:2)."

2.   A.   Another interpretation: "Hatred stirs up strife" (Prov. 10:12).

B.   [This refers to] the hatred which Aaron brought between Israel and their father in heaven.

C.   "Stirs up strife" (MDNYM) -- provoked judgments.

D.   Said R. Assi, "[Scripture] teaches that [Aaron] took a hammer and battered [the golden calf] before [the people] saying to them, 'See, there really is nothing in it.'

E.   "That is what the Holy One, blessed be he, told Moses: 'Him who has sinned against me shall I wipe out from my book' (Ex. 32:33).

F.   "That is in line with the following verse of Scripture: 'Moreover the Lord was very angry with Aaron, such as to destroy him' (Deut. 9:20)."

G.   Said R. Joshua of Sikhnin in the name of R. Levi, "The word, 'destroy,' used here means only the extinction of sons and daughters.

H.   "That is in line with the use of the same word in the following
      verse: 'And I destroyed his fruit from above and his root from
      beneath' (Amos 2:9).

I.   "'But love covers all offenses' (Prov. 10:12). [This refers to] the
      prayer that Moses said in [Aaron's] behalf [for he did have sons]."

J.   What prayer did he say in his behalf?

K.   R. Mana of Sha'ab and R. Joshua of Sikhnin in the name of R.
      Levi: "From the beginning of the scroll [of Leviticus] to this point,
      it is written, 'And the sons of Aaron will offer' (Lev. 1:5), 'The sons
      of Aaron will place...' (Lev. 1:7), 'The sons of Aaron will arrange'
      (Lev. 1:8), 'The sons of Aaron will burn' (Lev. 3:5).

L.   "Said Moses before the Holy One, blessed be he, 'Lord of the world,
      will the well be hated but its waters precious?

M.   "'You paid respect to trees because of their offspring [which would
      be valuable in the agricultural life of the holy land].'

N.   "as we have learned in the Mishnah: <u>'All trees may be used for
      burning on the altar-fire except the olive tree and the vine [which
      are too valuable for that purpose]</u> (M. Tam. 2:3).

O.   "'Will you not pay any honor at all to Aaron on account of his
      offspring?'

P.   "Said to him the Holy One, blessed be he, 'By your life, on account
      of your prayer I shall bring him back, and not only so, but I shall
      make him the main act and his sons the side-show:' 'Command
      Aaron and his sons, saying' (Lev. 6:2)."

VII:II

1.   A.   "[O Lord, open my lips, and my mouth shall show forth your praise.
            For you have no delight in sacrifice; were I to give a burnt
            offering, you would not be pleased.] The sacrifice acceptable to
            God is a broken spirit, [a broken and contrite heart, O God, you will
            not despise. Do good to Zion in your good pleasure; rebuild the
            walls of Jerusalem, then will you delight in right sacrifices, in
            burnt offerings and whole burnt offerings; then bulls will be offered
            on your altar" (Ps. 51:19-21 [RSV: 15-19]).

      B.   Zabdi [Zebedee] son of Levi and R. Yose b. Pertos [Peter] and
            rabbis:

      C.   The first of them [Zabdi] said, "David said before the Holy One,
            blessed be he, 'Lord of the world, If you accept me back as a
            penitent [of my sin with Bath Sheba], then I shall know that
            Solomon, my son, will build the house of the sanctuary and will
            build the altar and offer on it all of the sacrifices specified in the
            Torah.

D.   "[And it was from] the following verse of Scripture [that he derived the answer]: 'The sacrifice acceptable to God is a broken spirit.'" [So God did accept David's penitence.

E.   The second [Yose] said, "How do we know concerning one who has repented [his sin], that [Scripture] credits it to him as if he had gone up to Jerusalem, rebuilt the house of the sanctuary, built the altar, and offered on it all of the sacrifices that are specified in the Torah?

F.   "It is from the following verse of Scripture: 'The sacrifice acceptable to God is a broken spirit.'"

G.   And rabbis say, "How do we know that the one who goes before the ark [to lead the congregation in prayer] must make mention of the Temple service and kneel [at that point], as is done in saying this blessing: 'Accept, O Lord, our God and dwell in, Zion, your city?'

H.   "There is he who wishes to derive the answer from the verse: 'The sacrifice acceptable to God is a broken spirit, [a broken and contrite heart, O God, you will not despise. Do good to Zion in your good pleasure; rebuild the walls of Jerusalem, then will you delight in right sacrifices...] [The kneeling signifies the broken heart.]"

2.   A.   Said R. Abba bar Yudan, "Whatever [blemish God] declared invalid in the case of a beast, he declared valid in the case of a man.

     B.   "Just as he declared invalid in the case of a beast [to be brought for a sacrifice] 'one that was blind or broken' (Lev. 22:22), so he declared the same valid in the case of a man: 'A broken and contrite heart, O God, you will not despise' (Ps. 51:19)."

3.   A.   Said R. Alexandri, "In the case of an ordinary person, if he should make use of a broken pot, it is demeaning to him, but as to the Holy One, blessed be he, all the utensils that he uses are broken, as it is written, 'The Lord is near to those of broken heart' (Ps. 34:19), 'He heals broken hearts' (Ps. 11 147:3). 'I dwell in the high and holy place with him that is of a contrite and humble spirit' (Is. 57:15). 'The sacrifice acceptable to God is a broken spirit, a broken and contrite heart, O God, you will not despise' (Ps. 51:19)."

4.   A.   Said R. Abba bar Yudan, "The matter may be compared to the case of a king, whose courtier paid him honor by giving him a jug of wine and a basket of figs.

     B.   "Said the king to him, 'Is this a gift!'

     C.   "He said to him, "My lord, O king, this is how I can pay honor to you at the moment. But when you enter your palace, you will know how I can pay honor to you. [So this is just a gift for the moment.]"

D. "So the Holy One, blessed be he, said to Moses, 'This is the law of the burnt offering. [Is this] [sole lamb] a burnt offering...' (Lev. 6:9). [It is paltry.]

E. "[Moses] said before him, 'Lord of the world, for the moment this is what I can offer before you. But when "you do good to Zion in your good pleasure, rebuilding the walls of Jerusalem, then will you delight in right sacrifices, in burnt offerings and whole burnt offerings; then bulls [not merely lambs] will be offered on your altar" (Ps. 51:20-21).'"

VII:II

1. A. [To return to the] body [of the text, the topic of the burnt-offering:] R. Simeon b. Yohai taught, "A burnt-offering is brought only on account of what stirs up the heart [to sin]."

B. R. Levi said, "An available verse of Scripture makes that very point: 'The burnt-offering (^{C}olah) is on account of (^{C}al) your spirit' (Ez. 20:32)."

C. From whom do you derive [an example of that fact]? From Job's sons.

D. "His sons used to go and hold a feast in the house of each on his day; and they would send and invite their three sisters to eat and drink with them" (Job 1:4).

E. R. Meir said, "Princes commonly invite their brothers and sisters to a banquet."

F. R. Tanhum b. R. Hiyya said, "It was because they had betrothed wives for themselves, in line with the following verse of Scripture: 'And Job sent and sanctified [betrothed wives for] them' (Job 1:5).

G. What is the meaning of "sanctified?"

H. In the view of R. Meir, who said that princes commonly invite their brothers and sisters to a banquet, the meaning is that he invited them for a banquet on the following day [and they were to prepare for the event] in line with that which you find in Scripture: "And to the people say, 'Sanctify yourselves [and prepare] for the next day' (Num. 11:18)."

I. In the view of R. Tanhum bar Hiyya, who said that he sanctified [betrothed] wives for them, he took care of their affairs and they went their way.

J. That [proportion, stated at A,] is in line with the following verse of Scripture: "He would rise early in the morning and offer burnt offerings according to the number of them all [for Job said, 'It may be that my sons have sinned and cursed God in their hearts']" (Job 1:5).

K. R. Yudan raised the question, "Is it the number of his days or the number of his sons and daughters or the number of all the sacrifices that are listed in the Torah?"

L. And [as to the issue of Job as illustration of the proposition that the burnt-offering is on account of what stirs up the heart], that is in line with what Job said, "It may be that my sons have sinned and cursed God in their heart" (Job 1:5).

M. That then indicates that the burnt-offering is brought only on account of what stirs up the heart [to sin].

2. A. R. Aha in the name of R. Hanana bar Pappa, "Since when the Temple was standing, Israel would offer all of the offerings that are required in the Torah, what is the rule as to taking account of them at this time [at which there is no Temple]?

B. "Said to them the Holy One, blessed be he, 'Since you engage in studying their rules, I credit it to you as if you actually offered them.'"

3. A. R. Huna made two statements.

B. R. Huna said, "All of the communities of exiles will be gathered back into the land only on account of the merit of the passages of the Mishnah [that they have memorized].

C. "That is in line with the following verse of Scripture: 'Especially when they repeat [Mishnah-traditions and memorize them] among the gentiles, then will I gather them back' (Hos. 8:10)."

D. R. Huna made yet a second statement.

E. R. Huna said, "It is written, 'For from the rising of the sun even to the setting of the sun, my name is great among the nations, and in every place incense is offered to my name' (Mal. 1:11). Now in Babylonia is there [an incense offering accomplished by] the taking of a handful of incense and burning it up?

F. "Rather, the Holy One, blessed be he, has said, 'Since you engage in studying them, I credit it to you as if you offered them up.'"

4. A. Samuel said, "'[And you, son of man, describe to the house of Israel the temple and its appearance and plan, that they may be ashamed of their iniquities.] And if they are ashamed of all that they have done, [portray the temple, its arrangements, its exits and its entrances, and its whole form, and make known to them all its ordinances and all its laws; and write it down in their sight, so that they may observe and perform all the laws and all its ordinances]' (Ez. 43:10-11).

B. "Now at this time was the form of the temple house available?

C. "But the Holy One, blessed be he, has said, 'Since you engage in studying them, I credit it to you as if you built the Temple.'"

5.   A.   Said R. Issi, "What account do they start children's education in the Torah of the Priests [the book of Leviticus]? It would make more sense for them to start at Genesis.

     B.   "Said the Holy One, blessed be he, 'Since the sacrifices are pure and children are pure, let the pure come and engage in the study of the pure.'"

VII:IV

1.   A.   R. Berekhiah and R. Hanan in the name of R. Azariah of Kefar Hittaya, "[The matter may be compared] to [the case of] a king who had two cooks. The first of the two made a meal for him and he ate it and liked it, and the second made a meal for him and he ate it and liked it.

     B.   "Now we should not know which of the two he liked more, except that, since he ordered the second, telling him to make a meal like the one he had prepared, we know that it was the second meal that he liked more.

     C.   "So too, Noah made an offering and it pleased God, for it is said, 'And the Lord smelled the sweet smell' (Gen. 8:21).

     D.   "Israel made an offering to him and it pleased him, '[My offering, my food for my offerings by fire, my pleasing odor,] you shall take heed to offer to me in its due season' (Num. 28:2).

     E.   "Now we do not know which of the two he liked more, except that, since he commanded Moses, saying to him, 'This is the law of the burnt-offering, it is the burnt-offering' [repeating 'burnt-offering'] (Lev. 6:2), we know that the offering of Israel is the one that he liked more."

     F.   That is in line with the following verse of Scripture: "Then the offering of Judah and Jerusalem will be pleasing to the Lord as in the days of old and as in former years" (Mal. 3:4).

     G.   "As in the days of old" -- as in the days of Moses.

     H.   "And as in former years" -- as in the time of Solomon.

     I.   R. Ammi: "'As in the days of old' -- in the days of Noah. That is in line with the following verse of Scripture: 'For this is like the days of Noah to me' (Is. 54:9).

     J.   "'And as in former years' -- as in the time of Abel, when there was no idolatry in the world."

2.   A.   R. Abin made two statements.

     B.   R. Abin said, "The matter may be compared to the case of a king who was reclining at a banquet, and the servants brought him a dish, and he ate it and liked it. He began to wipe the dish. That is in line with the following verse of Scripture: 'I will offer you burnt-offerings which are to be wiped off' (Ps. 66:15) -- like one who wipes up his plate."

C. R. Abin made yet a second statement.

D. R. Abin said, "The matter may be compared to a king who was traveling in the wilderness. He came to the first stockade, and he ate and drank there. Then he came to the second stockade, and he ate and drank there, and also spent the night there" [and "the burnt-offering shall be upon the altar all night" (Lev. 6:3)].

E. Thus why does the formulation of the passage create a puzzle for us concerning the burnt-offering: "This is the Torah of the burnt-offering, it is the burnt-offering" (Lev. 6:2), [that is, by repeating the specification that we speak of the burnt-offering]?

F. "It is to indicate that the entire burnt-offering is to be consumed by the flames."

VII:V

1. A. "And the fire of the altar shall be kept burning in it" (Lev. 6:2).

B. Said R. Phineas, "'The fire of the altar shall be kept burning in it.' It is not written, '...shall be kept burning on it,' but '...in it.' [The meaning is that] the altar will be burning in the fire. [The altar itself burned.]"

C. It was taught in the name of R. Nehemiah, "For nearly a hundred and sixteen years, [the fire] kept hold of it, yet its wood was not burned up, and its copper did not melt."

D. If you say that it was a thick layer [and that is why it did not melt], it was taught in the name of R. Hoshaiah, "It was the thickness of a Gordian denar" [Y. Hag. 3:8].

E. Said R. Simeon b. Laqish, "'And you shall make an altar for the burning of incense' (Ex. 39:1). The altar was burning [and giving off a scent] like incense" [Y. Hag. 3:8].

F. And rabbis said, "[In the verse cited in a moment] it is not written, 'And in the utensils of the oxen the flesh was boiled,' but 'And as for the utensils of the oxen, the flesh made them boil' (1 Kgs. 19:20). The flesh [of the sacrifice] was boiled by the utensil [not requiring fire]."

VII:VI

1. A. Said R. Levi, "It is an ordinance and a decree that whoever is boastful before the Omnipresent is punished only by fire, [just as the fire-offering, ^colah, goes up on the fire and is burned up (Margulies)].

B. "As to the generation of the flood, because they were boastful and said, 'Who is the Almighty, that we should serve him' (Job 21:15), they were punished only by fire, as it is said, 'In time of heat they disappear, when it is hot, they vanish from their place' (Job 6:17)."

C. What is the meaning of the word "when it is hot?" When it is boiling.

D. <u>Said R. Yohanan</u>, "Every drop [of rain] which the Holy One, blessed be he, brought down on them, did he heat up in Gehenna [Y. San. 10:3].

E. "That is indicated by the statement, 'When it is hot, they vanish from their place' (Job 6:17)."

F. [Levi resumes,] "As to the Sodomites, because they were boastful and said, 'Let us go and cause the laws of hospitality to be forgotten from our midst,' they were punished only by fire.

G. "That is in line with the following verse of Scripture: 'And he made to rain on Sodom and Gomorrah brimstone and fire' (Gen. 19:24).

H. "As to Pharaoh, because he was boastful and said, 'And who is the Lord, that I should listen to his voice' (Ex. 5:2), he was punished only in fire, as it is written, 'So there was hail and fire flashing up amidst the hail' (Ex. 9:24).

I. "As to Sisera, because he was boastful and oppressed the Israelites, as it is written, 'And he oppressed the children of Israel forcefully' (Jud. 4:3) --

J. (what does "forcefully" mean? Said R. Isaac, "It means with blasphemy and cursing" --)

K. "'he was punished only with fire.'

L. "That is in line with the following verse of Scripture: 'From heaven they fought [against Sisera] (Jud. 5:20).

M. "As to Sennacherib, because he was boastful and said, 'Who are among the gods of these countries, who have delivered their country out of my hand' (Is. 36:20), he was punished only by fire.

N. "That is in line with the following verse of Scripture: 'And under his glory there shall be kindled a burning like the burning of fire' (Is. 10:16).

O. "As to Nebuchadnezzar, because he was boastful and said, 'And who is God, that he will deliver you out of my hands?' (Dan. 3:15), he was punished only by fire.

P. "That is in line with the following verse of Scripture: 'The flame of the fire slew those men that took up Shadrach, Meshach, and Abed-nego' (Dan. 3:22).

Q. "As to the wicked empire, because it is boastful and arrogant, saying, 'Whom have I in heaven, and Whom have I in heaven but you? And there is nothing on earth that I want besides you' (Ps. 73:25), it is destined to be punished by fire.

R. "That is in line with the following verse of Scripture: '[As to the fourth beast], as I looked, the beast was slain, and its body destroyed and given over to be burned with fire' (Dan. 7:11).

S.   "But as to Israel, because they are despised and humble in this
     world, they will be comforted only with fire.

T.   "That is in line with the following verse of Scripture: 'For I
     [Jerusalem shall be inhabited as villages without walls...] for I will
     be to her a wall of fire round about' (Zech. 2:9 [RSV: 2:5])."

Our first impression is that the proportion of materials shared between Leviticus
Rabbah and some other document is negligible. These materials, moreover, do not play an
important role in the articulation of the main points of the parashah. Those from the
Mishnah (VII.I.2N), as well as those common to our document and the Yerushalmi
(VII:V.1.D,E, VII:VL1.D) exhibit formal traits we associate with those other documents,
and not with this one.

The Mishnah's contribution is explicitly labeled. No one pretended it was part of
some vast shared corpus of available materials; it was a particular document that people
quoted and then explained.

What is shared with the Yerushalmi is not strikingly different. It consists of sayings
assigned to named authorities.

In all, it is difficult to see evidence for the view that the authors of Leviticus
Rabbah made use of sizable quantities of writings to which other authors or editors
resorted as well. No "Q" so far! As I said, the opposite proves to be our first impression.
What is not particular to Leviticus Rabbah, so far as Parashah 7 is concerned, is trivial
and merely illustrative. What is shared exhibits no traits distinctive to itself and
different from what is not shared.

iii. A Secondary Probe: Parashiyyot 12 and 18

The results of the first probe on the surface seem incredible. We should not have
expected, on the basis of the allegations so long in circulation about a vast corpus of
shared materials on which diverse editors drew promiscuously and constantly, so slight and
trivial a body of evidence for analysis. What taxonomy is possible on the basis of three
exempla, one of them from the Mishnah? And with so trivial a sample what proposition
can be proved about the relationship between, on the one side, materials shared by
Leviticus Rabbah and other documents, and, on the other, writings distinctive to Leviticus
Rabbah? It follows that a more substantial sample demands survey. Once more, the
reader will have patiently to consider the evidence of a complete statement, now
extended to two full parashiyyot. Once more I underline those sentences that appear,
more or less in the same wording, in other documents of the same time or prior to
Leviticus Rabbah.

PARASHAH TWELVE

XII:I

1.   A.   "[And the Lord spoke to Aaron, saying,] 'Drink no wine nor strong
          drink, [you nor your sons with you, when you go into the tent of

meeting, lest you die; it shall be a statute for ever throughout your generations]" (Lev. 10:9).

B. R. Azariah opened [discourse by citing the following verse:] "'Do not look upon wine when it is red [when it sparkles in the cup and goes down smoothly. At the last it bites like a serpent and stings like an adder]' (Prov. 23:31-2).

C. "'Do not look upon wine when it is red (YT'DM) -- for [when drunk] one will lust after blood (YT'W DM).

D. "One will lust after the blood of a menstruating woman or the blood of a woman subject to flux.

E. "'When it sparkles in the cup'. [The passage is written, not kos, cup, but] kis, at the bag.

F. "That is a euphemism [for the sexual organs], in line with the following verse of Scripture: 'If they say..., Cast in your lot among us, let us all have one purse [a gang-bang]' (Prov. 1:14).

G. "'...and goes down smoothly' (Prov. 23:31) -- In the end [even though] his wife does things smoothly, saying to him, 'I have seen something like a red lily [marking her menstrual cycle]' he will not desist [from sexual relations]."

H. Said R. Issi, "If he is a disciple of sages, he will end up declaring what is clean to be unclean, and what is unclean to be clean."

2. A. Another interpretation: "Do not look upon the wine when it is red." Certainly it makes one red.

B. "When it sparkles in the cup." It is written, "in the purse."

C. [The drinker] looks at the cup, the storekeeper at the purse.

D. "...and goes down smoothly" (Prov. 23:31). In the end he will make his house smooth [and bare].

E. R. Isaac b. R. Radipa in the name of R. Ami: "In the end he will sell everything in his house so as to drink wine with the proceeds.

F. "He will say, 'What this brass pot can do, a clay pot can do.' So he sells the brass pot and drinks wine with the proceeds. 'What this copper ladle can do, a clay ladle can do,' so he sells it and drinks wine with the proceeds."

3. A. Said R, Aha, "There is the case of a man who sold all his household goods to buy wine with the proceeds, the very beams of his house to buy wine with the proceeds.

B. "His children complained, saying, [in Aramaic:] 'Will this old man of ours leave the world without leaving us a thing after he dies? What can we do with him? Let's go and make him drink and get him drunk and put him on a slab and take him out and say he's dead and lay him on his bier in the graveyard.' They did just that, taking him and getting him drunk and bringing him out and leaving him in the cemetery.

C. "Wine merchants passed by the gate of the graveyard. Some of the wine merchants were passing by to go into that town. They heard that the corvee-tax [of personal labor] was being levied in that town. They said, 'Come and let's unload the wine skins in this grave and get out of here.' That's just what they did. They unloaded their burdens in the cemetery and went off to find out about the uproar in the town. Now that man was lying there, [and the merchants] saw him and took for granted that he was dead.

D. "When the man woke up from his sleep, he saw a skin of wine hanging above his head. He untied it and put the spout in his mouth and drank. When he was feeling good, he began to sing. After three days, his children said to one another, 'Shouldn't we go and see how father is doing, whether he's alive or dead?'

E. "They came and found him with a wine skin spout in his mouth, and he was sitting and drinking. They said to him, 'Even here your Creator has not abandoned you among the dead, but he has left you among the living. Since this is [the fate] that Heaven has given to you, we don't know what we can do to you.

F. "'Let's go and bring him back, and provide for him, and arrange some sort of permanent provision for him.' They set things up so that each one would provide him with drink for one day."

4. A. "You will be like one who lies down in the midst of the sea, like one who lies on the top of a mast. ['They struck me,' you will say, 'but I was not hurt; they beat me, but I did not feel it. When shall I awake? I will seek another drink]'" (Prov. 23:34-35).

B. "You will be like one who lies down in the midst of the sea" -- like a boat tossed on the high seas, going down and up, down and up.

C. Just as a ship is shaken in the ocean, so in the end a habitual drunkard is shaken out of his wits.

D. "Like one who lies on the top of a mast" -- like a helmsman who sits on top of the masthead and falls asleep, as the mast sways to and fro underneath him.

E. Another interpretation: "Like one who lies on top of a mast" -- like a cock which sits on the top of a pole and falls asleep, as the pole sways to and fro underneath it.

5. A. "They struck me, but I was not hurt" (Prov. 23:35). They hit him, but he did not feel it.

B. "They beat me, but I did not feel it" (Prov. 23:35).

C. They overcharge him, but he does not know it.

D. If he drank five xestes [of beer] they say to him, "You drank ten."

E. If he drank ten, they say to him, "You drank twenty."

F.   Should you wish to say, when he wakes up from his sleep, he will forget [wine], Scripture states, "When shall I awake? I will seek another drink" (Prov. 23:35).

6.   A.   "Who has woe? Who has sorrow? Who has strife? Who has complaining? Who has wounds without cause? Who has redness of eyes? Those who tarry long over wine, those who go to try mixed wine" (Prov. 23:29-30).

B.   Who has woe? Who has sorrow?

C.   R. Huna said, "He who does not enjoy studying Torah."

D.   "Who has strife? Who has complaining?" One who is sued, one who has quarrels.

E.   "Who has wounds without cause?" [In Aramaic:] one who has causeless injuries.

F.   "Who has redness of eyes?" [In Aramaic:] One who has irritated eyes.

7.   A.   There was a case of a man who would ordinarily drink twelve xestes of wine every day.

B.   One day he drank only eleven. He wanted to go to sleep, but sleep did not come. He got up in the darkness and went to the innkeeper, saying to him, "Sell me an xestes of wine."

C.   He said to him, "No. I'm not able to open for you, because it's already dark."

D.   He said to him, "If you don't give it to me, my sleep will not come to me."

E.   He said to him, "Just now the town watchmen went by here, and I am afraid on account of the watchmen, so I can't give you [what you want]."

F.   The man looked up and saw a hole in the door. He said to him, "Push a straw through that hole, then you pour on the inside, and I'll drink out here."

G.   The man pressed him. What did he do? He stuck a straw though the hole in the door, and as the innkeeper poured out wine inside, and the man drank it outside. When he finished, he fell asleep in a corner before the door.

H.   The watchman came upon him by the door and found him asleep. Thinking that he was a thief, they beat him, but he did not feel it, and they wounded him, but he did not know it. They reddened his eye, and he did not see a thing.

I.   People recited concerning him, "Who has wounds without cause?" Who has causeless injuries?

J.   "Who has redness of eyes?" Who has irritated eyes?

K.   Whom do such things afflict? "Those who tarry long over wine, those who go to try mixed wine" (Prov. 23:30).

8. A. "Those who tarry long over wine" (Prov. 23:30) -- they are the ones who get into the bar first and leave last.

    B. "Those who go to try mixed wine" -- these are people who go looking for wine.

    C. When they hear that someone has a fine vintage, they go running after him and say, "So-and-so's wine is great, So-and-so's wine is red. Give us some and let's drink. So-and-so's wine is sparkling, give us some and let's drink it."

9. A. "In the end it bites like a snake and stings [PRS, also: separates] like an adder" (Prov. 23:32).

    B. Just as a viper distinguishes (PRS) between death and life, so wine caused a separation (PRS) between Adam and Eve.

    C. That accords with what Judah b. R. Ilai said, "The tree from which Adam eat was a grape vine [Gen. R. 15:7].

    D. "That is in line with the following verse of Scripture: 'For their grapes are grapes of poison, their clusters are bitter; [their wine is the poison of serpents, and the cruel venom of asps]' (Deut. 32:32).

    E. "It follows that grape vines brought bitterness into the world."

10. A. Another interpretation: "It stings like an adder" (Prov. 23:32).

    B. Just as an adder distinguishes between death and life, so wine caused a separation between Noah and his sons in the matter of slavery.

    C. That is in line with the following verse of Scripture: "Noah was the first tiller of the soil. He planted a vineyard, and he drank of the wine, became drunk, and lay uncovered in his tent. And Ham, the father of Canaan, saw the nakedness of his father and told his two brothers outside. Then Shem and Japheth took a garment, laid it upon both their shoulders, and walked backward, and covered the nakedness of their father; their faces were turned away, and they did not see their father's nakedness. When Noah awoke from his wine and knew what his youngest son had done to him..."

    D. On that account: "He said, Cursed be Canaan; a slave of slaves shall he be to his brothers" (Gen. 9:20-25).

11. A. Another interpretation: "It stings like an adder" (Prov. 23:32).

    B. Just as an adder distinguishes between death and life, so wine caused a separation between Lot and his daughters in the matter of bastardy.

    C. That is in line with the following verse of Scripture: "Come, let us make our father drink wine, and we will lie with him, that we may preserve offspring through our father. So they made their father drink wine that night; and the first born went in and lay with her father; he did not know when she lay down or when she arose. And on the next day the first born said to the younger, Behold, I lay last night with my father; let us make him drink wine tonight also; then you go in and lie with him, that we may preserve offspring through our father. So they made their father drink wine that night also; and the younger arose and lay with him, and he did not know when she lay down or when she arose. Thus both the daughters of Lot were with child by their father" (Gen. 19:32-36).

D.   On that account: "No Ammonite or Moabite shall enter the assembly of the Lord" (Deut. 23:3).

12. A.   Another interpretation: "It stings like an adder" (Prov. 23:32).

B.   Just as an adder distinguishes between death and life, so did wine cause a separation between the ten tribes in the matter of the exile.

C.   That is in line with what is written: "Woe to those who rise early in the morning, that they may run after strong drink, who tarry late in the evening till wine inflames them" (Is. 5:11).

D.   "...who drink wine in bowls..." (Amos 6:6).

E.   On this account: "Therefore they shall now be the first of those who go into exile" (Amos 6:7).

13. A.   Another interpretation: "It stings like an adder" (Prov. 23:32).

B.   Just as an adder distinguishes between life and death, so did wine cause a separation between the tribes of Judah and Benjamin in the matter of the exile.

C.   For it is written, "These also reel with wine and stagger with strong drink; [the priest and the prophet reel with strong drink, they are confused with wine, they stagger with strong drink]" (Is. 28:7).

D.   These and also those [are subject to judgment].

14. A.   Another interpretation: "It stings like an adder" (Prov. 23:32).

B.   Just as an adder distinguishes between life and death, so did wine cause a separation between Ahasuerus and Vashti, the queen, in the matter of the death penalty.

C.   For it is said, "On the seventh day, when the heart of the king was merry with wine, he commanded Mehuman, Biztha, Harbona, Bigtha, Abagtha, Zethar, and Carkas, the seven eunuchs who served King Ahasuerus as chamberlains, to bring Queen Vashti before the king with her royal crown, in order to show the peoples and the princes her beauty. For she was fair to behold. But Queen Vashti refused to come at the king's command conveyed by the eunuchs. At this the king was enraged and his anger burned within him" (Est. 1:10-12).

D. He wanted to bring her in naked, but she did not accept his command. Therefore he became angry with her and killed her. After he had killed her, he began to wonder [at what he had done].

E. That is in line with the following verse of Scripture: "After these things, when the anger of King Ahasuerus had abated, he remembered Vashti and what she had done and what had been decreed against her" (Est. 2:1).

15. A. Another interpretation: "It stings like an adder" (Prov. 23:32).

B. Just as an adder distinguishes between life and death, so wine caused a separation between one reign and another in the matter of the death [of a reigning monarch].

C. For it is written: "King Belshazzar made a great feast for a thousand of his lords and drank wine in front of the thousand. Belshazzar, when he tasted the wine, commanded that the vessels of gold and of silver which Nebuchadnezzar his father had taken out of the temple in Jerusalem be brought, that the king and his lords, his wives, and his concubines might drink from them. Then they brought in the golden and silver vessels which had been taken out of the temple, the house of God in Jerusalem, and the king and his lords, his wives, and his concubines drank from them. They drank wine and praised the gods of gold and silver, bronze, iron, wood, and stone]" (Dan. 5:1-4).

D. On this account: "That very night Belshazzar the Chaldean king was slain, and [Darius the Mede received the kingdom...]" (Dan 5:30).

16. A. Another interpretation: "It stings like an adder" (Prov. 23:32).

B. Just as an adder distinguishes between life and death, so wine caused a separation between Aaron and his son in the matter of the death penalty.

17. A. R. Ishmael expounded, "The two sons of Aaron died only because they entered [the tent of meeting] when they were drunk."

B. R. Phineas in the name of R. Levi, in regard to this statement of R. Ishmael: "The matter may be compared to a king who had a reliable steward. But he observed the man standing at the doorway of a [wine] shop. He cut off his head without revealing the reason and appointed another one as steward in place of the first.

C. "Now we do not know on what account he killed the first. But from his instructions to the second, we may draw the proper conclusion, for he said, 'Do not go into that [wine] shop.' So we know on what account he killed the first.

D. "So here it is written, 'And fire came forth from the presence of the Lord and devoured them and they died before the Lord' (Lev. 10:2).

E. "Now we do not know on what account they were put to death. But from what the Holy One, blessed be he, instructed Aaron, saying to him, 'Drink no wine nor strong drink, [you nor your sons with you, when you go into the tent of meeting, lest you die]' (Lev. 10:8), we may draw the conclusion that they were put to death only on account of wine."

F. [Because Aaron remained silent at the death of his sons], he gained the merit of having the formulation of Scripture show him special regard, directing to him alone the divine instruction: "[And the Lord spoke to Aaron, saying,] Drink no wine nor strong drink" (Lev. 10:8-9).

XII:II

1. A. R. Isaac opened [discourse by citing the following verse:] "'Your words were found and I ate them, and your words became to me a joy and the delight of my heart, for I am called by your name, O Lord, God of Hosts. [I did not sit in the company of merrymakers, nor did I rejoice; I sat alone, because your hand was upon me]' (Jer. 15:16-17)."

2. A. Said R. Ishmael b. R. Nahman, "The Holy One, blessed be he, said to Moses, 'Moses, in the future, I am going to meet with Israel and to be sanctified by them in this house [Sifra 2:4, cf. also B. Zeb. 115b].

    B. "That is in line with the following verse of Scripture: 'There I will meet with the people of Israel, and it shall be sanctified by my glory; [I will consecrate the tent of meeting and the altar; Aaron also and his sons I will consecrate to serve me as priests]' (Ex. 29:43-4).

    C. "This statement was said to Moses at Sinai, but he was not informed [as to its meaning] until the matter was realized through his own action.

    D. "When did this take place? It was on the eighth day [of consecration of Aaron and the priesthood].

    E. "That is in line with the following verse of Scripture: 'And when all the people saw it, they shouted and fell on their faces' (Lev. 9:24).

    F. "Said Moses before the Holy One, blessed be he, "Lord of the ages! Who is more beloved than my brother Aaron and I, through whom this house is to be sanctified?'

    G. "When the two sons of Aaron went in to make an offering and came out burned up, Moses said to Aaron, 'Aaron, my brother! Your sons died only for the sanctification of the name of the Holy One, blessed be he. This is what the Lord has said, "I will show myself holy among those who are near me, [and before all the people I will be glorified]" (Lev. 10:3)."

3. A. Along these same lines, you find the following:

B. "There I will meet with the people of Israel, and it shall be sanctified by my glory" (Ex. 29:32).

C. This statement was said to Moses at Sinai, but he was not informed as to its meaning until the matter was realized through his own action.

D. But when the matter came to hand, he said to Aaron, "Aaron, my brother, at Sinai it was said to me, 'I am going to meet with Israel and to be sanctified by them in this house, and I shall sanctify [the house] through a great man.' Now I was supposing that it was either through me or through you that this house would be sanctified. But now it turns out that your two sons are more beloved than we."

E. When Aaron heard this, realizing that his sons had been God-fearing [lit.: known to Heaven], he kept silent [at their death].

F. He received a good reward for his humble silence.

G. That is in line with the following verse of Scripture: "And Aaron kept silent" (Lev. 10:3).

H. What reward did he receive for his silence? He gained the merit of having the formulation of Scripture show him special regard, directing to him alone the divine instruction: "And the Lord spoke to Aaron, saying, Drink no wine nor strong drink" (Lev. 10:8-9).

XII:III

1. A. "[The Torah of the Lord is perfect, reviving the soul; the testimony of the Lord is sure, making wise the simple;] the precepts of the Lord are right, rejoicing the heart; the commandment of the Lord is pure, enlightening the eyes; [the fear of the Lord is clean, enduring forever; the ordinances of the Lord are true and righteous altogether]" (Ps. 19:7-9).

B. Hezekiah taught, "Words of Torah are a crown for the head, a necklace for the neck, a balm for the heart, a salve for the eyes, an anointment for a wound, and a cup of root-drink for the bowels.

C. "'A crown for the head:' 'For they are a fair garland for your head' (Prov. 1:9).

D. "'A necklace for the neck:' 'And pendants for your neck' (Prov. 1:9).

E. "'A balm for the heart:' 'The precepts of the Lord are right, rejoicing the heart' (Ps. 19:8).

F. "'A salve for the eyes:' 'The commandment of the Lord is pure, enlightening the eyes' (Ps. 19:8).

G.   "'Anointment for a wound:' 'It will be a healing to your flesh' (Prov. 3:8).

H.   "'A cup of root-drink for the bowels:' 'And refreshment to your bones' (Prov. 3:8).

I.   "And how do we know that [words of Torah] are absorbed by the two hundred and forty-eight limbs which are in [the body]?'

J.   "Scripture says, '[For they are life to him who finds them,] and healing to all his flesh' (Prov. 4:22)."

2.   A.   Another interpretation: "The precepts of the Lord are right, rejoicing the heart" (Ps. 19:7) -- these are the sons of Aaron.

B.   "The commandment of the Lord is pure, enlightening the eyes" -- they had such merit that the divine speech focused upon them and upon their father while they were yet alive.

C.   He had such further merit that the Scripture showed him special favor by speaking about him all by himself: "[And God spoke to Aaron, saying,] 'Drink no wine nor strong drink'" (Lev. 10:8-9).

XII:IV

1.   A.   [To the] body [of the matter]: Said R. Tanhuma, "If one drinks the proper amount, that is wine-[drinking]. If one drinks more than the proper amount, that is [drunkenness and the drinker is an] ass."

2.   A.   Said R. Yudan, "All trees are called after the name of their fruit.

B.   "A fig-tree is called by the name of a fig, a pomegranate-tree is called by the name of its fruit, an apple tree is called by the name of its fruit.

C.   "But a vine has three names. It is called a vine, coming from it are grapes; and coming from grapes is wine.

D.   "That is to tell you, just as in the case of grapes, if you do not press them, you will not bring anything out of them, so he who drinks a great deal of wine in the end will vomit everything in his intestines."

3.   A.   Said R. Tanhuma, "[The prohibition of priests' drinking wine is based on the following reasoning:] The mother [of the wine, namely, the vine] cannot stand up [under its weight], so will you be able to stand up under it?

B.   "A vine without supports cannot stand up."

C.   Said R. Simon, "For offerings [of wine-libations], I have set a measure [of how much wine is to be used], but for you yourself you will not set a limit [but you may not drink at all].

D.   "For offerings [of wine-libations] I have set a measure: 'And their drink-offerings shall be half a hin of wine for a bullock, a third for a ram, and a fourth for a lamb' (Num. 28:14).

E.   "But for you yourself, you do not set any measure at all [but may not drink wine]."

4. A. Bar Qappara said, "When a substance [whose Hebrew name] stands for a numerical value of 70 goes in [to the mouth], a word with that same numerical value comes out [of the mouth]: 'When wine goes in [the Hebrew letters of which stand for 70], secrets come out,' [and the numerical value of the word secret also is 70]" [B. Er. 68a, San. 38a].

5. A. R. Abin made two statements.

    B. R. Abin said, "Why do they hold wine in goat-skins? To tell you [that] yesterday this skin was full of sinews and bones, but now it is utterly empty. So he who drinks too much wine will end up forgetting the two hundred forty-eight limbs that are in his body.

    C. "That is in line with the following verse of Scripture: 'Lest they drink and forget what has been decreed (MHWQQ) (Prov. 31:15).' The word is written MHQQ, [the numerical value of the letters of which is 248]."

    D. R. Abin said yet another saying: "Why do they hold wine in goat-skins?' To tell you [that] yesterday this skin was full of vein sinews and bones, and now it is a worthless piece of naked hide. So he who drinks too much wine will end up being made worthless on its account."

XII:V

1. A. Said R. Yudan, "During the entire seven-year period in which Solomon built the house of the sanctuary, he did not drink any wine.

    B. "When he had built the house of the sanctuary, and [in celebration] married Pharoah's daughter, that very night he drank some wine.

    C. "There were two dances in celebration that night, one, the rejoicing over the building of the house of the sanctuary, and the other, the rejoicing over the daughter of Pharoah.

    D. "Said the Holy One, blessed be he, 'Which one shall I accept, this or that?'

    E. "At that moment it entered God's mind to destroy the Temple.

    F. "That is in line with the following verse of Scripture: 'This city has aroused my anger ('P) and wrath (from the day it was built to this day, so that I will remove it from my sight because of all the evil of the sons of Israel and the sons of Judah, which they did to provoke me to anger] (Jer. 32:31)."

    G. Said R. Hillel b. R. Wallas, "It may be compared to someone who passes by a filthy place and turns up his nose ('P)."

2. A. Said R. Hunia, "Eighty different dances did Pharoah's daughter dance that night" [cf. B. Shab. 57b].

    B. R. Isaac b. Eleazar said, "Three hundred different dances did Pharoah's daughter dance that night."

3.   A.   Now Solomon slept to the fourth hour of the day, with the keys of the house of the sanctuary kept under his head.

     B.   That is in line with that which we have learned in the Mishnah [M. Ed. 6:1]: "The morning burnt offering is offered at the fourth hour."

     C.   Lo, what did [Pharoah's daughter] do for him? She made a kind of canopy and set stars and planets in its and spread it over his bed. When he wanted to get up, he saw it and supposed that it was still night, so he slept until the fourth hour.

     D.   His mother then came in and rebuked him.

     E.   And there is he who says that it was Jeroboam b. Nabat who came in and rebuked him.

     F.   And could [Jeroboam] have done any such thing?

     G.   R. Haggai in the name of R. Isaac: "He went and gathered eighty thousand men of his tribe [Ephraim] and went in and rebuked him.

     H.   "That is in line with the following verse of Scripture: 'When Ephraim spoke, people trembled. He was exalted in Israel. But he incurred guilt through Baal and died' (Hos. 13:1)."

     I.   "When Ephraim spoke, people trembled" -- when Jeroboam spoke of the incontinence of Solomon, the Holy One, blessed be he, said to him, "Why do you rebuke him?"

     J.   [God continues:] "'He was exalted in Israel' -- he is prince in Israel.

     K.   "By your life, I shall give you a taste of the kind of authority that he wields, and you will not be able to endure it."

     L.   When [Jeroboam] entered his dominion, forthwith: "He incurred guilt through Baal and died" (Hos. 13:1).

     M.   Rabbis say, "It was most certainly his mother who went in and rebuked him.

     N.   "She took her slipper and slapped him this way and that, saying to him, 'What my child' (Prov. 31:2)."

     O.   Said R. Oshaiah, "'What my son,' is not written, but 'What my child'.

     P.   "She said, 'My son, you are already grown up! Your father married many women and when Nathan, the prophet, came and said to him, "Behold, a son shall be born to you; he shall be a man of peace. I will give him peace from all his enemies round about; for his name shall be Solomon, and I will give peace and quiet to Israel in his days" (1 Chr. 22:9),

     Q.   "'then every one of David's wives [including me] said, "If I produce Solomon, I shall make an offering of every sacrifice that is listed in the Torah."

     R.   "'Now I am standing and my sacrifices are in my hand, but you are still sleeping!'"

S. "Give not your strength to women, your ways to those who destroy kings" (Prov. 31:3).

T. Said R. Yohanan, "His mother said to him, 'My son, the men of the generation of the flood were kings, but because they were drowning in pornographic filth, they were blotted up out of the world.'"

4. A. "It is not for kings, O Lemuel, [it is not for kings to drink wine or for rulers to desire strong drink, lest they drink and forget what has been decreed, and pervert the rights of all the afflicted]" (Prov. 31:4).

B. Said R. Abin, "They do not hand over the dominion to one who takes issue with the teachings of God, but with him who does the teachings of God."

C. "It is not for kings to drink wine."

D. Said R. Abin, "Let kings not drink wine, lest they forget and say something like him [i.e., Pharoah] who said, 'Who is the Lord, that I should listen to his voice' (Ex. 5:2)."

E. "Or for rulers to desire strong drink" (Prov. 31:4).

F. It is written, "Or" ('W), meaning woe to one on account of strong drink.

5. A. R. Hanana b. R. Pappa and rabbis:

B. R. Hanana b. R. Pappa said, "Said the Holy One, blessed be he, 'I had a great house, and I destroyed it only on account of wine.'"

C. Rabbis said, "Said the Holy One, blessed be he, 'I had two rulers, and I killed them only because of wine.'"

D. That is in line with the following teaching of R. Ishmael: "The two sons of Aaron died only because they went into the sanctuary when they were drunk.

E. R. Phineas in the name of R. Levi: "The matter may be compared to a king who appointed a reliable steward," etc., as stated above, up to "Drink no wine nor strong drink" (Lev. 10:9).

6. A. For in this world, wine is a stumbling block to the world. But in the time to come, the Holy One, blessed be he, will turn it into a source of joy.

B. That is in line with the following verse of Scripture: "And in that day the mountains shall drip sweet wine, and the hills shall flow with milk, and all the stream beds of Judah shall flow with water; and a fountain shall come forth from the house of the Lord, and water the valley of Shittim" (Joel 3:18).

PARASHAH EIGHTEEN

XVIII:I

1. A. "[The Lord said to Moses and Aaron, 'Say to the people of Israel,]

"When any man has a discharge from his body, [his discharge is unclean]"" (Lev. 15:1-2).

B. "Remember your creator in the days of your youth" (Qoh. 12:1).

C. We have learned in the Mishnah [M. Abot 3:1]: "Aqabiah b. Mehalalel says, 'Contemplate three things, and you will not come to commit a transgression. Know whence you have come, from a fetid drop; and where you are going, to worms and corruption; and before whom you are going to have to give a full accounting of yourself, before the King of kings of kings, the Holy One, blessed be he.'"

D. R. Abba b. R. Kahana in the name of R. Pappi and R. Joshua of Sikhnin in the name of R. Levi: "All three matters did Aqabiah derive by exegesis from a single word [i.e. BWR'K, "your Creator"]:

E. "Remember your well (be'erka), your pit (BRK), and your Creator (BWR'K).

F. "'Remember your well' -- this refers to the fetid drop.

G. "'Remember your pit' -- this refers to worms and corruption.

H. "'Remember your Creator' -- this refers to the King of kings of kings, the Holy One, before whom one is destined to render a full accounting" [Y. Sot. 2:2].

2. A. "In the days of your youth" (Qoh. 12:1) means in the days when you are young, while your strength is yet with you.

B. "[Remember your Creator in the days of your youth,] before the evil days come" (Qoh. 12:1) -- this refers to the time of old age.

C. "When the years draw near, when you will say, 'I have no pleasure in them' (Qoh. 12:1). This refers to the time of the coming of the Messiah, at which there will no longer be consideration either of merit or of liability."

D. "Before the sun and the light and the moon and the stars are darkened" (Qoh. 12:2). [The sun] refers to the appearance of the face.

E. "The light" (Qoh. 12:2) refers to the forehead.

F. "The moon (Qoh. 12:2) refers to the nose.

G. "The stars" (Qoh. 12:2) refers to the protruding cheek bones.

3. A. "And the clouds return after the rain" (Qoh. 12:2).

B. R. Levi made two statements on this matter, one with reference to colleagues, the other in reference to the ignorant.

C. The one with reference to colleagues: "When one comes to weep, his eyes will overflow with tears."

D. The one with reference to the ignorant: "When one comes to urinate, feces will come out first [for one will not control his natural functions]."

4. A. "In the day when the keepers of the house tremble, and the strong men are bent, and the grinders of grain cease because they are few, and those that look through the windows are dimmed" (Qoh. 12:3).

    B. "In the day when the keepers of the house tremble" refers to one's knees.

    C. "And the strong men are bent" refers to one's ribs.

    D. R. Hiyya b. R. Nehemiah says, "This refers to his arms."

    E. "And the grinders of grain cease" refers to the stomach.

    F. "For they are few" refers to the teeth.

    G. "And those that look through the windows are dimmed" refers to the eyes [B. Shab. 152a].

    H. R. Hiyya b. R. Nehemiah says, "This refers to the laps of the lungs, from which sound comes forth."

5. A. "And the doors on the street are shut, when the sound of the grinding is low" (Qoh. 12:4).

    B. "And the doors on the street are shut" refers to the joints.

    C. "When the sound of the grinding is low" refers to the fact that the stomach is not grinding.

6. A. "And one rises up at the voice of a bird" (Qoh. 12:4). When an old man hears the sound of birds chirping, he thinks, "Robbers have come to attack me."

    B. "And all the daughters of song are brought low" refers to one's lips.

    C. R. Hiyya b. R. Nehemiah said, "This refers to the kidneys, which propose, while the heart disposes."

7. A. "they are afraid also of what is high, and terrors are in the way; the almond tree blossoms, and the grasshopper is a burden" (Qoh. 12:5).

    B. "They are afraid also of what is high." When people call an old man to go to such-and-such a place, he asks, "Are there steps to go up there? Are there steps to go down there?"

    C. "And terrors are in the way."

    D. R. Abba b. R. Kahana and R. Levi:

    E. R. Abba bar. R. Kahana said, "Fear of travelling falls on him."

    F. The other said, "He begins to set limits to a journey, saying, 'Up to such-and-such a place I have the strength to go, but to such-and-such a place I have not got the strength to go.'"

    G. "The almond tree blossoms." This refers to his ankles.

    H. "And the grasshopper is a burden." This refers to the nut of the spinal column [that is, a vertebre].

8. A. Hadrian (may his bones be crushed) asked R. Joshua b. Hananiah, saying to him, "From what part of the body will the Holy One, blessed be he, cause a person to sprout in the age to come?"

B. He said to him, "From the nut of the spinal column."

C. He said to him, "Prove it."

D. He brought one before him. He put it in water, but it did not dissolve. He ground it in grinding wheels, but it was not pulverized. He put it into fire, but it was not burned. He put it on an anvil and began hitting it with a hammer. The anvil split and the hammer broke, but nothing came of it.

9. A. "And desire fails" (Qoh. 12:4). This refers to that desire which brings peace between man and wife.

10. A. R. Simeon b. Halputa would customarily go up to greet Rabbi [Judah the Patriarch] at the beginning of each lunar month. When [Simeon] grew old, he remained at home for he could not go up to see him any longer. But one day he did go. [Rabbi] said, "What has so engaged you that you have not come up to see me as you used to do?

B. He said to him, "What was once near is now far, what was once far is now near. Two things have become three. What brought peace at home has now failed" [B. Shab. 152a].

C. "What was once near is now far" -- this refers to the eyes, which could see things from afar, but now, even things near at hand they do not see.

D. "What was once far is now near" -- this refers to the ears, which used to hear things when they were said only once or twice, but now do not hear things even if they are said a hundred times.

E. "Two things have become three" -- [once two legs, now] a staff and the two legs.

F. "What brought peace at home has now failed" -- this refers to the [physical] desire which brings peace between man and wife.

11. A. "Because man goes to his eternal home" (Qoh. 12:5).

B. Said R. Simeon b. Laqish, "This teaches that each and every righteous person has an eternal home [designated for him in particular].

C. "[The matter may be compared] to the case of a king who came into a town, with his generals, hyparchs, and soldiers. Even though the entire unit enters by the same gate, each unit is encamped in accord with its standing.

D. "Likewise even though every individual tastes the flavor of death, every righteous person has an eternal home [designated for him in particular]."

12. A. "And the mourners go about the streets" (Qoh. 12:5) -- this refers to the worms.

B. "Before the silver cord is snapped [or the golden bowl is broken or the pitcher is broken at the fountain or the wheel is broken at the cistern" (Qoh. 12:6).

C. "Before the silver cord is snapped" refers to the backbone.

D. "Or the golden bowl is broken" refers to the skull.

E. R. Hiyya b. R. Nehemiah said, "This refers to the gullet, which rejects gold and lets silver run."

F. "Or the pitcher is broken at the fountain" (Qoh. 12:6) -- this refers to the belly.

G. R. Abba b. R. Pappi and R. Joshua of Sikhnin in the name of R. Levi: "After three days [in the grave] a person's belly bursts open and erupts into the mouth and says [to the person], 'Here is what you stole, grabbed, and put into me!'" [Y. M.Q. 3:5, Yeb. 16:3].

H. R. Haggai in the name of R. Isaac finds proof for that proposition from the following verse: "And I will spread shit on your faces, the shit of your sacrifices" (Mal. 2:3) -- even the shit of your sacrifices.

I. Bar Qappara said, "For three days the spirit of deep mourning seizes the mourner. Why? Because the features of the deceased's face still are to be discerned.

J. "For it has been taught [in the Mishnah, M. Yeb. 16:3:] 'They adduce evidence as to a corpse's identity only from the features of the face, including the nose, and they give testimony only within three days [of the deceased's death].'"

13. A. "Or the wheel is broken at the cistern" (Qoh. 12:6).

B. Two Amoraic-teachers [explained the word for wheel, GLGL, variously]:

C. One said, "[The word GLGL refers to] something comparable to the boulders (GLYLY') of Sepphoris."

D. The other said, "[It refers to] something like the clods of Tiberias.

E. "That is in line with the following verse of Scripture: 'The clods of the valley are sweet to him' (Job 21:33)."

14. A. "And the dust returns to the earth as it was, but the spirit returns to God, who gave it" (Qoh. 12:7).

B. R. Phineas and R. Hilkiah in the name of R. Simon: "When does the spirit return to God? When the dust has returned to the earth as it was.

C. "But if not: 'The souls of your enemies he shall sling out as from the hollow of a sling' (I Sam. 23:29)."

D. R. Ishmael b. R. Nehemiah taught the following in the name of R. Abdimi of Haifa, "[The matter of the disposition of the soul] may be compared to the case of a priest who ate his cultic food in a state of cultic cleanness. He handed over to a priest who did not observe the rules of cultic cleanness with regard to consecrated food a loaf of bread in the status of heave-offering [hence, consecrated food].

E.   "What did he say to him?

F.   "'See that I am in a state of cultic cleanness, and so too are my house and utensils. So too this loaf of bread that I am handing over to you is in a state of cultic cleanness. Now if you hand it back to me in the condition in which I am giving it over to you, lo, that is well and good, but if not, I shall simply throw it in your face [since you will have ruined it by violating its condition of cultic cleanness.'

G.   "So did the Holy One, blessed be he, say to this man, 'See here, I am in a state of cultic cleanness, and the place of my dwelling [the Temple] is in a state of cultic cleanness, and my servants are in a state of cultic cleanness, and the soul that I am handing over to you is in a state of cultic cleanness. If you return it to me in the condition in which I hand it over to you, well and good, but if not, I am going to burn it in your very presence.'"

15. A.   All of these matters [Qoh. 12:1-7] pertain to the time of a person's old age. But as to one's youth, if a person sins, he is smitten with a flux [Lev. 15:1] or with leprosy.

B.   Therefore Moses admonished Israel, saying to them, "When any man has a discharge from his body, his discharge is unclean" (Lev. 15:2).

XVIII:II

1. A.   "Dread and terrible are they; their justice and dignity proceed from themselves" (Hab. 1:7).

B.   "Dread and terrible" refers to the first Man.

C.   R. Judah b. R. Simon in the name of R. Joshua b. Levi: "When the Holy One, blessed be he, created the first man, he created him so that he filled the entire world.

D.   "Whence [do we know that it was] from east to west? 'Back and front [KDM, also meaning east] have you formed me' (Ps. 139:5).

E.   "From north to south? 'From one end of the heaven to the other end' (Deut. 4:32).

F.   "In the space of the universe? 'You placed your hand upon me [indicating that the first man's body reached to God's hand in the heaven]' (Ps. 139:5)" [Gen. R. 8:1].

G.   "Their justice and dignity proceed from themselves" (Hab. 1:7).

H.   This refers to Eve.

I.   That is in line with the following verse of Scripture: "The woman whom you gave to be with me is the one who gave me of the tree, and I ate" (Gen. 3:2).

2. A. Another interpretation: "Dread and terrible" refers to Esau.

B. That is in line with the following verse of Scripture: "And Rebecca took the most coveted garments of Esau, her elder son" (Gen. 27:15). [This clothing came from Nimrod, so Esau was more of a hunter than he, hence, "dread and terrible" (Israelstam, p. 228, no. 2).]

C. "Their justice and dignity proceed from themselves" (Hab. 1:7).

D. This refers to [the prophet] Obadiah.

E. Said R. Isaac, "Obadiah was a proselyte of Edomite origin, and he gave a prophecy concerning Edom, 'And there shall not be any remnant of the house of Esau for the mouth of the Lord has spoken it' (Ob. 1:18)."

3. A. Another interpretation: "Dread and terrible" refers to Sennacherib.

B. "Who among all the gods of the lands has saved their country from my hand" (Is. 36:20).

C. "Their justice and dignity proceed from themselves" (Hab. 1:7).

D. This refers to his sons: "And it came to pass, as Sennacherib was worshipping in the house of Nisroch, his god, [that Adrammelech and Sarezer, his sons, smote him with the sword]' (2 Kgs. 19:37).

4. A. Another interpretation: "Dread and terrible" refers to Hiram, king of Tyre.

B. "Son of man, say to the prince of Tyre, thus says the Lord God, "Because your heart was lifted up, and you said, I am God..." (Ez. 28:2).

C. "Their justice and dignity proceed from themselves" (Hab. 1:7).

D. This refers to Nebuchadnezzar.

E. Said R. Simon, "There is a tale that Hiram was the husband of Nebuchadnezzar's mother. He rose against him and killed him [which explains how the justice owing to Hiram came out of his own fold]."

F. That is in line with the following verse of Scripture: "And I brought fire out of your midst and it consumed you" (Ez. 28:18).

5. A. Another interpretation: "Dread and terrible" refers to Nebuchadnezzar: "And you said, I shall go up to heaven" (Is. 14:13).

B. "Their justice and dignity proceed from themselves" (Hab. 1:7).

C. This refers to Evil Merodach.

D. They say, "During those seven years which passed over Nebuchadnezzar [Dan. 4:22], they took Evil Merodach and made him king in the other's place. When he came back, he took him and imprisoned him. And whoever went into that prison never came out, as it is said, "He did not open the house of his prisoners" (Is. 14:17).

E. Then, when Nebuchadnezzar died, they went back to Evil to make him king. He said to them, "I shall not listen to your proposal. At

the outset I did listen to you, and he took me and put me into
prison, and now [when he comes back] he will kill me."

F.   He did not believe them [that the former had died] until they
dragged [Nebuchadnezzar's corpse] and threw it before him.

G.   That is in line with the following verse of Scripture: "And you are
cast forth, away from your grave like an abhorred offshoot" (Is.
14:19).

H.   Said R. Eleazar b. R. Abina, "And furthermore, each of his enemies
came and speared him with a sword, fulfilling that which is stated
in the following verse: 'In the garment of the slain ones, thrust
through with the sword' (Is. 14:19)."

6.   A.   Another interpretation: "Dread and terrible" refers to Israel.

B.   "I said, You are God[-like beings]' (Ps. 82:6).

C.   "Their justice and dignity [or swelling] proceed from themselves"
(Hab. 1:7).

D.   For Israelites may be smitten with flux and with leprosy [which
punishes them for their sins, and comes from their very bodies].

E.   Therefore Moses admonished Israel, saying to them, "When any man
has a discharge from his body" (Lev. 15:2).

XVIII:III

1.   A.   "In the day on which you planted, you acted basely; [in the morning
your seed germinated]' (Is. 17:11, following Israelstam's rendering).

B.   [God speaks:] "On the day on which I planted you for myself as a
nation, you turned into dross."

C.   "You are the dross of silver" (Ez. 22:18). This refers to the dross.

D.   "You put on a false face."

E.   "Like the silver of dross plating of an earthen vessel [are the
smooth lips with an evil heart]' (Prov. 26:23).

F.   This refers to the base metal, for you acted basely against me.

G.   "But they flattered him with their mouths; they lied to him with
their tongues; their heart was not steadfast toward him; [they were
not true to his covenant]' (Ps. 78:37).

H.   "In the morning your seed sprouted up" (Is. 17:11).

I.   R. Hama b. R. Hanina and R. Ishmael b. R. Nehemiah:

J.   R. Hama b. R. Hanina said, "[The matter may be compared] to
someone who had a field with vegetables. He got up in the morning
and found that the entire field had withered."

K.   R. Ishmael b. R. Nahman said, "[It may be compared] to someone
who had a field full of flax. He got up in the morning and found
that the entire crop had turned to capsules [no longer good for
linen (Israelstam)]."

2.   A.   "Yet the harvest will flee away (ND)" (Is. 17:11).

B. You have brought (NDYTM) on yourselves the harvest of the foreign governments, the harvest of violating prohibitions, the harvest of the angel of death.

C. For R. Yohanan in the name of R. Eliezer, son of R. Yose the Galilean, said, "When the Israelites stood before Mount Sinai and said, 'All that the Lord has said we shall do and we shall hear' (Ex. 24:7). At that very moment the Holy One, blessed be he, called the angel of death and said to him, 'Even though I have made you world ruler over all of my creatures, you have no business with this nation. Why? For they are my children.' That is in line with the following verse of Scripture: 'You are the children of the Lord your God' (Deut. 14:1)."

D. And it says, "And it happened that when you heard the voice out of the midst of the darkness" (Deut. 5:20).

E. Now was there darkness above? And is it not written, "And the light dwells with Him" (Dan. 2:22)?

F. That (D) refers to the angel who is called, "Darkness."

G. That is in line with the following verse of Scripture:

H. "And the tablets were the word of God... engraven (HRWT) on the tablets" (Ex. 32:16). Read not "engraven" but "freedom" (HYRWT) [B. Erub. 54a].

I. R. Judah, R. Nehemiah, and rabbis:

J. R. Judah says, "Freedom from the angel of death."

K. And R. Nehemiah said, "Freedom from the gentile kingdoms."

L. And rabbis said, "Freedom from suffering."

3. A. "In a day of inheritance (NHLH) [and incurable pain]" (Is. 17:11).

B. "On the day on which I gave you the Torah as an inheritance."

C. "And unbearable pain" (Is. 17:11).

D. R. Yohanan and rabbis:

E. R. Yohanan said, "You have brought on yourselves an ailment that causes pain and discharges."

F. And rabbis say, "You have brought on yourself an ailment that is overwhelming and saps strength.

G. "What is it? It is flux and leprosy."

4. A. Therefore Moses admonished Israel, saying to them, "When any man has a discharge from his body" (Lev. 15:2).

XVIII:IV

1. A. R. Simeon b. Yohai taught, "When the Israelites stood before Mount Sinai and said, 'All that the Lord has spoken we shall do and we shall hear' (Ex. 24:7), among them there were no people afflicted with flux, no lepers, no cripples, no blind, no dumb, no deaf, no idiots, no imbeciles, no fools.

B.   "Concerning that hour Scripture says, 'You are wholly fair, my beloved, and there is no blemish in you' (Song 4:7).

C.   "When they had sinned, not many days passed before there were found among them people afflicted with flux, lepers, cripples, blind, dumb, deaf, idiots, imbeciles, and fools.

D.   "Concerning that hour what does Scripture then state? 'And they shall send out of the camp every leper and everyone afflicted with flux' (Num. 5:2)" [cf. Sifre Num. 1].

2.   A.   On what account were the Israelites declared liable for flux and leprosy?

B.   R. Honia in the name of R. Hoshiah: "It was because they maligned their great men, saying, 'So-and-so's family -- what do they amount to? Aren't they just a bunch of lepers?'

C.   "This is meant to teach you that leprosy-spots come only on account of gossip.

D.   "It was on that account that the Israelites became liable to suffer from flux and leprosy."

E.   R. Tanhuma said, "It was because they were maligning the ark and saying, 'That ark slays the people who carry it.'

F.   "And leprosy-spots come only on account of gossip. On that acount the Israelites became liable to suffer from flux and leprosy."

G.   Rabbis say, "It was on account of the calf, for it was written in that regard, 'And Moses saw the people, that it had broken out' (Ex. 32:25) -- that among the people flux and leprosy had broken out.

H.   "How do we know? For it is said, 'His [the leper's] clothing will be disheveled and his hair will be broken out' (Lev. 13:45)."

I.   R. Judah b. R. Simon said, "It was on account of the complainers, for it is said, 'But at a whole month, until it comes out at your nostrils and becomes loathsome to you, [because you have rejected the Lord who is among you] (Num. 11:20)."

J.   What is the meaning of "loathsome (LZR')?"

K.   R. Huna said, "Vomiting (LZWRN') and swelling."

L.   R. Simeon b. Laqish said, "Croup."

M.   R. Abbahu said, "It served as a warning (L'ZHRH)."

N.   R. Abiathar said, "A grating abdominal pain [so Israelstam]."

O.   R. Simeon b. Yohai said, "[The word, _lezara_, means (Israelstam)] 'Only in respect thereof, you must keep at a distance more than you draw near.'" [Israelstam, p. 232, n. 4: "Referring, apparently, to lepers, who are to be removed from the camp or city. Or perhaps: the quails to which the passage refers will eventually become more loathsome to you than they are now desirable in your eyes."]

P.   Said R. Judah b. R. Simon, "From that time [that they were told it would become loathsome,] they became strangers (ZRYM) (zarim) to the tent of meeting."

XVIII.V

1.   A.   R. Joshua of Sikhnin in the name of R. Levi: "Just as a mortal [king] imposes the sentence of exile, so the Holy One, blessed be he, imposes the sentence of exile.

B.   "'Command the children of Israel, that they expel from the camp [every leper, etc.]' (Num. 5:2).

C.   "A mortal [king] imposes imprisonment, and the Holy One, blessed be he, imposes imprisonment: 'And the priest will lock up the one afflicted with a leprosy-spot' (Lev. 13:4).

D.   "A mortal [king] decrees banishment, and the Holy One, blessed be he, decrees banishment: 'All by himself he will dwell outside the camp' (Lev. 13:46).

E.   "A mortal [king] imposes the penalty of flogging, and the Holy One, blessed be he, imposes the penalty of flogging: 'Forty stripes will he smite him' (Deut. 25:3).

F.   "A mortal [king] collects a fine, and the Holy One, blessed be he, collects a fine: 'And he will punish him with a fine of a hundred pieces of silver' (Deut. 22:19).

G.   "A mortal [king] gives a royal donation, and the Holy One, blessed be he, gives a royal donation: 'Lo, I bring rain for you, bread from heaven' (Ex. 16:4).

H.   "A mortal [king] passes out rations, and the Holy One, blessed be he, passes out rations: 'Take a census' (Num. 1:2).

I.   "A mortal [king] imposes a head-tax, and the Holy One, blessed be he, imposes a head-tax: 'An omer for a head for the entire number of your souls' (Ex. 16:16).

J.   "A mortal [king] imposes a flogging on account of the testimony of witnesses, but the Holy One, blessed be he, will impose a penalty on the basis of his own view: 'I have wounded, and I heal, and none besides me can save' (Deut. 32:39)."

K.   R. Berekhiah in the name of R. Levi said, "A mortal [king] wounds with a scalpel and heals with a salve.

L.   "But the Holy One, blessed be he, heals with that with which he wounds: 'For I shall restore your health, and from out of your wounds I shall bring healing to you, says the Lord' (Jer. 30:17)" [Mekhilta Beshallah 8].

Our first, and disbelieving, impression proves accurate. Of the four marked items in Parashah 12, one intersects with the Bavli, another with the Mishnah. So only two items,

one in Leviticus Rabbah and also in Genesis Rabbah, the other shared by Leviticus Rabbah
with Sifra, prove pertinent to our problem. Once more we find ourselves lacking all
reason to undertake a classification of data. Consequently no interpretation proposes
itself; there is nothing to explain. While Parashah 18 appears to make room for a more
sizable corpus of shared materials, first impressions prove deceiving. Among the eight
items I have marked, three are shared with the Bavli, therefore on temporal grounds are
not relevant. Another appears, also, in the Mishnah. That leaves for analysis four items,
two found also in the Yerushalmi, one in Genesis Rabbah, and one in the Mekhilta. None
of these items takes a critical role in the exposition of the ideas of the subunit in which it
appears. To be sure, it is the fact that the items shared by Leviticus Rabbah with other
documents would fall into the category of miscellanies. Why so? Because none exhibits
those, formal or redactional, traits we regarded as distinctive to our authors. Indeed all
are so brief as to defy formal classification other than as miscellanies. But the sample is
so slight that we can draw no conclusions from that fact.

iv. Not Unique, Not Important

It remains to ask what proportion of the three parashiyyot is made up of the shared
materials I have identified. For this purpose I count up the number of stichs encompassed
by the materials at hand and also the number of stichs shared by Leviticus Rabbah and
documents prior to its time or contemporaneous with it. A stich for this rough estimate is
constituted by a lettered unit, whether that unit is made up of one sentence or several.

	Particular to Leviticus Rabbah	Shared	
Parashah 7	103	4	96.2%
Parashah 12	172	4	97.7%
Parashah 18	152	12	92.8%

The analysis for Parashah 18 omits reference to items that occur also in the Mishnah, on
the one side, or the Bavli, on the other. If we add these to the totals, we have another 13
stichs, thus 85.8%.

In all, the results are one-sided. While rough, they confirm the impression of the
essential autonomy of Leviticus Rabbah. How so? Nearly everything, that is, something
like 95% of all stichs, in our composition, from the viewpoint of the extant canon in hand
prior to the redaction of, or contemporary with, Leviticus Rabbah is unique.

To conclude: when we asked about the integrity of the document as a whole, we
took up the encompassing traits, the definitive literary and redactional characteristics.
Accordingly, we asked whether Leviticus Rabbah is an anthology or a sustained composition. On formal grounds we concluded that it constitutes a text with its own
integrity, not merely a collection of this and that. Now that we have examined a sample
of the smallest components of the document, brief sayings of various kinds, we have found
two facts.

First of all, our probe of three <u>parashiyyot</u> yields an astonishingly small proportion of materials that are not unique. We may conclude that, in the context of the whole document, what is not unique takes up a very minor place and contributes episodic and unsustained supplements.

Second, much of that shared component turns out to be formally diverse. Little indicates that the items shared with other documents fit well into Leviticus Rabbah. Why not? Within Leviticus Rabbah, the shared items do not conform to the formal preferences, as to the construction of large-scale discourse, dominant in the document as a whole.

Accordingly, our probe leaves no doubt that a catalogue of phrases and sentences or even groups of sentences -- from two to ten stichs -- that occur in both Leviticus Rabbah and another document of its own time or earlier would list little more than editorial detritus. Such a catalogue of all of the passages shared with documents other than Scripture and the Mishnah, at the beginning, through to the Yerushalmi and other contemporary writings, at the end, would prove a random collection of this and that. That is to say, all we should turn up is lists of items shared by Leviticus Rabbah and, e.g., Sifra, the two Sifres, the Yerushalmi, and the like. If our now-completed probe is suggestive, such lists by themselves would not tell us anything we wish to know.

For our question is not whether our document is mostly original ("unique"). That we may now take for granted is readily demonstrated simply on the criterion of the volume and proportion of shared materials. By that criterion, Leviticus Rabbah appears to be "original" in 95% of its volume, in that what we find here we find nowhere else. Nor do we ask whether Leviticus Rabbah is made up of materials less or more suited to its authors' editorial preferences than to those of the writers of, e.g., Tosefta, Sifra, the two Sifres, the Yerushalmi, or other prior or contemporary writings. As I shall explain below, I see little at stake in settling that question. What we ask, I emphasize, is whether we deal with a text, like the Mishnah, or a scrapbook, like the Tosefta, a document of integrity and proportion, like Sifra, or a convenient receptacle in which to collect diverse materials, like the Fathers according to R. Nathan. And that question will not be settled merely by what has now been shown to be highly probable, which is one simple fact. What is not unique to Leviticus Rabbah also turns out to be not important in Leviticus Rabbah. The more interesting question lies ahead of us. But we must conduct a far more thorough probe, in Chapter Four, before we answer those questions, as we shall in Chapter Five.

Chapter Four

UNITS OF DISCOURSE COMMON TO LEVITICUS RABBAH AND OTHER TEXTS

i. The Problem

Brief sayings in our probes in sayings shared among Leviticus Rabbah and various other documents prove too few in number and too slight in structural weight to settle any questions. In numbers and importance they surely do suggest that Leviticus Rabbah constitutes much more than a collection of this and that. The shared corpus of brief sayings, after all, plays no role whatsoever in constituting the characteristic literary structures of the document. So we cannot conclude that diverse materials, flowing hither and yon, by chance coalesced in Leviticus Rabbah in an essentially random way. Leviticus Rabbah, we have seen, is not a document formed in a random way but in accord with a large plan, and materials flowing into the document from some common heritage play no definitive role in Leviticus Rabbah at all. But the sample proved too negligible, the data altogether too episodic, to demonstrate the contrary proposition. That is to say, because of their unimportance to the whole, the brief sayings do not demonstrate that the vast stretches of the document at hand not shared with other rabbinic writings do follow cogent programs and intelligible patterns. On the basis of what we have examined, we simply do not know whether or not the shared materials in our particular document are so worked out as to serve cogent and encompassing purposes distinctive to our document or constitute episodic and inconsequential accretions.

Let me expand on that last point, because it is critical to defining the real problem of analysis and interpretation before us. As we shall now see, Leviticus Rabbah does encompass important units of discourse not unique to its authorship. These sizable statements appear in other writings, generally thought to be contemporary or nearly contemporary with Leviticus Rabbah, namely, Pesiqta de R. Kahana, Genesis Rabbah, and the Yerushalmi. We shall review a large population, not merely a sample. Numerous instances of these larger compositions, those encompassing more than a few stichs and constituting whole and cogent units of discourse, common to one or more of the writings of the fourth and fifth centuries, will come before us. In our inquiry we must find guidance in a very specific question. The alternative is to lose sight of our fundamental purpose and wander about in a morass of subjective impressions meant to settle objective questions. The question demanding attention is simple. Leviticus Rabbah does share with the listed compositions sizable and significant units of discourse. That fact generates two questions, one to be dealt with here, the other not relevant to our inquiry. What is relevant is how an item shared between Leviticus Rabbah and, e.g., Pesiqta de R. Kahana or Genesis Rabbah, serves the purpose in particular of Leviticus Rabbah and its editors. The answer to the question will emerge in some simple and objective facts. Does the shared item (however it fits elsewhere) fit into the larger literary constructions of

Leviticus Rabbah? Does it advance the interests of the framers of the discussion in which it finds its location (however it advances the work of other authors)? Or does the shared item prove incongruous to its larger setting? And does it set down in splendid isolation from its context formal constructions at best congruent with, but not particular to, its present context? If the answer is that the shared item (however it serves its other contexts) has been made to fit well into our setting, then we may judge Leviticus Rabbah to be a text. It is a composition in which available materials are purposefully shaped for a cogent and coherent program. If the shared item (however it contributes to other discussions) clearly takes up the specific concerns of the framer of the setting in which the item is located in Leviticus Rabbah, then we may deem Leviticus Rabbah to present a cogent and sustained discussion, and note merely a sequence of random, if loosely connected, thoughts. Let me state with emphasis: the criterion is whether the shared item is continuous with its larger setting here, in both its literary and its intellectual aspects, or whether it is merely connected to that larger setting, but autonomous in both its literary and its intellectual aspects. Thus, in a word: continuous or merely connected.

The negatives hardly require extensive amplification. If an item is formally incongruous, then no one has revised the item in light of the definitive requirements of Leviticus Rabbah. If its contents prove connected only in a general or thematic way, then no one has selected the item or recast it, so as to fit tightly and uniformly into Leviticus Rabbah. Then Leviticus Rabbah will appear, at the point at hand, to be not cogent and not sustained. In the given instance, the document comprises a mere sequence of expressions of related but essentially episodic entries, a scrapbook. In other words a rabbinic text is merely a context for the localization of distinct and finished pieces of discourse. These are the choices, to be settled by the facts surveyed in this Chapter and analyzed in Chapter Five.

What is not relevant to our discussion, and a point we shall never pursue, proves more familiar from existing literature. In the available scholarly discussion we find long debates on whether or not a given passage is "original to" or finds its "more natural place in" Leviticus Rabbah than in Genesis Rabbah, or in Leviticus Rabbah than in Pesiqta de R. Kahana. These debates yield no useful results. What is at stake, after all, in an argument about whether a given passage is "primary to" Genesis Rabbah or to Leviticus Rabbah? Is it that the people who wrote it were the editors of Genesis Rabbah or had in mind the interests of Genesis Rabbah? What does that tell me about Leviticus Rabbah? I find the issue murky. What we know about the passage at hand, that we did not know before, I cannot say. But still less can I suggest what we know that we did not know before about either Genesis Rabbah or Leviticus Rabbah. True, if we can demonstrate that a given passage is "primary" to Genesis Rabbah, then we can claim that Leviticus Rabbah (at that point) is secondary to Genesis Rabbah. What we then have is a self-evident statement.

But the upshot yields slight meaning. Why so? For if the authors of Genesis Rabbah have made up a sizable discussion, and those of Leviticus Rabbah have taken it over, then the latter have done so either for cause or purposelessly. But it is always their literary and intellectual program that we seek to grasp. What we want to know is not whether or not they derived useful materials from earlier writers. We know that they did. After all, they quote not only the Mishnah, but also Scripture! What we want to know is about not their sources but their authorship and composition, not where they got what they used but how they so recast everything they borrowed as to produce a composition -- if that is what Leviticus Rabbah turns out to have been. So at issue is whether shared materials serve the purposes of the authorship of Leviticus Rabbah. If the shared materials exhibit a strong connection with the context, in Leviticus Rabbah, in which they are used, then the fact that the materials proved useful elsewhere means little. If the shared materials appear to be parachuted down, with slight relationship to the context defined by the setting in Leviticus Rabbah, then the fact that the materials served a different authorship, another document, means much. It means that Leviticus Rabbah has admitted materials without much reason. That is to say, Leviticus Rabbah at the point at hand proves miscellaneous and lacking in clear purpose, a mere compilation, an anthology, a scrapbook, not a text, not a composition. At issue at each point, therefore, is the simple criterion of relevance to the context defined by Leviticus Rabbah. That question I systematically address to each item in the survey that follows.

In the present chapter, as in the preceding, we simply review an important sample of the shared sources, now the large and sustained compositions, whole units of discourse or sizable components of units of discourse. In Chapter Five we analyze the results of the work of collection accomplished in Chapters Three and Four.

ii. Units of Discourse Common to Leviticus Rabbah and the Yerushalmi

We shall review a sizable repertoire of items appearing in both the Yerushalmi and Leviticus Rabbah. I include not only the item, but some lines fore and aft, so we can see how the shared passage fits. My appended comments in one way or another deal with the stated questions: why is the item introduced? Does it advance the discussion in context? Or does it prove incongruous and irrelevant?

III:II

1. A. "You who fear the Lord, praise him! All you seed of Jacob, [glorify him and stand in awe of him, all you seed of Israel! For he has not despised or abhored the affliction of the afflicted, and he has not hid his face from him but has heard, when he cried to him]" (Ps. 22:23-24).

   B. "You who fear the Lord, praise him!"

   C. R. Joshua b. Levi said, "This refers to those who fear Heaven."

   D. R. Ishmael b. R. Nehemiah said, "This refers to righteous converts."

2. A. R. Hezekiah, R. Abbahu in the name of R. Eleazar [= Y. Meg. 1:10]: "If the righteous converts enter [into the world to come], Antoninus will enter at the head of all of them..." "This passage is not fully spelled out.]

3. A.   What is the meaning of the verse, "All you seed of Jacob, glorify him"?

    B.   This refers to the ten tribes.

III:II.1 speaks of righteous converts, and then No. 2 illustrates that notion with reference to a specific figure. The passage therefore is continuous with the foregoing. No. 3 reverts to No. 1.

III:III

1. A.   "Let the wicked abandon his way, and the man of evil his thoughts" (Is. 55:7).

    B.   Said R. Biba b. R. Abina [= Y. Yoma 8:7], "How should a person recite the confession on the eve of the Day of Atonement?

    C.   "A person has to say, 'I acknowledge everything that I did in the evil way in which I was standing, and the like of whatever I did I shall never do again. May it be your will, O Lord, my God, to forgive me for all my sins, and to bear with me for all my transgressions, and to atone for me for all my wicked deeds.'

    D.   "That is in line with the following verse of Scripture: 'Let the wicked abandon his way, and the man of evil his thoughts' (Is. 55:7)."

    E.   It is written, "Let [him] abandon..."

III:III.1.B-C provides a substantial example of how the "man of evil" must abandon his way and his thoughts. The passage is integral to its setting.

V:IV

2. A.   "A man's gift makes room for him and brings him before great men" (Prov. 18:16).

    B.   [Y. Hor. 3:4:] M^CSH B: R. Eliezer, R. Joshua, and R. Aqiba went to the harborside of Antioch to collect funds for the support of sages.

    C.   [In Aramaic:] A certain Abba Yudan lived there.

    D.   He would carry out his religious duty [of philanthropy] in a liberal spirit, but had lost his money. When he saw our masters, he went home with a sad face. His wife said to him, "What's wrong with you, that you look so sad?"

    E.   He repeated the tale to her: "Our masters are here, and I don't know what I shall be able to do for them."

    F.   His wife, who was a truly philanthropic woman -- what did she say to him? "You only have one field left. Go, sell half of it and give them the proceeds."

G. He went and did just that. When he was giving them the money, they said to him, "May the Omnipresent make up all your losses."

H. Our masters went their way.

I. He went out to plough. While he was ploughing the half of the field that he had left, the Holy One, blessed be he, opened his eyes. The earth broke open before him, and his cow fell in and broke her leg. He went down to raise her up, and found a treasure beneath her. He said, "It was for my gain that my cow broke her leg."

J. When our masters came back, [in Aramaic:] they asked about a certain Abba Yudan and how he was doing. They said, "Who can gaze on the face of Abba Yudan [which glows with prosperity] -- Abba Yudan, the owner of flocks of goats, Abba Yudan, the owner of herds of asses, Abba Yudan, the owner of herds of camels."

K. He came to them and said to them, "Your prayer in my favor has produced returns and returns on the returns."

L. They said to him, "Even though someone else gave more than you did, we wrote your name at the head of the list."

M. Then they took him and sat him next to themselves and recited in his regard the following verse of Scripture: "A man's gift makes room for him and brings him before great men" (Prov. 18:16).

3. A. R. Hiyya bar Abba called for charity contributions in support of a school in Tiberias. A member of the household of Siloni got up and pledged a litra of gold.

B. R. Hiyya bar Abba took him and sat him next to himself and recited in his regard the following verse of Scripture: "A man's gift makes room for him and brings him before great men" (Prov. 18:16).

4. A. [In Aramaic:] R. Simeon b. Laqish went to Bosrah. A certain Abba [Lieberman deletes: Yudan], "the Deceiver," lived there. It was not -- Heaven forfend -- that he really was a deceiver. Rather, he would practice [holy] deception in doing the religious duty [of philanthropy].

B. [In Aramaic:] He would see what the rest of the community would pledge, and he would then pledge to take upon himself [a gift equivalent to that of the rest of the] community.

C. R. Simeon b. Laqish took him and sat him next to himself and recited in his regard the following verse of Scripture: "A man's gift makes room for him and brings him before great men" (Prov. 18:16).

V:IV.1 introduces the notion that the gifts to the Levites are the cause for the increase in Israel's territory in the land (Deut. 12:19 and Deut. 12:20 being linked as cause and effect): "In accord with your gifts they will enlarge your place." Then No. 2's citation of Prov. 18:16 delivers the same message. The extended case, shared with Y. Hor. 3:4, makes that same point. While formally autonomous, the story in substance is entirely integral to the point that the framer of the passage wishes to make. The same is to be said for Nos. 3 and 4, which are continuous both here and in Y. Hor. 3:4.

V:VI

4. A.   Said R. Aibu [Y. Ter. 8:3, A.Z. 2:3], "M^CSH B: Once there was a butcher in Sepphoris, who fed Israelites carrion and torn-meat. On the eve of the Day of Atonement he went out drinking and got drunk. He climbed up to the roof of his house and fell off and died. The dogs began to lick him.

    B.   "[In Aramaic:] They came and asked R. Hanina the law about moving his corpse away from the dogs [on the Day of Atonement].

    C.   "He said to him, '"You will be holy people to me, therefore you shall not eat any meat that is torn of beasts in the field, you shall cast it to the dogs" (Ex. 22:30).

    D.   "'This man robbed from the dogs and fed carrion and torn-meat to Israelites. Leave him to them. They are eating what belongs to them.'"

The context is established at V:VI.1, reference to Lev. 4:3, if the anointed priest sins. The issue then is how an anointed priest can sin, so V:VI.2. Levi then comments, "Pity the town whose physician has gout [and cannot walk to visit the sick]." No. 3 speaks of the anointed priest's bringing guilt on the people. Then, as we see, No. 4 speaks of a butcher who supplies improper meat and is punished. In context, the story illustrates the main point at hand, concerning a public official who causes the community to sin. The thematic link is continuous.

IX:VI

1. A.   [Y. Megillah 1:11.IV:] R. Eleazar and R. Yose b. Haninah:

    B.   R. Eleazar said, "Peace-offerings did the children of Noah offer up."

    C.   R. Yose b. Haninah said, "Burnt-offerings did the children of Noah offer up."

    D.   R. Eleazar objected to R. Yose b. Haninah, "[And has it not been written,] 'And Abel brought of the firstlings of his flock and of their fat portions. [And the Lord had regard for Abel and his offering]' (Gen. 4:4)? [This indicates that the animals were offered as peace-offerings, of] which the fat portions are offered, [not the whole beast]."

    E.   How does R. Yose b. Haninah [interpret] this [verse]? He offered up their fat parts [along with the whole beast].

F.   R. Eleazar objected to R. Yose b. Haninah, "[And lo, it is written,]
      'And he sent young men of the people of Israel, [who offered
      burnt-offerings and sacrificed peace-offerings of oxen to the Lord]'
      (Ex. 24:5). [This verse explicitly refers to peace-offerings.]"

G.   How does R. Yose b. Haninah interpret this verse? He reads it in
      accord with the view of him who said that they were whole in their
      body [reading the word for peace-offerings as "whole"], meaning
      that they were not flayed or chopped up.

H.   R. Eleazar objected to R. Yose b. Haninah, "[And lo, it is written],
      'And Jethro, Moses' father-in-law, offered a burnt-offering and
      sacrifices to God, [and Aaron came with all the elders of Israel to
      eat bread with Moses' father-in-law before God]' (Ex. 18:12). [This
      indicates that there were peace-offerings as well as burnt-offer-
      ings.]"

I.   How does R. Yose b. Haninah deal with this? He concurs with him
      who says that it was only after the giving of the Torah that Jethro
      converted.

J.   R. Huna said, "Judah b. Rabbi and R. Yannai differed. One said, 'It
      was after the giving of the Torah that Jethro converted.' The
      other said, 'It was before the giving of the Torah that Jethro
      converted."

K.   He who maintains that it was prior to the giving of the Torah that
      Jethro converted concurs with him who says that the children of
      Noah offered peace-offerings.

L.   He who says that it was after the giving of the Torah that Jethro
      converted concurs with him who said that the children of Noah
      offered burnt-offerings.

M.   The following supports the position of R. Yose b. Haninah:
      "Awake, O north wind, and come, O south wind! [Blow upon my
      garden, let its fragrance be wafted abroad. Let my beloved come
      to his garden, and eat its choicest fruits]' (Song 4:16).

N.   "Awake, O north wind" refers to the burnt-offering, which is
      slaughtered at the north side of the altar.

O.   And why does scripture call it [the burnt offering] Uri [Awake]? It
      means that this is something that was sleeping [prior to the coming
      of Israel] and was then awakened [at the building of the Israelite
      cult].

P.   "And come, O south wind" refers to peace-offerings, which are
      slaughtered at the south side of the altar. And why does Scripture
      call it [the peace-offering] "come, south wind"? It speaks of
      something that was an innovation. [This then refutes Yose's view
      after all.]

Q.   Also this verse of Scripture supports the view of R. Yose b.
     Haninah: "This is the law of the burnt-offering, this is [that same]
     burnt-offering" (Lev. 6:9) that the children of Noah had been
     offering. Now when [Scripture] came to peace-offerings, it said,
     'And this is the law of the sacrifice of peace-offerings [which they
     will offer to the Lord]' (Lev. 7:11).

R.   "Which they offered" is not written here, but rather, "which they
     will offer." The meaning then is, from now on. [That supports
     Yose's view that in olden times peace-offerings were not offered.]

S.   How does R. Eleazar deal with the verse that supports the position
     of R. Yose b. R. Haninah, that is, "Awake, O north wind, [and
     come, O south wind]?"

T.   ["Awake, O north wind"]: When the exiles who are located in the
     north will awake, they will come and make camp in the south.

U.   "Lo, I shall bring them from the north country" (Jer. 31:8).

V.   When Gog, who is located in the north, will awake, he will come
     and fall in the south.

W.   That accords with the following verse of Scripture: "I will turn you
     about and lead you on and will bring you up from the uttermost
     parts of the north" (Ez. 39:2).

X.   When the anointed king [or: King Messiah], who is now located in
     the north, will awake, he will come and rebuild the house of the
     sanctuary, which is located in the south.

Y.   That accords with the following verse of Scripture: "I have roused
     up one from the north and he has come" (Is. 41:25).

Z.   R. Yose in the name of R. Benjamin b. R. Levi: "Now in this world,
     when the north wind blows, the south wind does not blow, and when
     the south wind blows, the north wind does not blow. But in the
     world to come, the Holy One, blessed be he, will say, 'I shall bring
     an argestes-wind into the world, which blows from two directions
     at once.'

AA. "That is in line with the following verse of Scripture: 'I will say to
     the north, "Give up," and to the south, "Keep not back" (Is. 43:6)'"

BB. R. Yohanan said, "The Torah teaches you proper conduct. For a
     bridegroom does not enter into the marriage canopy until the bride
     gives him permission to come in. That is in line with the following
     verse of Scripture: 'Let my beloved come into my garden and
     enjoy his precious fruits' (Song 4:16), and afterward, 'I have come
     into my garden, my sister, my bride' (Song 4:17)."

1.A-R occurs with minor changes at Y. Meg. 1:11.IV, as indicated. The reason for
including the passage is the shared theme of the thanksgiving offering. I see no message

distinctive to the present context. The framer reveals no effort to demonstrate that the thanksgiving offering is superior in its moral character to any other offering. Lev. 7:11 is not the base-verse but merely a proof-text. Here is a case in which the shared pericope is parachuted down into Leviticus Rabbah. I see no substantial links to the larger context. The thematic tie is most general; the details of the theme of the larger parashah, the thanksgiving offering, are ignored. So the reason for inclusion is that the base-verse of the larger parashah appears here as proof-text. To be sure, we can point to numerous instances in Leviticus Rabbah in which a base-verse or an intersecting-verse is subjected to sustained exegesis on its own. But the present passage finds its place in the larger construction solely because of a connection, via the common reference, to a given verse of Scripture. We cannot claim that the statement at hand is continuous with the larger context.

IX:IX

1. B.   [Y. Meg. 1:4:] R. Meir would sit and expound [the Torah] on Sabbath nights. A certain woman would attend regularly. [Once] when his exposition ran on, she remained until he was finished. When she got home, she found that the lamp had gone out. Her husband said to her, "Where were you?"

    C.   She said to him, "I was in the session and listening to the exposition."

    D.   He said to her, "You will not come in here until you go and spit in the face of the expositor."

    E.   She stayed away [from home] one week, then a second, then a third. Her neighbors said to her, "Are you people still mad at one another? Let us go with you to the expositor."

    F.   When R. Meir saw them, he understood through the Holy Spirit [what was going on]. He said to the women, "Among you is there a woman who is knowledgeable about whispering over [treating] a sore eye?"

    G.   Her neighbors said to her, "If you go and spit in his face, you will be permitted to go back to your husband."

    H.   But when the woman sat down before him, she became afraid of him. She said to him, "My lord, I am not really an expert at whispering over a sore eye."

    I.   He said to her, "Spit in my face seven times, and I'll get better."

    J.   She spit in his face seven times. He said to her, "Go and tell your husband, 'You said to do it once, but I did it seven times.'"

    K.   His disciples said to him, "My lord, is that the way people should abuse the Torah? Could you not have told one of us to whisper [over your eye] for you?"

    L.   He said to them, "Is it not sufficient [honor] for Meir to be merely equal to his Creator?

M.   "For R. Ishmael has taught, 'The greatness of peace is shown in
that the great name [of God], which is written in a state of
sanctification, did the Holy One, blessed be he, instruct to have
blotted out in water, if only to bring peace between a man and his
wife.'"

The context is a sequence of autonomous units illustrating the same point, how great
or important peace is. Some of these passages appear, in the extant canon, only here.
Others occur elsewhere, e.g., IX:IX.3 is shared with Gen. R. 48:18, No. 4, Gen. R. 100:8.
The story at hand, of which I have given only part, is shared with Y. Meg. 1:4, as
indicated. The entire construction therefore constitutes a miscellany on a common
theme, and, in that context, the passage used also in the Yerushalmi fits as well, or as
poorly, as any other. It is part of an anthology on a theme.

X:VI

1.   A.   "[The Lord said to Moses, 'Take Aaron and his sons with him,] and
the garments [and the anointing oil and the bull of the sin-offering,
the two rams, and the basket of unleavened bread, and assemble all
the congregation at the door of the tent of meeting]" (Lev. 8:1-3).

B.   R. Simon said, "Just as the sacrifices effect atonement, so
[wearing of the] garments effects atonement.

C.   "This is in accord with the following teaching, which we have
learned in the Mishnah [M. Yoma 7:5]: 'The high priest serves in
eight garments, and an ordinary priest in four: tunic, underpants,
headcovering, and girdle. The high priest in addition wears the
breastplate, apron, upper garment, and frontlet.'

D.   [Y. Yoma 7:3:] "The tunic serves to effect atonement for those
who wear garments made up of mixed fabrics [deriving from both
vegetable matter and animal matter, such as linen and wool].

E.   "That is in line with the following verse of Scripture: 'And he
made from him a tunic of many colors' (Gen. 37:3).

F.   "Underpants serve to effect atonement for licentiousness.

G.   "That is in line with the following verse of Scripture: 'And you
shall make linen underpants for them to cover the flesh of
nakedness' (Ex. 28:42).

H.   "The headcovering serves to effect atonement for arrogance.

I.   "That is in line with the following verse of Scripture: 'And you will
set the headcovering on his head' (Ex. 29:6).

J.   "The girdle: There is he who maintains that it is on account of
deceivers, and he who holds it is on account of thieves."

K.   (Said R. Levi, "The girdle was thirty two cubits, and he wound it
towards the front and the back.")

L. [Simon continues:] "The breastplate serves to effect atonement for those who corrupt justice.

M. "This is in line with the following verse of Scripture: 'And you shall put in the breastplate of judgment' (Ex. 28:30).

N. "The apron serves to effect atonement for idolatry.

O. "This is in line with the following verse of Scripture: '[For the children of Israel shall dwell many days without king or prince without sacrifice or pillar,] without apron or teraphim. [Afterward the children of Israel shall return and seek the Lord]' (Hos. 3:4)."

P. The upper garment: R. Simon in the name of R. Nathan said, "For two matters there is no possibility of atonement, yet the Torah has [still] assigned a mode of atonement to them, and these are they: gossip and unintentional manslaughter.

Q. "What is it that serves as atonement in the view of him who maintains that while there is no real possibility of atonement for gossip, yet the Torah has assigned to it a mode of atonement?

R. "It is the little bells of the priest's robe.

S. "That is in line with the following verse of Scripture: 'A golden bell and a pomegranate, a golden bell and a pomegranate, round about on the skirts of the robe. And it shall be upon Aaron when he ministers, and its voice shall be heard when he goes into the holy place before the Lord, and when he comes out, lest he die' (Ex. 28:34-5).

T. "Said the Holy One, blessed be he, 'Let the voice come and effect atonement for what the voice has done.'

U. "He who commits unintentional manslaughter has no means of atonement, yet the Torah has assigned atonement to such a deed. And what is that means of atonement? It is the death of the high priest.

V. "That is in line with the following verse of Scripture: 'But after the death of the high priest the one guilty of manslaughter may return to the land of his possession' (Nm. 35:28).

W. "The frontlet:

X. "There is he who maintains that it serves to make atonement for those who are shameless, and there is he who holds that it serves to make atonement for one who those who blaspheme.

Y. "He who holds that it serves to make atonement for those who are shameless derives evidence from the case of the daughters of Zion.

Z. "Here it is written, 'It shall be upon Aaron's forehead' (Ex. 28:38).

AA. "There it is written, 'You [daughters of Zion] had a harlot's forehead, but you refused to be ashamed' (Jer. 3:3).

BB. "He who maintains that it serves to attain atonement for those who blaspheme draws evidence from the case of Goliath.

CC. "Here it is written, 'It will be on his forehead forever' (Ex. 28:38).

DD. "And in regard to Goliath it is written, 'and the stone sand into his forehead' (1 Sam. 17:49)."

The systematic exegesis serves not Lev. 8:1-3 but M. Yoma 7:5. The entire construction is inserted, therefore, solely for thematic reasons. In fact, the whole occurs at Y. Yoma 7:3. As we see, the list of the garments, supplied by the Mishnah, is then provided with both the theological-moral exegesis and secondary proof-texts in support of the proposed exegesis. The purpose is to show that each garment serves to expiate some specific sin, and then the proof-texts serve the successive allegations, all in within the agendum of M. Yoma 7:5. I see no point of intersection with Lev. 8:1-3, and, it goes without saying, the texts cited do not constitute intersecting verses. The composition is not continuous but thematically connected.

X:VIII

1. A. "[The Lord said to Moses, Take Aaron and his sons with him, and the garments,] the anointing oil, [the bull of the sin-offering, the two rams, and the basket of unleavened bread] (Lev. 8:1-2).

   B. R. Judah b. R. Ilai said, "With the anointing oil which Moses made in the wilderness were miracles done from beginning to end [Y. Hor. 3:2, Y. Sheq. 6:13.]

   C. "[For at the outset] there were only twelve logs, as it is said, '...and of olive oil, a hin' (Ex. 30:24).

   D. "Now if there was not sufficient oil for putting oil on the wood, how much the more so [that the oil was insufficient for much else]:

   E. "For how much did the fire, the wood, the pot feed on it,

   F. "with it were anointed Aaron and his sons for all the seven days of consecration, the golden altar and all its utensils,

   G. "with it were anointed the copper altar and all its utensils, the table and all its utensils, the lampstand and all its utensils, the laver and its base,

   H. "from it were anointed high priests and kings. [And yet it sufficed!]"

   I. Even a high priest son of a high priest requires anointing, even down to the tenth successive generation.

   J. [A king [anointed] at the outset [of a dynasty] requires anointing.] But the son of an anointed king does not, [for it is said, "Arise, anoint him; for this is he" (1 Sam. 16:12).] [This one requires anointing. But his son does not require anointing.]

   K. [They anoint a king who is son of a king only on account of dissension.] Why was Solomon anointed at all? Because of the struggle with Adonijah; Joash, because of Athaliah;

L.   Jehoahaz, because of Jehoiakim, his brother, who was two years older than he, [was anointed].

M.   Now the whole [of the twelve hin of oil] will remain for the age to come, for it is said, "It will be holy [anointing oil for all your generations]" (Ex. 30:31).

N.   They anoint kings only over a spring: "Cause Solomon my son to ride on my own mule, and bring him down to Gihon: [and let Zadok the priest and Nathan the prophet there anoint him king over Israel]" (1 King 1:33-34).

O.   [You must say, they anointed him with oil from a balsam tree.]

P.   They anoint kings only from a horn. Saul and Jehu, who were anointed from a cruse, had a transient reign. David and Solomon, who were anointed from a horn, had an enduring reign.

The passage, which occurs with slight variations at the places of Y. indicated, serves as an anthology on the anointing oil and in no way intersects with the passage at hand.

XVI:VIII

2.   B.   [Y. Shab. 14:3:] R. Jacob b. R. Aha in the name of R. Yohanan: "'And the Lord will remove from you every ailment' (Deut. 7:15) This refers to depressing thoughts."

C.   And R. Abin said, "This refers to the evil impulse. For in the beginning it is sweet but at the end it is bitter."

D.   R. Tanhuma in the name of R. Eleazar, and R. Menahama in the name of Rab: "'And the Lord will remove from you every ailment' This refers to bile."

E.   This is in line with the view of R. Eleazar: "Ninety-nine die of bile and one by the hands of Heaven."

F.   Rab and R. Hiyya the Elder both say, "Ninety-nine die of the evil eye and one at the hands of Heaven."

G.   R. Haninah and R. Nathan both say, "Ninety-nine die of cold, and one at the hands of Heaven."

H.   Rab is consistent with his setting, and R. Haninah likewise is consistent with his setting.

I.   Rab is consistent, for Rab lived in Babylonia, where the evil eye was commonplace.

J.   R. Haninah is consistent, because he lived in Sepphoris, where it was very cold.

3.   A.   Antoninus said to Our Holy Rabbi [Judah the Patriarch], "Pray for me."

B.   He said to him, "May you be saved from cold."

C.   He said to him, "That's no prayer. With one extra cover, the cold goes its way."

D.   He said to him, "May you be saved from heat."

E.   He said to him, "Lo, that is the prayer that you should say for me.

F.   "For it is said, 'There is no hiding from his heat' (Ps. 19:7)."

4.   A.   R. Samuel b. R. Nahman in the name of R. Nathan, "Ninety-nine
          die of heat, and one at the hands of Heaven."

     B.   And rabbis say, "Ninety-nine die of transgression, and one at the
          hands of Heaven."

The bulk, serving Deut. 7:15, is at Y. Shab. 14:3, with very minor changes and
rearrangements. Inclusion here in no way serves the exegesis of the passage at hand.

XIX:V

6.   A.   And there is the following verse: "If a woman has a discharge of
          blood for many days" (Lev. 15:25).

     B.   R. Hiyya taught [Y. Yoma 2:4], "The reference to 'days' is to two
          days, and to 'many' means that three days in all [are under
          discussion].

     C.   "From that time onward [if a woman continues to produce blood],
          the woman is not regarded as a menstruant, but as a 'sick' woman
          [that is, afflicted by flux in line with Lev. 15:25]."

This passage is integral to the exegesis of the base-verse, Lev. 15:25. The passage is
continuous, not merely connected.

XXI:X

1.   A.   R. Hananiah, associate of the rabbis: "On what account does the
          high priest serve in eight garments [Y. Yoma 7:3]? It is for the
          circumcision, which is eight days [after birth], in line with the
          following verse of Scripture: '[So shall you know that I have sent
          this command to you, that] my covenant with Levi may hold, [says
          the Lord of hosts]'" (Mal. 2:4).

     B.   R. Simon in the name of R. Joshua: "Why does not the high priest
          serve in golden garments? It is because the prosecution cannot
          become the defense, so as not to give Satan an opening [following
          Y.:] 'Yesterday in their regard it is written concerning them, 'So
          Moses returned to the Lord and said, Alas, this people have sinned
          a great sin; they have made for themselves gods of gold' (Ex.
          32:31). Today is he going to stand and serve in golden garments?!'"

     C.   R. Joshua of Sikhnin in the name of R. Levi: "To spare Israel
          excessive expense."

     D.   R. Levi said, "On account of excessive pride.

     E.   "'Do not put yourself forward in the king's presence or stand in the
          place of the great' (Prov. 25:6)."

None of this has any bearing on our passage. The passage is thematically connected.

XXII:IX

1. A. [Y. Meg. 1:11-12:] Said R. Yose b. R. Haninah, "Sacrifice on a high place [once the prohibition had taken effect] could be permitted only by a prophet.

    B. "What is the Scriptural basis for that view?

    C. "'Take heed that you do not offer your burnt-offerings [at every place that you see,] but at the place which the Lord your God will choose' (Deut. 12:13)."

    D. Did Elijah make an offering on a high place at the time that the high places were forbidden?

    E. Said R. Simlai, "The Divine Word had told him [that it was all right to do so.]

    F. "[That is in line with the following verse of Scripture: 'And at the time of the offering of the oblation Elijah the prophet gave ear and said, 'O Lord, God of Abraham, Isaac, and Israel, and that I am your servant,] and that I have done all these things at your word' (1 Kgs. 18:36).

    G. "It was on account of your word that I have done so."

    H. R. Yohanan b. R. Mareh derived that proposition from the following: "Then Joshua built [an altar in Mount Ebal to the Lord, the God of Israel as Moses, the servant of the Lord, had commanded the people of Israel] (Josh. 8:30)."

    I. I know only that that is the case [that the high place was built at the word of a prophet] of Joshua [Mount Ebal]. How do we know [that the same is so of that built by] Gideon?

    J. "And it came to pass that same night that the Lord said to him, 'Take your father's bullock [...and build an altar... on the top of this stronghold]'" (Jud. 6:25).

    K. R. Abba bar Kahana said, "Seven transgressions were permitted through the bullock offered by Gideon: the wood came from an Asherah; the stones on which it was offered were invalid; the beast had been designated for idolatry; it had been worshipped; it was done by a non-priest; it was at night; and it was at the time at which high places were prohibited."

    L. I know only that that is the case in respect to Gideon.

    M. How do I know [that it applies also to the altar built by] Samuel?

    N. "So Samuel took a sucking lamb [and offered it as a whole burnt-offering to the Lord and Samuel cried to the Lord for Israel, and the Lord answered him]" (1 Sam. 7:9).

    O. Said R. Ba bar Kahana, "Three transgressions were committed through the lamb offered by Samuel: It and its hide [were offered up, without flaying]; it was yet too young; and Samuel was a Levite [not a priest]."

P.   Said R. Jonah, "As to that matter, there is nothing to be derived from the case."

Q.   And he who wants to derive a lesson should accord with that which was said by R. Samuel bar Nahman, "'Then he would come back to Ramah, for his home was there, [and there also he administered justice to Israel. And he built there an altar to the Lord]' (1 Sam. 7:17)."

The general theme of sacrificing on the high places unites the construction at hand to Lev. 17:3. But nothing in the base-verse interests the framers, whose materials are not particular to the present collection at all but occur at Y. Meg. 1:11-12.

XXV:I

4.   A.   "For wisdom is a defense as money is a defense" (Qoh. 7:12).

B.   [Y. Sot. 7:4:] R. Aha in the name of R. Tanhum b. R. Hiyya: "If one had learned Torah and taught it, kept and done [its teachings], but had the power to protest [wrongdoing] and did not protest, or to support [disciples of sages] and did not support them, lo, this one falls into the category of cursed.

C.   "That is in line with the following verse of Scripture: '[Cursed be he] who does not confirm...' (Deut. 27:26)."

D.   R. Jeremiah in the name of R. Hiyya: "If one did not study [Torah] and did not carry out [its teachings], did not keep them and did not teach them to others, and did not have the power to support [disciples of sages] but [nonetheless] he did so, [or] did not have the power to protest [wrongdoing] but nonetheless he did so, lo, this one falls into the category of blessed."

The exposition of the base-verse, Lev. 19:23, rests upon its reference to a "tree," and in the intersecting verse, Prov. 3:18, that is understood to invoke the theme of the Torah, "the tree of life." Accordingly, here we have the case of an intersecting verse which, to the rabbinical exegetes in general, makes explicit reference to the theme of the base-verse. The sense of No. 1 is that the Torah should be regarded as a desirable bride, and not as the leftover. The point now is that the Torah protects Israel. Perhaps that reinforces the notion that the Torah is very valuable and not to be viewed as something forced upon Israel. Nos. 2, 3, and 4 go over the notion that people who do not study the Torah should at least support those who do. This rather general notion does not carry forward the proposition of No. 1, only the theme.

XXXII:VII

1.   A.   When R. Zeira came up here, he heard people saying, "Mam-

zer-boy" and "Mamzer-girl." He said to them, "[Why is this? Lo,
note] that which R. Huna stated, 'A mamzer does not live more
than thirty days.'"

B. Said to him R. Jacob bar Aha, "I was with you when R. Ba and R.
Huna in the name of Rab stated, 'A mamzer does not live more
than thirty days. Under what circumstances? When the matter is
not known. But if the matter is known, he may live [a good long
life]'"

2. A. That accords with what happened in the time of R. Berekhiah. A
Babylonian came up here, and it was known of him that he was a
mamzer. He came to him. He said to him, "Rabbi, give me
[charity]."

B. R. Berekhiah said to him, "Go, but tomorrow appear in the
congregation, and I shall publicly provide you something from the
community chest."

C. The next day he came to him and found him in session expounding
lessons in the synagogue. He waited until he finished. When he had
finished his exposition, he came to him. Then R. Berekhiah said to
them, "Brethren, provide for this one, who is a mamzer." They
allotted him [what he needed].

D. When the congregation had gone out, he said to him, "Rabbi, I
asked you for sustenance for this life, and you have cut off the life
of that man [me]."

E. He said to him, "By your life! I have given you life. For R. Ba in
the name of R. Huna in the name of Rab stated, 'A mamzer lives
only thirty days. Under what circumstances? When the matter is
not known. But if the matter is public, he lives a good long life.'"

3. A. R. Meir and R. Yose:

B. R. Meir says, "Mamzers will never be clean in the world to come.
What is the proof-text? 'A mongrel people [mamzer] shall dwell in
Ashdod' (Zech. 9:6). They bring mud to a muddy place and thorns
to thorns."

C. R. Yose said, "They will be clean in the world to come. Lo,
Scripture says, 'I will sprinkle clean water upon you, and you shall
be clean' (Ez. 36:25).

D. Said to him R. Meir, "Lo, it says, 'And you shall be clean from
[some of] all your uncleannesses, and from all your idols I will
cleanse you' (Ez. 36:25)."

E. Said to him R. Yose, "Rabbi, if Scripture had said, '...all your
uncleannesses and from all your idols,' and then nothing more, I
should have ruled in accord with your view. When Scripture says, 'I
shall clean you,' it means, even from the mamzers."

F.   Said R. Huna, "If the law is not in accord with R. Yose, generations
      to come will be destitute."

The entire section consists of an anthology of materials on the theme of the
mamzer. These materials are shared, nearly verbatim, with Y. Qid. 3:13. The context of
XXXII:VII is a still longer composition on the same theme.

XXXIII:V.

1.   A.   [Y. Yeb. 16:3:] "Abijah and his people slew them with a great
            slaughter; [so there fell slain of Israel five hundred thousand picked
            men]' (2 Chr. 13:17).

      B.   What is the meaning of a great slaughter?"

      C.   Said R. Aba b. Kahara, "He removed [the Israelite's] noses."

      D.   That is in line with what is written, "The point of recognition of
            their faces witnesses against them" (Is. 3:9). [This refers to the
            nose.]

      E.   R. Issi said, "He set up guards over them for three days [so that
            they could not be buried], until their faces were disfigured. [Y.
            Yeb. 16:3.II adds: That is in line with what is written, 'I have made
            their widows more in number than the sand of the seas; (I have
            brought against the mothers of young men a destroyer at noonday; I
            have made anguish and terror fall upon them suddenly)' (Jer. 15:8)."

      F.   And so we learned there [M. Yeb. 16:3A-B, E]: "They derive
            testimony concerning the identity of a corpse only from the
            appearance of the whole face with the nose even though there are
            signs of the corpse's identity on his body or garments... They give
            testimony about the identity of a corpse only during a period of
            three days after death."

2.   A.   "Jeroboam did not recover his power in the days of Abijah; and the
            Lord smote him and he died [2 Chr. 13:20]"

      B.   Said R. Samuel bar Nahman, "Do you think that this refers to
            Jeroboam? It refers only to Abijah."

      C.   And why was he smitten?

      D.   R. Yohanan, R. Simeon b. Laqish, and rabbis.

      E.   R. Yohanan said, "Because he humiliated Jeroboam in public. This
            is in line with the following verse of Scripture: '[And now you
            think to withstand the kingdom of the Lord in the hand of the sons
            of David,] because you are a great multitude and have with you the
            golden calves which Jeroboam made you for Gods' (2 Chr. 13:8)."

      F.   R. Simeon b. Laqish said, "It was because he despised Ahihah the
            Shileonite: 'And certain worthless scoundrels gathered about him

[and defiled Rehoboam the son of Solomon, when Rehoboam was young and irresolute and could not withstands them] (2 Chr. 13:7).'
[It was because he cried out against Ahijah the Shilonite.]"

G. Rabbis say, "It was because idolatry came about through his deed, and he did not wipe it out. That is in line with what is written, 'And Abijah pursued Jeroboam, and took cities from him, Bethel with its villages [and Jeshanah with its villages and Ephron with its villages] (2 Chr. 13:19).' And it is written, 'And he set one in Bethel, and the other he put in Dan' (I Kings 12:29)."

H. Now it is an argument a fortiori: Now if a king humiliated another king, Scripture indicates he was punished, he who humiliates his fellow, how much the more so [will be punished].

I. Therefore Moses admonishes Israel: "You shall not wrong one another" (Lev. 25:14).

Nos. 1 and 2 form a whole, inserted here because of 2.E, which then is served by the editorial subscript, 2.H-I. The sense of "wronging" then is public humiliation, and the rest follows. The version at Y. Yeb. 16:3 lacks 2.H-I, but otherwise is virtually identical. But that point is important, because it indicates that the editors, who added 2.H-I, made such an addition as was needed to legitimate including the entire construction. They did not simply insert whole what was thematically relevant but tried to make the passage fit in an explicit and articulated way.

XXXIV:XIV

1. A. "When you see the naked to cover him" (Is. 58:7).

    B. R. Abba bar Zabeda, Rab, and R. Yohanan:

    C. One said, "When it comes to providing funds for clothing, they carefully look into the matter [to ascertain the worthiness of the beggar], but when it comes to providing the necessities of life, they do not carefully look into the matter."

    D. Another said, "Even when it comes to providing clothing, they do not carefully look into the matter, on account of the covenant of Abraham our father."

2. A. "And not to hide yourself from your own flesh" (Is. 58:7):

    B. Bar Qappara said, "Regard his flesh as equivalent to your own flesh."

    C. For Bar Qappara taught, "There is no one who does not come to that condition [of poverty]. If he does not become impoverished, it will be his son, if not his son, then his grandson."

3. A. "And not to hide yourself from your own flesh" (Is. 58:7).

    B. R. Jacob bar Aha in the name of R. Eleazar: "This refers to a woman whom one has divorced. [A man must continue to care for her.]"

4. A.   Y. Ket. 11:3: R. Yose the Galilean had a bad wife, who humiliated him in front of his disciples.

B.   His disciples said to him, "Master, divorce her, for she does not respect you."

C.   He said to them, "I should then owe her a considerable sum for maintenance, and I therefore cannot divorce her."

D.   One time he and R. Eleazar b. Azariah were in session and studying [the law]. When they had completed their studies, [Yose] said to [Eleazar], "Master, listen to [me] and come to my house."

E.   He said to him, "All right."

F.   When they got to his house, [the wife] turned her face and left the room.

G.   [Yose] saw a pot set on the stove and said to her, "Is there anything in the pot?"

H.   She said to him, "Vegetable stew."

I.   He went and uncovered it and found chickens.

J.   R. Eleazar b. Azariah understood the implications of what he was sitting and hearing. He said to him, "Rabbi, she said there was only vegetable stew, but lo, we find chickens."

K.   He said to him, "Master, it was a miracle."

L.   When they had finished eating and drinking, he said to him, "Master, divorce this wife of yours, for she does not respect you."

M.   He said to him, "I should then owe her a considerable sum for maintenance, so I can't be rid of her."

N.   He said to him, "But we shall provide the money for her maintenance, so you can let her go." He provided the necessary sum for her maintenance, and he divorced her. He married a woman much better than she.

O.   The sins of that other woman whom he had divorced caused her [grief,] for she went and married the town watchman. After some time he fell into suffering, being blinded. She would lead him through the whole town [in search of alms], but she did not bring him to the neighborhood in which R. Yose the Galilean lived. Since that man knew the town very well, he said to her, "What do you not lead me into the neighborhood in which R. Yose the Galilean lives? For I hear that he carries out many religious duties [and supports the poor]."

P.   She said to him, "I am his divorced wife, and I don't have the strength to look at his face."

Q.   One time they came to that neighborhood. The man began to beat her, and they humiliated themselves in the marketplace. R. Yose the Galilean looked out and saw them disgracing themselves in the

marketplace. He took them and settled them in a house that he
owned, and he provided them with food all the rest of their lives.

R.   This was on the count of the verse, "And not to hide yourself from
your own flesh" (Is. 58:7).

5.   A.   In the time of R. Tanhuma, the Israelites needed rain. They came
to him, saying to him, "Master, make a decree of a fast, so that it
will rain."

B.   He made a decree of a fast one time, then a second, and it did not
rain.

C.   On the third occasion, he went up and preached to them, saying,
"Let the entire people give out [charity and so carry out that]
religious duty."

D.   One man went and took what he had in the house and he went out
to give it away in the market place. His former wife, whom he had
divorced, met him and said to him, "Acquire merit through me, for
from the day on which you put that woman out of your house, she
has not seen any pleasure."

E.   He saw that she was in tatters and in great distress, and he was
filled with pity for her and gave her [charity], on the count, "And
not to hide yourself from your own flesh" (Is. 58:7).

F.   Someone saw the incident and he went and told R. Tanhuma, saying
to him, "While you're sitting here, a great sin is being committed
there."

G.   He said to him, "What did you see?"

H.   He said to him, "I saw Mr. So-and-so tarrying with a woman whom
he divorced and [even] giving her some coins. Now if he were not
suspect on her account, he would not have tarried with her and
given her money!"

I.   R. Tanhuma sent and summoned him. He said to him, "My son,
don't you know that the whole world is in trouble? Human beings
are in trouble, cattle are in trouble, and [yet] you go and tarry with
the woman you divorced [and so bring sin on the community as a
whole], and not only so, but you give her money! Don't you know
that that is improper?"

J.   He said to him, "But are you not the one who preached, 'And not to
hide yourself from your own flesh' (Is. 58:7)? And you furthermore
said for everyone to go out and share [the wealth, and so carry out]
the religious duty [of charity]. So I took what I had in my house
and I went out to give it away as a religious duty in the market
place, and the woman whom I had divorced met me and said to me,
'Acquire merit through me, for from the day that I left your house,
I have not seen any pleasure.' Since I saw her in tatters and in

great distress, I was filled with pity for her, and I gave her [what I had], on the count of, 'And not to hide yourself from your own flesh' (Is. 58:7)."

K. At that moment R. Tanhuma raised his face to heaven and said, "Now if this mean-spirited mortal, who does not owe maintenance [to his former wife], when he saw her in tatters and in great distress, was filled with pity for her and so gave her [what she needed],

L. "we, who are your children, descendants of your tried and true servants, children of Abraham, Isaac, and Jacob, whose maintenance you do owe, how much the more so [should you be filled with mercy pity for us and give us what we need]."

M. At that moment the rains came and the world found relief.

The entire construction, devoted to the exegesis of Is. 58:7, spells out the meaning of not hiding oneself from his own flesh, meaning, the woman whom he has divorced. The several stories have been strung together whole and complete; there is no point at which the ultimate redactor of Leviticus Rabbah has made any contribution whatsoever.

XXXVI:VI

1. A. [Returning to] the body [of the matter:] [Y. San. 10:1.VI:] How long does the merit of the patriarchs endure?

    B. R. Tanhuma made this statement, Rab in the name of R. Hiyya the Elder, R. Menehama said it, R. Berekhiah and R. Helbo in the name of R. Abba bar Zabeda: "Down to Jehoahaz. 'But the lord was gracious to them and had compassion on them [and he turned toward them, because of his covenant with Abraham, Isaac, and Jacob, and would not destroy them; nor has he cast them from his presence until now]' (2 Kgs. 13:23).

    C. "Until now [the time of Jehoahaz, 2 Kgs. 13:22] the merit of the patriarchs has endured."

    D. R. Joshua b. Levi said, "Until the time of Elijah: 'And it came to pass at the time of the evening offering, that Elijah the prophet came near and said, 'O Lord, [the God of Abraham, Isaac, and Israel, this day let it be known that you are God' (1 Kgs. 18:36). Thus, to this day the merit endured, but not afterward.]'"

    E. Samuel said, "Down to the time of Hosea: 'Now will I uncover her shame in the sight of her lovers, and no man will [ever again] deliver her out of my hand' (Hos. 2:12).

    F. "'Man' refers then to Abraham, as it is said in Scripture: 'And now, return the wife of the man' (Gen. 20:7).

    G. "'Man' refers only to Isaac, as it is said, 'Who is this man?' (Gen. 24:65).

H.   "'Man' refers only to Jacob, as it is said, 'Jacob, a quiet man, dwelling in tents' (Gen. 28:27)."

I.   R. Yudan said, "Down to the time of Hezekiah: 'That the government may be increased [and of peace there be no end... the zeal of the Lord of hosts [thus: not the merit of the patriarchs] does this' (Is. 9:6)."

J.   R. Yudan bar Hanan in the name of R. Berekiah said, "If you see that the merit of the patriarchs is slipping away, and the merit of the matriarchs is trembling, then go and cleave to the performance of deeds of loving kindness.

K.   "That is in line with the following verse of Scripture: 'For the mountains will melt (YMWSW), and the hills will tremble, [but my love will not depart from you]' (Is. 54:10).

L.   "'Mountains' refers to the patriarchs, and 'hills' to the matriarchs.

M.   "Henceforward: 'But my love will not (YMWS) depart from you' (Is. 54:10)."

N.   Said R. Aha, "The merit of the patriarchs endures forever. Forever do people call it to mind, saying, 'For the Lord your God is a merciful God. He will not fail you nor destroy you nor forget the covenant he made with your fathers' (Deut. 4:31)."

The theme of the patriarchs, occurring at Lev. 26:42, accounts for the inclusion of this elegant exercise. But the passage in no way serves the concrete interests of the larger context of Leviticus Rabbah; the only reason it is inserted is the shared theme. I do not see a clear allusion to the base-text, Lev. 26:42.

XXXVII:I

1.   A.   "It is better that you not vow than that you vow and not pay" (Qoh. 5:5).

     B.   R. Meir and R. Judah:

     C.   [Y. Ned. 1:1] R. Meir said, "'It is better that you should not vow' but better still is he who vows and pays.'"

     D.   "What is the proof text? 'Vow and pay to the Lord your God' (Ps. 76:12)."

     E.   R. Judah says, "'It is better that you should not vow' but better still is he who does not vow at all.

     F.   "But one brings his lamb to the Temple court [not in advance making a vow to do so], and [only] there he declares it to be consecrated and slaughters it as an offering [without prior commitments, which he may not be able to carry out].

The base-verse, Lev. 27:2, "When a person makes a special vow of persons...," generates interest in verses about vowing, hence Qoh. 5:5. Then the exegetical debate on the matter generated by Qoh. 5:5 is integral to the composition as a whole.

XXXVII:III

1. A. [Back to] the body [of the matter]:

    B. [Y. A.Z. 2:19:] The story is told of Rabban Gamaliel, who was going on the road from Acre to Akhzib, and Tabi, his servant, was walking in front of him, and R. Ilai was walking behind him.

    C. He found a loaf of cheap bread on the road. [He said to Tabi, his slave, "Take the loaf." (Y. A.Z. 1:9)]

    D. He saw a gentile coming toward him. He said to him, "Mabgai, Mabgai, take this loaf of bread."

    E. R. Ilai ran after [Mabgai] and said to him, "What is your name?"

    F. He said to him, "Mabgai."

    G. "And where do you come from?"

    H. "From one of the [nearby] station-keeper's villages."

    I. "Now did Rabban Gamaliel ever in your whole life meet you?"

    J. He said to him, "No."

    K. And from what he said we learn three things:

    L. We learn that the leaven of a gentile is permitted immediately after Passover [cf. M. Pes. 2:2].

    M. [On the basis of this event we learn that] Rabban Gamaliel divined by the Holy Spirit that his name was Mabgai.

    N. And that they do not pass by food [but pick it up].

    O. [Y. A.Z. 1:9 adds:] And that they follow the status of the majority of those who travel the roads [in a given place, in this instance, gentile] [T. Pes. 2:15].

    P. R. Jacob bar Zabedai in the name of R. Abbahu: "That rule [about not walking past food, but stopping and picking it up] was valid in the past, but now they do pass by foodstuffs because of the possibility of witchcraft."

    Q. When they reached Akhzib, they ate and drank there.

    R. When he was leaving Akhezib, someone came along and besought from him [absolution of] his vow. Rabban Gamaliel said to Ilai [who was with him], "Do you reckon that we have drunk so much as a quarter-log of Italian wine?"
        He said to him, "Yes." He said to the one who asked the question, "Travel with us until the effect of our wine has worn off." He walked with them to the Ladder of Tyre.

    S. Once they got to the Ladder of Tyre, Rabban Gamaliel got off [his ass] and wrapped himself in his cloak and sat down and declared his vow to be absolved.

T. From these statements of his we learn three things: [that a quarter-log of wine causes drunkenness; (Y.A.Z. 1:9)]

U. [that traveling wears down the effects of wine; (Y.A.Z. 1:9)]

V. that [sages] do not grant absolution from vows or give decisions when they are drunk;

W. and that they do not absolve vows either while riding on an ass or while walking or while standing,

X. but only sitting down and wrapped in a cloak [T. Pes. 2:16].

Y. On what grounds did he unbind him?

Z. Said R. Yohanan, "Thus he opened the discourse for him: 'There is one whose rash words are like sword thrusts but the tongue of the wise brings healing' (Prov. 12:18). Whoever takes a vow is worthy of being thrust through with a sword!

AA. "'But the tongue of the wise brings healing.' [This may be compared] to one who has taken a vow not to eat bread. Woe to him if he eats, woe to him if he does not eat. If he eats, he violates his vow. If he does not eat, he sins against his soul. What should he do? Let him go to sages and beseech absolution from his vow, as it is written, 'But the tongue of the wise brings healing.'"

The sole reason for including this item is the theme shared with Lev. 27:2, taking vows. But at issue here is not taking but remitting them, so the connection is remote.

Most of the long passages shared with the Yerushalmi appear to serve no purpose intimate to the discourse of Leviticus Rabbah. To the contrary, as we have seen, the larger number of passages shared with the Yerushalmi appear inserted whole and complete. In some instances we can find thematic connections to the setting in Leviticus Rabbah that absorbs the Yerushalmi's saying or story. In others the connection is at best tenuous. We shall consider in Chapter Five the meaning of these facts for the assessment of the character of Leviticus Rabbah.

iii. Units of Discourse Common to Leviticus Rabbah and Genesis Rabbah

We turn to Genesis Rabbah and assemble a large repertoire of those passages that occur in both of the Rabbah-collections. Here again we wish to know why a given item appears in Leviticus Rabbah, and whether and how it advances the discussion of the context in which it makes its appearance. Again, we shall postpone until Chapter Five analysis of the results.

Genesis Rabbah 44:14 (trans. H. Freedman, p. 370):

"And he took him all these," etc. R. Simeon b. Yohai said: The Holy One, blessed be He, showed Abraham all the atoning sacrifices save the tenth of an ephah [of fine meal]. The Rabbis said: He showed him the tenth of an ephah [of fine meal] also; for "all these" is stated here, while elsewhere it is said, "And thou shalt bring the meal-offering that is made of these things" (Lev. 2:8).

III:III

3.   A.   "And let him return to the Lord, that he may have mercy on him" (Is. 55:7).

     B.   Rabbis and R. Simeon b. Yohai:

     C.   Rabbis say, "All forms of atonement-[offerings] did the Holy One, blessed be He, show to Abraham, our father, [at the covenant 'between the pieces,' Gen. 15] except for the form of atonement gained through offering a tenth of an ephah of fine flour [Lev. 2:1]."

     D.   R. Simeon b. Yohai said, "Also the form of atonement-offering of the tenth of an ephah of fine flour did the Holy One, blessed be He, show to Abraham, our father.

     E.   "The word, 'these' is used here [with reference to the meal offering, at Lev. 2:8: 'The meal-offering that is made out of these'], and the same word occurs elsewhere [with reference to the account of the covenant 'between the pieces': 'And he took him all these' (Gen. 15:10)].

     F.   "Just as the word, 'these,' used in the present context refers to the tenth of an ephah of fine flour, so the word, 'these' used with reference to [the modes of expiatory offering described at Gen. 15] likewise encompasses the tenth of an ephah of fine flour."

4.   A.   "...and to our God, for he will abundantly pardon."

     B.   R. Judah b. R. Simon in the name of R. Zeirah: "The Holy One, blessed be He, further gave us a mode of attaining forgiveness out of what, in fact, belongs to him, namely, the tenth of an ephah of fine flour.

     C.   "When any one brings a cereal offering as an offering to the Lord..." (Lev. 2:1).

This pastiche of materials relevant to Is. 55:7 aims, if not very directly, at Lev. 2:1. We have a systematic construction addressed to Is. 55:7. Nos. 3 and 4 alone intersect with the present passage. If we did not have No. 3, No. 4 would be perfectly comprehensible on its own, that is, as a comment not pertinent to Gen. 15 but solely to Lev. 2:1. In the balance, it is difficult to demonstrate that at the foundation lay a citation of Is. 55:7 followed by the substance of No. 4. It seems plausible to see Nos. 3 and 4 as the base. Here is a clear case in which what is shared with Gen. R. -- namely, No. 3, is entirely out of place. Why so? Because the intersecting-verse, Is. 55:7, in no way relates to the passages subject to discussion, which is Gen. 15:1ff. No. 4, by contrast, clearly does relate to Is. 55:7. It further relates to the topic of the foregoing, namely, forgiveness attained through the offering of the ephah of fine flour. So what has been joined -- Nos. 3, 4 -- has come together prior to insertion here. Part of the composition, No. 4, surely belongs. Then the whole has been inserted on that account. That is not an uncommon phenomenon.

What it shows is that the authors of Leviticus Rabbah selected what they required and used what they chose without totally revising the whole. But when we review the version of the part of the passage that occurs, also, at Gen. R., we see what they have been prepared to do. At 3.A they have introduced the whole with their own inter-secting-verse. They have reordered and recast what they wished (assuming the passage of Gen. R. was before them). Then, at No. 4, they made ample use of what was important for their larger purpose. As we note, Gen. R. does not contain No. 4. The upshot is that the authors of Leviticus Rabbah have intervened in a decisive way to revise what they chose, so that what is shared with Genesis Rabbah has now been made to serve the purposes of Leviticus Rabbah. That is quite a new result, when we reflect on how little was done to naturalize to Leviticus Rabbah materials shared with the Yerushalmi.

Genesis Rabbah 36:1 (Freedman, pp. 287-8):

"And the sons of Noah, that went forth from the ark, were Shem, and Ham, and Japhet" (Gen. 9:18). It is written, "When He giveth quietness, who then can condemn," etc. (Job 34:29)? R. Meir interpreted it: He quieteneth Himself from His world, like a judge before whom a curtain is spread, so that he does not know what is happening without. Let that suffice thee, Meir, said they to him. Then what is meant by, "When He giveth quietness, who can condemn?" he demanded. Was not ease given to the generation of the Flood; who then can condemn them? they replied. And what ease was given to them? "Their seed is established (nakon) in their sight with them, and their offspring before their eyes (ib. 21:8); They send forth their little ones like a flock," etc. (ib. 2). R. Levi said: Their wives were pregnant but three days and then bore: for "nakon" is stated here, whilst elsewhere it is said, "Be ready (nekonim, pl. of nakon) against the third day" (Ex. 14:15): just as "nakon" there means for three days, so "nakon" here means for three days. The Rabbis said: Even after one day, for "nakon" occurs here, while elsewhere it is said, "And be ready (nakon) by the morning" (ib. 34:2): just as "nakon" there means in one day, so here too it means one day. "And their offspring before their eyes" means that they saw their children's children. "They send forth their little ones ('awilehem) like a flock": R. Levi said: In Arabia a child is called "awila. And their children dance (ib.)" -- like demons, as you read, "And satyrs shall dance there" (Isa. 13:21). When one of them gave birth by day she would say to her son, "Go and bring me a flint to cut your navel cord."

If at night, she would say to her son, "Go and light a lamp to cut [burn] through your navel cord." It once happened that a woman who gave birth at night said to her son, "Go and light me a candle to cut through your navel cord." He went out, and the demon Shimadon [lit. "Destruction"] met him and said to him, "Go and inform your mother that the cock has crowed, but if the cock had not crowed yet, I would have smitten and killed you." "Go and inform your mother that my mother had not yet cut my navel cord," he retorted, "but had my mother cut my navel cord, I would have smitten and killed you." Thus it is written, "Their houses are safe, without fear" (Job 21:9) -- of demons: "Neither is the rod of God upon them (ib.)" -- they are spared sufferings. Yet when He hid His face from them, who said to Him, "Thou hast not done well"? And why did He hide his face from them? [Because as it is written], "Whether it be done unto a nation or unto a man, alike" -- yahad (Job 34:29): "Unto a nation" refers to the generation of the Flood; "And unto a man," to Noah; "alike": for from him [Noah] was the world established, and He can set up His world from a nation, and He can establish His word from a single person, as it is written, "And the sons of Noah," etc.

V:I

1.   A.   "If it is the anointed priest who sins, [thus bringing guilt on the people, then let him offer to the Lord for the sin which he has committed a young bull without blemish]" (Lev. 4:3).

     B.   "When he is quiet, who can condemn? When he hides his face, who can set him right [RSV: behold him] [whether it be a nation or a man? that a godless man should not reign, that he should not ensnare the people]" (Job 34:29-30).

     C.   R. Meir interpreted [the matter] [Gen. R. 36:1], "'When he is quiet' -- in his world, 'when he hides his face' -- in his world.

     D.   "The matter may be compared to the case of a judge who draws a veil inside and so does not see what goes on outside.

     E.   "So the people of the generation of the flood thought: 'The thick clouds cover him, so he will not see [what we do]' (Job 22:14)."

     F.   They said to him, "That's enough from you, Meir."

2.   A.   Another interpretation: "When he is quiet, who can condemn? When he hides his face, who can set him right?" (Job 34:29)

     B.   When he gave tranquility to the generation of the flood, who could come and condemn them?

     C.   What sort of tranquility did he give them? "Their children are established in their presence, and their offspring before their eyes. [Their houses are safe from fear, and no rod of God is upon them]" (Job 21:8).

     D.   R. Levi and rabbis:

E. R. Levi said, "A woman would get pregnant and give birth in three days. [How do we know it?] Here, the word, 'established,' is used, and elsewhere: 'Be established in three days' (Ex. 19:15). Just as the word, 'established,' used there involves a span of three days, so the word, 'established,' used here means three days."

F. Rabbis say, "In a single day a woman would get pregnant and give birth.

G. "Here, the word, 'established,' is used, and elsewhere: 'And be established in the morning' (Ex. 34:2). Just as the word 'established' stated there involves a single day, so the word 'established' used here involves a single day."

3. A. "And their offspring before their eyes" -- for they saw children and grandchildren.

B. "They send forth their little ones like a flock, [and their children dance]' (Job 21:11).

C. [The word for "children" means] "their young."

D. Said R. Levi, "In Arabia for children they use the word 'the young.'"

4. A. "And their children dance" (Job 21:11) --

B. ["they dance"] like devils.

C. That is in line with the following verse of Scripture: "And satyrs will dance there" (Is. 13:21).

5. A. They say: When one of them would give birth by day, she would say to her son, "Go and bring me a flint, so I can cut your umbilical cord."

B. If she gave birth by night, she would say to her son, "Go and light a lamp for me, so I can cut your umbilical cord."

C. M^{C}SH B: A woman gave birth by night and said to her son, "Go and light a lamp for me, so I can cut your umbilical cord."

D. [In Aramaic:] When he went out to fetch it, a devil, Ashmadon [Asmodeus], head of the spirits, met him. While the two were wrestling with one another, the cock crowed. [Ashmadon] said to him, "Go, boast to your mother that my time has run out, for if my time had not run out, I could have killed you."

E. He said to him, "Go, boast to your mother's mother that my mother had not cut my umbilical cord, for if my mother had cut my umbilical cord, I would have beaten you."

F. This illustrates that which is said: "Their houses are safe from fear" (Job 21:9) -- from destroying spirits.

6. A. "And no rod of God is upon them" -- [for their houses are free from suffering.

B. [And this further] illustrates that which is said: "When he is quiet, who can condemn,] when he hides his face, who can put him right" (Job 34:30).

C.   When [God] hides his face from them, who can come and say to him, "You have not done right."

D.   And how, indeed, did he hide his face from them? When he brought the flood on them.

E.   That is in line with the following verse of Scripture: "And he blotted out every living substance which was upon the face of the earth" (Gen. 7:23).

7. A.   "Whether it be to a nation [or a man together]' (Job 34:29) -- this refers to the generation of the flood.

B.   "Or to a man" -- this refers to Noah.

C.   "Together" -- he had to rebuild his world from one man, he had to rebuild his world from one nation.

Let us treat Leviticus Rabbah first. On the surface, the sole point of contact between the base-verse and the intersecting verse, Lev. 4:3 and Job 34:29-30, is in the uncited part of the passage of Job, "that he should not ensnare the people." The anointed priest has sinned and in so doing has brought guilt on the entire people. If, however, that is why the entire assembly of exegeses of Job has been inserted here, that theme plays no role in making the collection of materials on Job. For at no point in the present unit (or in the next one) does the important segment of the passage of Job come under discussion. The interpretation of Job 34:29 in light of the story of the flood predominates here. No. 1 has Meir's view that the entire passage refers to God's failure to intervene, with special reference to the flood. No. 2 pursues the same line of thought. No. 3 illustrates the notion that their children "are established in their presence," and Nos. 3-4 continue to spell out the phrase-by-phrase exegesis of the same verse. No. 5 pursues the same line of thought. No. 6 shifts the ground of interpretation. Now God is "quiet," but later, in "hiding his face," he brings punishment on them. No. 7 completes the exegesis of the cited passage of Job in line with the view that Job was a contemporary of Noah and spoke of his ties. Noah might then serve as the counterpart and opposite of the priest who brings guilt on the people. But that is by no means the clear intent of the passage at hand. As to the relevance of Leviticus Rabbah to Genesis Rabbah and vice verse, we see that the authors of Leviticus Rabbah have used materials pertinent to their inter- secting-verse, Job 34:29, just as the authors of Genesis Rabbah have used the same materials for the same intersecting-verse. The two have in common the fact that Job 34:29 serves both Lev. 4:3 and Gen. 9:18. Once more, the passage works well in its context here.

Genesis Rabbah 48:18 (Freedman, p. 417)

"And the Lord said unto Abraham: 'Wherefore did Sarah laugh, saying... "seeing that I am old"'" (XVIII, 13). Bar **Kappara** said: Great is peace, for even Scripture made a mis-statement in order to preserve peace between Abraham and Sarah. Thus, it is written, "Wherefore did Sarah laugh, saying: 'Shall I of a surety bear a child?'" It does not say, "Since my lord is old," but "Seeing that I am old."

Genesis Rabbah 100:8 (Freedman, p. 999)

"And they sent a message unto Joseph, saying: 'Thy father did command... forgive... the transgression of thy brethren'" (L, 16f.). R. Simeon b. Gamaliel taught: Great is peace, for even the tribal ancestors resorted to a fabrication in order to make peace between Joseph and themselves. Thus it says, "And they sent a message unto Joseph, saying: 'Thy father did command,'" etc. Yet when did he command thus? We do not find that he did so.

IX:IX

3. A.   Bar Qappara made three statements [about peace].

    B.   [Gen. R. 48:18:] Bar Qappara said, "The greatness of peace is shown in that the Scripture used misleading language in the Torah so as to bring peace between Abraham and Sarah.

    C.   "That is in line with the following verses of Scripture: '[So Sarah laughed to herself, saying, After I have grown old and my husband is old, shall I have pleasure?' (Gen. 18:12). But this was not what [God] told Abraham. Rather: '[Why did Sarah laugh, and say, Shall I indeed bear a child,] now that I am old?' (Gen. 18:13)."

4. A.   [Gen. R. 100:8:] Said Rabban Simeon b. Gamaliel, "The greatness of peace is shown in that Scripture used misleading language in order to bring peace between Joseph and his brothers.

    B.   "That is in line with the following verse of Scripture: ['And they sent a message to Joseph, saying, "Your father commanded before he died, saying,] 'So shall you say to Joseph, Forgive, I pray you, the sin of the servants of the God of your father'"' (Gen. 50:16-17).

    C.   "But we do not find in Scripture that Jacob had given any such instructions."

The items common to Leviticus Rabbah and Genesis Rabbah serve the former as part of a long composition of miscellaneous materials on the importance of peace.

Genesis Rabbah 39:16 (Freedman, p. 315):

R. Azariah commenced in R. Aha's name thus: "Thou hast loved righteousness, and hated wickedness," etc. (Ps. 45:8). R. Azariah in R. Aha's name referred the verse to our father Abraham. When Abraham our father stood to plead for mercy for the Sodomites, what is written there? "That be far from Thee to do

after this manner" (Gen. 18:25). R. Aha explained this: Thou hast sworn not
to bring a deluge upon the world. Wouldst Thou evade Thine oath! Not a
deluge of water wilt Thou bring but a deluge of fire? Then Thou hast not been
true to Thine oath. R. Levi commented: "Shalt not the Judge of all the earth
do justly (ib.)?" If thou desirest the world to endure, there can be no absolute
justice, while if Thou desirest absolute justice the world cannot endure, yet
Thou wouldst hold the cord by both ends, desiring both the world and absolute
justice. Unless Thou forgoest a little, the world cannot endure. Said the Holy
One, blessed be He, to Abraham: "Thou hast loved righteousness, and hated
wickedness; therefore God, thy God, hath anointed thee with the oil of
gladness above thy fellows (ib.): from Noah until thee were ten generations,
and out of all of them I spoke with thee alone"; hence, "Now the Lord said unto
Abraham."

X:I

1.   A.   "[The Lord said to Moses,] 'Take Aaron [and his sons with him, and
            the garments, the anointing oil, the bull of the sin-offering, the
            two rams, and the basket of unleavened bread, and assemble all the
            congregation at the door of the tent of meeting]' (Lev. 8:1-3).

      B.   [Gen. R. 39:6:] "You love righteousness and hate wickedness,
            [therefore God, your God, has anointed you with the oil of gladness
            above your fellows]' (Ps. 45:7).

      C.   R. Yudan in the name of R. Azariah interpreted the verse to speak
            of Abraham, our father:

      D.   "When [Abraham] was pleading for mercy for the people of Sodom,
            he said before him, 'Lord of the world! You have taken an oath
            that you will not bring a flood upon the world.'

      E.   "That is in line with the following verse of Scripture: 'For this is
            like the days of Noah to me; as I swore that the waters of Noah
            should no more go over the earth, so I have sworn that I will not be
            angry with you and will not rebuke you.' (Is. 54:9).

      F.   "'Now [Abraham continued], it is a flood of water that you will not
            bring, but a flood of fire you will bring! Then you turn out to
            practice deception with regard to the oath.

      G.   "'If so, you will not carry out the obligation of your oath.'

      H.   "That is in line with the following verse: 'Far be it from you to do
            such a thing!' (Gen. 18:25).

      I.   "He said before him, 'Far be it from you... shall not the judge of all
            the earth do justly' (Gen. 18:25).

      J.   "'If [Abraham continued], you want true justice, there will be no
            world left, and if you want a world, there can be no strict justice.

K. [In Aramaic:] "'You hold the rope by both ends: You want a world, and you want true justice. If you don't let go a little, your world cannot endure.'

L. "He said to him, 'Abraham, you have loved righteousness' (Ps. 45:7). You love to show my creatures to be righteous.

M. "'You have hated wickedness.' You hate declaring them to be guilty.'

N. "'Therefore God, your God, has anointed you with the oil of gladness above your fellows.'

O. "What is the meaning of 'above your fellows'?

P. "He said to him, 'By your life, among the ten generations from Noah to you, I shall not speak with any one of them, but one with you shall I speak.'

Q. "'After these things, the word of the Lord came to Abraham' (Gen. 15:1)."

The intersecting text proves appropriate because of the shared reference to anointing someone with oil. Then the first focus of exegesis is not on a priest, such as Aaron, but on Abraham. The passage shared with Genesis Rabbah has been inserted because it supplies an exegesis of Ps. 45:7-8. While the passage obviously has been framed to serve Gen. 15:1, in fact in its setting in Leviticus Rabbah it fits quite smoothly. What the authors of our composition have added is the base-text, Lev. 8:1-3, which will in due course make its appearance. In gathering exegeses of the intersecting-verse, the authors of Leviticus Rabbah thus found entirely serviceable the passage shared with Genesis Rabbah. The fact that it serves elsewhere has no bearing on its integrity in this context.

Genesis Rabbah 5:7 (Freedman, pp. 37-8):

In human practice, a man empties a full vessel into an empty one; does he ever empty a full vessel into a full vessel? Now the world was full of water everywhere, yet you say, "Unto one place!" In truth, from this we learn that the little held the much. Similarly, "And Moses and Aaron gathered the assembly together before the rock" (Num. 20:10). Now R. Hanina said: It was but the size of the opening of a small sieve, yet all Israel stood there! In truth, from this we learn that the little held the much. Similarly, "Take to you handfuls of the soot of the furnace" (Ex. 9:8): said R. Hana, Could then one fistful of Moses contain eight handfuls! For a fistful is not the same as a handful, one fistful equaling two handfuls, yet it is written, "And let Moses throw it (ib.)," so that one fistful of Moses actually contained eight handfuls! From this, however, we learn that the little held the much. Similarly R. Jose b. Halafta observed: "The length of the court shall be a hundred cubits," etc. (Ex. 27:18), yet all Israel stood there! In fact, from this we learn that the little held the much. Similarly, "And Joshua said unto the children of Israel: Come hither," etc. (Josh. 3:9). R. Huna said: He made them stand between the staves of the Ark. R. Hama said: He crowded them between the staves of the Ark; our Rabbis said: He squeezed them between the two staves of the Ark. Said Joshua to them: "Hereby ye shall know that the living God is among you (ib. 10)." And in Jerusalem, too, they stood pressed together, yet when they prostrated themselves they had ample room. R. Samuel b. R. Jonah said: Each had four cubits, a cubit on each side, so that none should hear his neighbour's prayer. And in the future, too, it shall be thus, viz. "At that time they shall call Jerusalem 'The Throne of the Lord,' and all the nations shall be gathered unto it" (Jer. 3:17). R. Johanan went up to inquire after the wellbeing of R. Hanina, and he found him sitting and lecturing on this verse: "At that time they shall call Jerusalem 'The throne of the Lord,' and all the nations shall be gathered unto it." Said he to him: Can it then hold [them all]. It is amazing! -- The Holy One, blessed be He, will order it: "Lengthen [thy boundaries], enlarge [thy space], and receive thy hosts," as it is said, "Enlarge the place of thy tent" (Is. 54:2).

X:IX

1. A. ...and the bull of the sin offering and the two rams" (Lev. 8:2).

   B. R. Huna in the name of R. Abba bar Kahana said, "He arranged them like a kind of a hill, with a ram on one side and the other, and the bull in the middle."

2. A. "...and assemble all the congregation at the door of the tent of meeting" (Lev. 8:3).

   B. [Gen. R. 5:7] Said R. Eleazar, "All of the Israelites added up to six hundred thousand, so how can you say, '...at the door of meeting'?

   C. "But this is one of the [miraculous] instances in which what is less was able to contain what is more."

3. A. Along these same lines: "Let the waters under the heavens be gathered together into one place" (Gen. 1:9).

   B. Ordinarily someone will pour the contents of a jug full of water into an empty one. But who can pour a full jug into a full jug? Now the whole world was full of water, and yet you say, "...let the waters under the heavens be gathered together"?

   C. But this is one of the [miraculous] instances in which what is less was able to contain what is more.

4. A. Along these same lines: "Fill your two hands with soot of the furnace" (Ex. 9:8).

   B. Said R. Huna, "The volume of a handful is not the same as the volume of a fistful. The handful's volume is twice that of a fistful, four handfuls are the same as eight fistfuls. The handfuls of Moses would then hold eight fistfuls, and yet you say, "And Moses threw it [all -- his and Aaron's] up to heaven" (Ex. 9:8). [This would indicate that Moses' hand held eight fistfuls.]

C. But this is one of the [miraculous] instances in which what is less was able to contain what is more.

5. A. Along these same lines: "The length of the court was a hundred cubits..." (Ex. 27:18).

B. Said R. Yose b. R. Halapta, "The length of the courtyard was [only] a hundred cubits, and yet all of the Israelites were able to stand in it."

C. But this is one of the [miraculous] instances in which what is less was able to contain what is more.

6. A. Along these same lines: "And Moses and Aaron gathered the assembly on the rock" (Num. 20:10).

B. Said R. Hanan, "[The rock] was no larger than a sieve, and yet all Israel were able to stand on it!"

C. But this is one of the [miraculous] instances in which what is less was able to contain what is more.

7. A. Along these same lines: "Joshua said to the children of Israel, 'Come here and hear the word of the Lord your God' (Jos. 3:9).

B. R. Hunia said, "He set them between the two staves of the ark."

C. R. Huna said, "He stood them between the two staves of the ark."

D. Rabbis said, "He crowded them in between the two staves of the rock."

E. "And Joshua said, "This is how you will know that the living God is in your midst" (Jos. 3:10).

F. Because the space between the two staves of the ark holds [you all], you should know that the living God is in your midst.

8. A. So too was the case in Jerusalem, for we have learned in the Mishnah: "They were crowded when they were standing, but had plenty of room to prostrate themselves" (M. Abot 5:5).

B. What is the meaning of "plenty of room"?

C. R. Ishmael b. R. Onia in the name of R. Aha: "There was a space of four cubits between each one and the next, and a cubit on each side, so that no one should hear the sound of the prayer of his fellow."

D. So too will matters be worked out in the age to come, for it is written, "In that time they shall call Jerusalem the throne of the Lord, and all the nations shall be gathered into it, [to the name of the Lord, to Jerusalem]' (Jer. 3:17).

E. R. Yohanan went up to pay a call on R. Hanina. He found him occupied with the study of the cited verse: "In that day they shall call Jerusalem the throne of the Lord..."

F.   He said to him, "My lord, how can Jerusalem hold them all?"

G.   He said to him, "The Holy One, blessed be he, will say to them,
      'Stretch out, expand, and receive your population.' Thus: 'Enlarge
      the place of your tent, [and let the curtains of your habitations be
      stretched out, hold not back, lengthen your cords and strengthen
      your stakes] (Is. 54:2)? Why? 'For you will spread abroad to the
      right and to the left, and your descendants will possess the nations,
      and will people the desolate cities' (Is. 54:3)."

Once more the text at hand, Lev. 8:3, finds a place in a miscellany, organized to
make a single important point. The composite has certainly not been assembled for the
purposes of amplification of Lev. 8:3; rather, our passage serves the interests of the
compositor who wishes to point to certain miraculous events of a single category or
classification. The order of items varies from one version to the next. Our compositor
set No. 2 at the head, for obvious reasons. I see no other contribution particular to the
exegesis of Leviticus. Here is an excellent example of how, in using materials shared with
other compositions, the authors of Leviticus Rabbah have shaped matters to suit their own
purpose. Since they wished to speak of the tent of meeting, they put No. 2 where they
did, as I said, leaving for the miscellany, "along these same lines," No. 3ff., the remainder
of the illustrative materials. By contrast, we note, Gen. R. 5:7 begins with what is
relevant to its proof-text, "Unto one place." For both sets of authors, the rest proves
random.

Genesis Rabbah 60:7 (Freedman, pp. 531-2):

"And he said: Come in thou blessed of the Lord" (Gen. 24:31): he thought him
to Abraham, because his features were similar to his. R. Jose b. R. Dosa said:
Canaan was Eliezer, yet because he faithfully served that righteous man, he
passed from the category of the accursed into that of the blessed, as it says,
"And he said: Come in, thou blessed of the Lord." R. Jacob b. R. Yohai said:
R. Johanan of Beth Gubrin utilized this as a farewell address: If Eliezer
passed from the category of the cursed into that of the blessed through
faithfully serving that righteous man, how much the more Israel who show
kindness [hospitality] to their leaders with their hands and feet!

XVII:V

3.   A.   Said R. Yose b. Dosa, "Eliezer [Abraham's associate] was a
            Canaanite, and because he faithfully served that righteous man
            [Abraham], he was removed from the category of those who were
            cursed and placed into the category of those who were blessed.

      B.   "That is in line with the following verses of Scripture: 'And he
            said, 'Cursed be Canaan' (Gen. 9:25)."

C.   "And he said, 'Come in [Eliezer], you who are blessed by the Lord'
      (Gen 24:31)."

D.   R. Jacob b. R. Judah in the name of R. Nathan of Bet Gubrin made
      use of the following for his leave-taking: "Now if Eliezer, because
      he faithfully served that righteous man, was removed from the
      category of those who were cursed and placed into the category of
      those who were blessed, our brothers, O Israel, who pay honor to
      their great masters, all the more so [will be blessed]."

The reference to the land of Canaan, Lev. 14:34, at the base-verse, accounts for the
inclusion of materials on Canaan. No. 3 then provides yet further information on that
subject. The item, in context in Leviticus Rabbah, simply enriches a catalogue of
information. It is part of a construction of miscellanies.

Genesis Rabbah 47:1 (Freedman, pp. 399-400):

"Thou shalt not call her name Sarai, but Sarah shall her name be" (Gen. 17:15).
R. Joshua b. Karhah said: The "yod" which the Lord took from Sarai soared
aloft before God and protested: "Sovereign of the Universe! Because I am the
smallest of all letters, Thou hast withdrawn me from the name of that
righteous woman!" Said the Holy One, blessed be He, to it: "Hitherto thou
was in a woman's name and the last of its letters; now I will set thee in a
man's name and at the beginning of its letters," as it says, "And Moses called
Hoshea the son of Nun Joshua" (Num. 13:16). R. Mana said: Formerly she was
a princess [Sarai] to her own people only, whereas now she is a princess [Sarah]
to all mankind.

XIX:II

6.   A.   R. Huna in the name of R. Aha, "The Y that the Holy One, blessed
            be he, took out of the name of Sarah [when he changed it from
            Sarai (SRY) to Sarah (SRH)] he divided into two. Half of it went to
            Abraham, and half to Sarah."

      B.   Said R. Joshua b. Qorhah, "The Y that had belonged to Sarah went
            up and prostrated itself before the Holy One, blessed be he. It said
            before him, 'Lord of the World, You have pulled me up out of the
            name of that righteous woman.'

      C.   "Said the Holy One, blessed be he, 'Go in peace. In the past, you
            were located in the name of a woman, and at the end of the name
            at that, but now, lo, I shall put you in the name of a man, and at
            the beginning of his name. That is in line with the following verse
            of Scripture: 'And Moses called Hoshea ben Nun Joshua [Yehoshua]
            (Num. 13:16).'"

Leviticus Rabbah XIX:IL6 is part of a miscellaneous collection on the theme of how various letters of the Hebrew alphabet play a role in the framing of the Torah's rules. There is nothing that distinguishes No. 7 from its companions, fore and aft. All are miscellaneous and all illustrate the same basic proposition.

Genesis Rabbah 36:5 (Freedman, pp. 213-214):

R. Huna said in R. Joseph's name: The generation of the Flood were not blotted out from the world until they composed nuptial songs in honor of pederasty and bestiality. R. Simlai said: Wherever you find lust, an epidemic visits the world which slays both good and bad. R. Azariah and R. Judah b. R. Simeon in R. Joshua's name said: The Holy One, blessed be He, is long-suffering for everything save immorality. What is the proof? "The sons of men saw," etc., which is followed by, "And the Lord said: I will blot out man" (Gen. 6:7). R. Joshua b. Levi said in Bar Padiah's name: the whole of that night Lot prayed for mercy for the Sodomites. They [the angels] would have heeded him, but as soon as they [the Sodomites] demanded, "Bring them out unto us, that we may know them (ib. 19:5)" -- for intercourse -- they [the angels] said, "Hast thou here any besides (ib. 12)?" Hitherto you may have pleaded in their defense, but you are no more permitted to do so."

XXIII:IX

3. B.   Said R. Simlai, "In every case in which you find prostitution, mass slaughter comes into the world and kills the good and the bad."

   C.   R. Huna in the name of R. Yose said, "The Generation of the Flood were blotted out of the world only because they composed hymeneal songs even for pederasty and bestiality."

   D.   R. Azariah in the name of R. Joshua b. R. Simon and R. Joshua b. Levi in the name of Bar Qappara: "We find that with all things the Holy One, blessed be he, is long-suffering, except for prostitution.

   E.   "And there are many verses of Scripture [that prove that fact]:

   F.   "'When men began [to multiply on the face of the ground]... the sons of God saw that the daughters of men were fair... The Lord saw that the wickedness of man was great [in the earth]... So the Lord said, I will blot out [man, whom I have created... for I am sorry that I ever made them' (Gen. 6:1-7)]."

4. A.   As to the Sodomites:

   B.   R. Joshua b. Levi in the name of Bar Pedaiah: "That entire night Lot was standing and marshalling arguments in their defense. When they came and said to him, 'Where are the men... bring them out, that we may know them' (Gen. 19:5) sexually,

   C.   "forthwith: 'The men said to Lot, Whom else do you have here?' (Gen. 19:12). Up to this point you had an opening to marshall

arguments in their defense. But from this point you have no more
opening to marshall arguments in their defense. Rather: 'Your
son-in-law, sons, daughters... for we will destroy this place' (Gen.
19:13)."

The context in which the materials common to Leviticus Rabbah and Genesis
Rabbah occur is defined by the theme of the deeds of Egypt and of Canaan which the
Israelites were not to imitate (Lev. 18:3-4). The passage at hand fits very well into the
exegesis of the base-verse, as part of a systematic catalogue following a cogent program.

Genesis Rabbah 46:4-5 (Freedman, pp. 391-392):

"And I will make my covenant," etc. (Gen. 17:2). R. Huna said in Bar
Kappara's name: Abraham pondered and drew an inference: "orlah" (foreskin)
is said here (V.II), and "orlah" occurs in reference to a tree (Lev. 19:23): just
as "orlah" in the case of trees refers to the place where it yields fruit, so
"orlah" employed in reference to man means the member which produces
offspring [fruit]. Said R. Hanina to him: Had then reasoning by analogy
already been given to Abraham? Surely not! But [he learned it from God's
promise]: "And I will make my covenant between me and thee, and will
multiply thee exceedingly:" hence, with [that member through which] "I will
multiply thee exceedingly, I will make my covenant between me and thee."

R. Ishmael and R. Akiba [reasoned as follows]. R. Ishmael said: Abraham was
a High Priest, as it says, "The Lord hath sworn, and will not repent: Thou art a
priest for ever after the manner of Melchizedek" (Ps. 110:4). Again it is said,
"And ye shall be circumcised in the flesh of your 'orlah'" (Gen. 17:2). If he
circumcised himself at the ear, he would be unfit to offer; at the heart, he
would be unfit to offer. Hence, where could he perform circumcision and yet
be fit to offer? Nowhere else than at the "orlah" of the body [the foreskin].
R. Akiba said: There are four kinds of "orlah." Thus, "orlah" is used in
connection with the ear, viz. "Behold, their ear is" "orlah" -- E.V. "dull" (Jer.
6:10); the mouth, "Behold, I am" aral [E.V. "uncircumcised"] "of lips" (Ex. 6:30);
the heart: "For all the house of Israel are" arle [E.V. "uncircumcised"] "in the
heart" (Jer. 9:25). Now, he was ordered, "Walk before me, and be thou
whole." If he circumcised himself at the ear, he would not be "whole"; at the
mouth, he would not be "whole"; at the heart, he would not be "whole". Where
could he circumcise himself and yet be "whole"? Nowhere else than at the
"orlah" of the body.

Nakdah said: It is written, "And he that is eight days old shall be circumcised
among you, every male" (Gen. 17:12). Now if he is circumcised at the ear, he

cannot hear; at the mouth, he cannot speak; at the heart, he cannot think. Where then could he be circumcised and yet be able to think? Only at the "orlah" of the body. R. Tanhuma observed: This argument of Nakdah is logical.

XXV:VI

1. A. R. Huna in the name of Bar Qappara said, "Abraham, our father, sat and constructed an argument a fortiori [as follows]:

   B. "The matter of uncircumcision is stated with regard to a tree [Lev. 19:23] and the matter of uncircumcision is stated with regard to a man.

   C. "Just as the matter of uncircumcision stated with regard to a tree applies to the place at which it produces fruit,

   D. "so the uncircumcision stated with regard to a man applies to the place in which he produces progeny."

   E. Said R. Hanan b. R. Pazzi, "And did Abraham, our father, actually know anything about constructing arguments a fortiori or arguments based on analogy?

   F. "But he found an intimation of the matter in the following verse of Scripture: 'And I will set my covenant between me and you, [and I will make you multiply very much]' (Gen. 17:2).

   G. "[The mark of the covenant is to be] in the place at which a man is fruitful and multiplies."

2. A. R. Ishmael taught, "The Holy One, blessed be he, wanted to take the priesthood away from Shem [as its progenitor], as it is said, 'And Melchizedek, king of Salem, brought out bread and wine; he was priest of God Most High. [And he blessed [Abraham] and said, "Blessed be Abram by God Most High, maker of heaven and earth, and blessed be God Most high who has delivered your enemies into your hand"]' (Gen. 14:18-19).

   B. "Since he placed the blessing of Abraham before the blessing of the Omnipresent, Abraham said to him, 'Now does one place the blessing of the servant before the blessing of his master?'

   C. "The Omnipresent removed [the priesthood] from Shem and handed it over to Abraham, as it is said, 'The Lord says to my lord, [Sit at my right hand.]' (Ps. 110:1). And after that statement it is written, 'The Lord has sworn and will not change his mind, You are a priest forever after the matter of Melchizedek' (Ps. 110:4). It is on account of the matter of Melchizedek.

   D. "That is in line with the following verse of Scripture: 'He was priest of God Most High' (Gen. 14:18)."

3. A. R. Ishmael and R. Aqiba:

B. R. Ishmael said, "Abraham was high priest, as it is said, 'The Lord has sworn and will not change his mind. [You are a priest forever] (Ps. 110:4).

C. "And it is written, 'And you will circumcise the flesh of your foreskin' (Gen. 17:11).

D. "Now where was he to make the mark of circumcision [since as we now see, it could apply to the ear, mouth, heart, and body equally, so far as biblical usage is concerned]?

E. "If he were to circumcise his ear, he would then not be fit to make an offering.

F. "If he were to circumcise his mouth, he would not be fit to make an offering.

G. "If he were to circumcise his heart, he would not be fit to make an offering.

H. "At what point, then, could he make the mark of circumcision and yet be [unblemished and thus] fit to make an offering? It could only be circumcision of the body [at the penis]."

The materials shared between Genesis Rabbah and Leviticus Rabbah find a natural place in the latter composition as part of a large anthology on the theme of circumcision. The reason that the theme occurs is the reference of the base-verse to the "uncircumcision of trees," Lev. 19:23. XXV:VI.1 alludes to the base-verse at B. That is why the entire composition has been introduced. But I see nothing in the passage that exhibits marks of revision to serve the interests of Leviticus Rabbah in particular. The list is miscellaneous, composed on a merely thematic basis.

Genesis Rabbah 90:2 (Freedman, pp. 827-828):

"Only (Rak) in the throne will I be greater than thou." Resh Lakish said: Two things our Teacher Moses stated in the Torah, and we learn their meaning from the passage about that wicked man [Pharaoh]. (i) "And thou shalt be above only" -- rak (Deut. 28:13): You might actually think, like Myself! Therefore "rak" is inserted which means, My greatness will be higher than your greatness. Now we learn this interpretation from the present passage: "Thou shalt be over my house, and according unto thy word shall all my people be ruled." Yet lest you should think that you will be as great as I, it states, "Only (rak) in the throne will I be greater than thou": my greatness is above yours. Again, (ii) "Speak unto all the congregation of the children of Israel, and say unto them: Ye shall be holy" (Lev. 19:2). Lest you should think, like Myself, the text adds, "For I the Lord your God am holy (ib.)" -- My holiness is above your holiness. Now this interpretation we learn from the passage about this wicked man: "And Pharaoh said unto Joseph: I am Pharaoh" (Gen. 41:44) -- for lest you should think that you will be as great as I, it says, "I am Pharaoh," which means, my greatness is above yours. R. Aha said: From the "I" spoken by a mortal you may learn the force of the "I" spoken by the Holy One, blessed be He. If Joseph attained to all this greatness because Pharaoh said to him, "I am Pharaoh," how much the more will it be thus when the "I" of the Holy One, blessed be He, comes to pass, viz. "I have made, and I will bear; yea, I will carry, and will deliver" (Isa. 46:4).

XXIV:IX

1. A. Said R. Simeon b. Laqish, "There are two lessons that Moses gave us in writing in the Torah, and we may derive both [lessons] from the passage dealing with the wicked Pharaoh.

   B. "[The first lesson:] A verse of Scripture states, 'And you shall be only above' (Deut. 28:13).

   C. "May one suppose, [as high] as I [God]?

   D. "Scripture says, 'Only,' which serves to limit the matter. 'My rank is above your rank.'

   E. "We learn that fact from the passage dealing with the wicked Pharaoh: 'You shall be over my house' (Gen. 31:30).

   F. "May one suppose [that Joseph will be] equivalent to me [Pharaoh]? Scripture says, 'Only in the throne shall I be greater than you' (Gen. 41:40). 'My rank will be greater than yours.'

   G. "[The second lesson is] in the following verse: 'Say to all the congregation of the people of Israel, You shall be holy' (Lev. 19:2).

   H. "Is it possible that [Israel will be holy] like me?

   I. "Scripture says, 'For I am holy' (Lev. 19:2).

   J. "'My level of holiness is above your level of holiness.'

   K. "And we learn that fact from the passage dealing with the wicked Pharaoh: 'And Pharaoh said to Joseph, I am Pharaoh' (Gen. 41:44).

   L. "Is it possible [that Joseph would be] equivalent [to him]?

   M. "Scripture states, 'I am Pharaoh.' 'My rank will be higher than your rank.'"

2. A. R. Joshua of Sikhnin in the name of R. Levi: "From the 'I' stated by a mortal you may learn the meaning of the 'I' stated by the Holy One, blessed be he.

   B. "Just as through the 'I' used by mortal, when Pharaoh said to Joseph, 'I am the Pharaoh,' [Joseph] acquired all that glory,

   C. "when the 'I' of the Holy One, blessed be he, is realized, how much the more so [will Israel be glorified]!

   D. "[It is as in these verses:] 'Until old age, I am he' (Is. 46:4).

   E. "'Thus said the Lord, king of Israel and its redeemer, "I am the first"' (Is. 44:6).

   F. "'[I the Lord, am the first,] and with the last, I am he' (Is. 41:4)."

The exercise of XXIV:IX.2 is repeated here, now with the somewhat more complicated exegetical problem of deriving the positive lessons from the negative example of Pharaoh's discourse with Joseph. The reason the passage is included is clear at 1.G-I. None of these materials was formed for the particular purpose of stringing together exegeses of Lev. 19:2ff.; all of them take up the contents or the themes that occur in a variety of biblical passages. The passage forms part of a miscellany for Leviticus Rabbah.

Genesis Rabbah 32:4 (Freedman, p. 251):

"That are not clean" (Gen. 7:2). R. Judan said: Even when [Scripture] comes to enumerate the signs of unclean animals, it commences first with the signs of cleanness [which they possess]: it is not written, "The camel, because he parteth not the hoof," but "Because he cheweth the cud but parteth not the hoof" (Lev. 11:4); "The rock-badger, because he cheweth the cud but parteth not the hoof" (ib. 5); "The hare, because she cheweth the cud but parteth not the hoof" (ib. 6); "The swine, because he parteth the hoof, and is cloven-footed, but cheweth not the cud" (ib. 7).

XXVI:I

2. D. "'And from every unclean beast' is not what is written here, but rather, 'Of every beast that is not clean, two, male and female' (Gen. 7:2)."

    E. Said R. Yudan b. R. Manasseh, "Even when Scripture came to introduce the signs of unclean beasts, the Scripture commenced only with the signs of clean [beasts], as in the following cases:

    F. "'The camel, because it does not part the hoof' is not what is written here, but rather, 'Because it chews the cud [but does not...]' (Lev. 11:4).

    G. "'The rock-badger, because it does not part the hoof' is not what is written here, but rather, 'Because it chews the cud [but does not...]' (Lev. 11:5).

    H. "'The hare, because it does not part the hoof' is not what is written here, but rather, 'Because it chews the cud [but does not...]' (Lev. 11:6).

    I. "'The pig, because it does not chew the cud' is not what is written here, but rather, 'Because it parts the hoof [but does not...]' (Lev. 11:7)."

The intersecting text of Parashah XXVI is Ps. 12:7, which refers to the purity of God's speech. The passage at hand illustrates that proposition and fits well into the exegetical program of the authors. That is the case, even though, as is clear, the interests of Gen. 7:2 are what define the matter.

<u>Genesis Rabbah 1:15 (Freedman, pp. 13-14)</u>:

"The heaven and the earth" (Gen. 1:1). Beth Shammai maintain: The heaven was first created; while Beth Hillel hold: The earth was first created. In the view of Beth Shammai this is parallel to the case of a king who first made his throne and then his footstool, for it is written, "The heaven is My Throne, and the earth is My footstool" Isa. 66:1). On the view of Beth Hillel this is to be compared to a king who builds a palace; after building the nether portion he builds the upper, for it is written, "In the day that the Lord God made earth and heaven" (Gen. 2:4). R. Judah b. R. Ilai said: This supports Beth Hillel, viz. "Of old Thou didst lay the foundations of the earth," which is followed by, "And the heavens are the work of Thy hands" (Ps. 102:26). R. Hanin said: From the very text which [apparently] supports Beth Shammai, Beth Hillel refute them, viz. "And the earth was" (Gen. 1:2), meaning that it had already existed [before heaven], R. Johanan, reporting the Sages, said: As regards creation, heaven was first; as regards completion, earth was first. Said R. Tanhuma: I will state the grounds [of this opinion]: as regards creation heaven was first, as it is written, "In the beginning God created the heaven;" whereas in respect of completion earth took precedence, for it is written, "In the day that the Lord God made earth and heaven." R. Simeon observed: I am amazed that the fathers of the world engage in controversy over this matter, for surely both were created [simultaneously] like a pot and its lid, [as it is written], "When I call unto them" [sc. heaven and earth], "they stand up together" (Isa. 48:13). R. Eleazar b. R. Simeon observed: If my father's view is right, why is the earth sometimes given precedence over the heaven, and sometimes heaven over earth? In fact it teaches that they are equal to each other.

<u>XXXVI:I</u>

1.   A.   "Of old you laid out the foundation of the earth, and the heavens are the work of your hands" (Ps. 102:25).

      B.   The House of Shammai and the House of Hillel:

      C.   <u>The House of Shammai say, "The heaven was created first, and then the earth."</u>

      D.   <u>The House of Hillel say, "The earth was created first, then the heaven."</u>

      E.   <u>This party brings a proof-text for its opinion, and that party brings a proof-text for its view.</u>

      F.   <u>In the view of the House of Shammai, who maintain that the heaven was created first and then the earth, we may make a comparison. To what is the matter comparable?</u>

G. To the case of a king who made a throne. Only after he made the throne did he make its footstool. Thus: "So says the Lord, 'The heaven is my throne, and the earth the dust at my feet'" (Is. 66:1).

H. In the view of the House of Hillel, who maintain that the earth was created first and then the heaven, we may make a comparison. [To what is the matter comparable?]

I. To the case of a king who built himself a palace. Only after he builds the lower floors does he build the upper floors.

J. So it is written, "My hand laid the foundation of the earth, and my right hand [then] spread out the heaven" (Is. 48:13).

K. Said R. Haninah, "Also the following verse of Scripture supports the position of the House of Hillel: 'Of old you laid out the foundations of the earth,' and afterward: 'and the heavens are the work of your hands' (Ps. 102:25)."

L. Said R. Judah, "From the very passage of Scripture which is adduced in support of the position of the House of Shammai, the House of Hillel find proof to dismiss that same position.

M. "In the view of the House of Shammai, who maintain that the heaven was created first and then the earth, [the following proof-text confirms their position:] 'In the beginning God created the heaven and the earth' (Gen. 1:1).

N. "In the view of the House of Hillel, who say that the earth was created first, then the heaven: 'And the earth was unformed and void' (Gen. 1:2), indicating that the earth already was in being."

2. A. R. Yohanan said in the name of sages, R. Yohanan said, "As to the act of creation, heaven came first. As to the process of finishing off creation, the earth came first.

B. "As to the act of creation, the heaven came first: 'In the beginning God created [the heaven and the earth]' (Gen. 1:1).

C. "As to the process of finishing off creation, the earth came first: 'On the day on which the Lord God made heaven and earth' (Gen. 2:4)."

3. A. Said R. Simeon b. Yohai, "I am amazed that the fathers of the world [the Houses of Shammai and Hillel] were split on the question of the creation of the world, for I say, Heaven and earth were created only like a pot and its lid [that is, in a single act].

B. "That is in line with the following verse of Scripture: 'My hand established the earth, and my right hand spread out the heaven. When I call them, they stand up together' (Is. 48:13)."

C. Said R. Eleazar b. R. Simeon, "According to this opinion of my father, sometimes heaven precedes earth, sometimes earth precedes heaven. But he [really] teaches that they are both equal [having been created at the same instant]."

4.   A.   [T. Ker. 4:14: R. Simeon says,] "In every place [Scripture] has given precedence to the creation of heaven over the creation of earth. In one place, however, it says, 'On the day of the Lord God's creating of earth and heaven' (Gen. 2:4), teaching that the two are deemed equivalent.

B.   "In every place Scripture has given precedence to Moses over Aaron. But in one place it says, 'It is Aaron and Moses' (Ex. 6:26). This teaches that the two are deemed equivalent.

C.   "In every place Scripture has given precedence to Joshua over Caleb. But in one place it says, 'Except for Caleb, the son of Jephunneh the Kenizzite, and Joshua, the son of Nun' (Num. 32:12). This teaches that the two are deemed equivalent.

D.   "[M. Ker. 6:9I-L:] In every place Scripture has given precedence to the honor of the father over that of the mother. In one place, however, it says, 'You shall fear every one his mother and his father' (Lev. 19:3). This teaches that the two are deemed equivalent.

E.   "In every place Scripture has given precedence to doves before young pigeons. But in one place it says, 'A young pigeon or a dove for a sin-offering' (Lev. 12:6). This teaches that the two of them are deemed equivalent.

F.   "In every place Scripture has given precedence to Abraham over the other patriarchs. But in one place it says, 'And I remembered my covenant with Jacob, [...Isaac... and Abraham...]' (Lev. 26:42). This teaches that the three are deemed equivalent to one another."

Since the base-verse, Lev. 26:42, is cited at the end, we can see the principle by which the redactor selected the materials at hand. The principle of aggregation comes at the end, 4.E-F. The point the compositor wished to make is that various important things, occurring in a given order, in fact are equivalent to one another. A reversal, even one time only, of the established order in which they are ordinarily listed, indicates that fact. Then No. 1's dispute, joined to its complements at Nos. 2, 3, is presented whole. There is no intersecting verse: the proof-texts themselves are not worked out, but only cited in a context they do not define. But 3.C is the bridge to No. 4. No. 4 is given whole, as it occurs at Tosefta and Mishnah, with only F, the concluding lines added and pertinent here. To achieve the required effect, however, the framer has had to reorganize the order in which the items appear in the Tosefta's and Mishnah's versions. Obviously, the authors of Leviticus Rabbah have imposed their own program on the chosen materials.

Genesis Rabbah 40:3 (Freedman, pp. 526ff.):

"Behold, I stand by the fountain of water, etc... so let it come to pass, that the damsel to be chosen shall be she to whom I shall say: Let down thy pitcher" (Gen. 24:13-14).

Four asked improperly: three were granted their request in a fitting manner, and the fourth, in an unfitting manner. They are: Eliezer, Caleb, Saul, and Jephthah. Eliezer: "So let it come to pass, that the damsel" -- even a bondmaid! Yet God prepared Rebekah for him and granted his request in a fitting manner. Caleb: "He that smiteth Kiriath-sepher, and taketh it, to him will I give Achsah my daughter to wife" (Judg. 1:12) -- it might even be a slave! But God chose Othniel for him. Saul: "And it shall be, that the man who killeth him, the king will enrich him with great riches, and will give him his daughter" (1 Sam. 17:25) -- it might even be a slave! But God prepared David for him. Jephthah asked in an unfitting manner, and God answered him in an unfitting manner. He asked in an unfitting manner, as it says, "And Jephthah vowed a vow unto the Lord, and said: Then it shall be, that whatsoever cometh forth... it shall be the Lord's and I will offer it up for a burnt-offering" (Judg. 11:30f.). Said the Holy One, blessed be He, to him: "Then had a camel or an ass or a dog come forth, thou wouldst have offered it up for a burnt-offering!" What did the Lord do? He answered him unfittingly and prepared his daughter for him, as it says, "And Jephthah came... and, behold, his daughter came out to meet him" (ib. 34).

"And it came to pass, when he saw her, that he rent his clothes" (ib. 35). R. Johanan and Resh Lakish disagree. R. Johanan maintained: He was liable for her monetary consecration; Resh Lakish said: He was not even liable for her monetary consecration. For we learned: If one declared of an unclean animal or an animal with a blemish: "Behold, let these be burnt-offerings, his declaration is completely null. If he declared: "Let these be for a burnt-offering," they must be sold, and he brings a burnt-offering for their money. Yet was not Phinehas there to absolve him of his vow? Phinehas, however, said: He needs me, and I am to go to him! Moreover, I am a High Priest and the son of a High Priest; shall I then go to an ignoramus? While Jephthah said: Am I, the chief of Israel's leaders, go to Phinehas! Between the two of them the maiden perished. Thus people say: "Between the midwife and the woman in travail the young woman's child is lost!" Both were punished for her blood. Jephthah died through his limbs dropping off: wherever he went a limb would drop off from him, and it was buried there on the spot. Hence it is written, "Then died Jephthah the Gileadite, and was buried in the cities of Gilead" (ib. 12:7). It does not say, "In a city of Gilead," but "In the cities of Gilead." Phinehas was deprived of the divine afflatus. Hence it is written, "And

Phinehas the son of Eleazar had been ruler over them," but "Had been ruler in time past, [when] the Lord was with him" (ib.).

XXXVII:IV

1.   A.   Four opened [their prayers of petition] by taking vows, three asking not in the proper way, while the Holy One, blessed be he, responded to them in the proper way, and one asking not in the proper way, and the Holy One, blessed be he, responded to him not in the proper way.

     B.   These are they: Eliezer, servant of Abraham; Caleb; Saul; and Jephthah.

     C.   Eliezer asked not in the proper way, for it is written, "Let the maiden to whom I shall say, ['Pray, let down your jar that I may drink,' and who shall say, 'Drink, and I will water your camels' -- let her be the one whom you have appointed for your servant Isaac. But this I shall know that you have steadfast love to my master]' (Gen. 24:14).

     D.   Said to him the Holy One, blessed be he, "If a serving girl, a gentile girl, or a whore, should come forth, would you turn out even then to say, "Let her be the one whom thou hast appointed for thy Servant Isaac" (Gen. 24:14)?

     E.   What did the Holy One, blessed be he, do? He appointed Rebecca for him: "Before he had done speaking, [behold, Rebekah, who was born to Bethuel... came out with her water jar upon her shoulder]' (Gen. 24:15).

     F.   Caleb asked in an improper way, but the Holy One, blessed be he, responded to him in a proper way.

     G.   "And Caleb said, 'Whoever smites Kiriath sepher [and takes it -- to him will I give Achsah my daughter as wife]'" (Josh. 15:16).

     H.   Said he to him the Holy One, blessed be he, "If a gentile, a slave, or a mamzer [should take the city], would you give him your daughter [as a wife]?"

     I.   What did the Holy One, blessed be he, do? He responded to him in a proper way and appointed for him Othniel, son of Kenaz, for it is written, "And Othniel, son of Kenaz, son of Caleb, took it" (Josh. 15:17).

     J.   Saul asked in an improper way, but the Holy, One, blessed be he, responded to him in a proper way.

     K.   For it is written, "And the men of Israel said, 'Have you seen this man who has come up? Surely he has come up to defy Israel; and the man who kills him the king will enrich with great riches and will give him his daughter [and make his father's house free in Israel]'" (1 Sam. 17:25).

L.   Said the Holy One, blessed be he, "If a slave, or a gentile [should smite him], would you give him your daughters?"

M.   What did the Holy One, blessed be he, do? He responded to him in a proper way and appointed David for him, as it is said, "And David said to the men [who stood by him, 'What will be done for the man who kills this Philistine]'" (1 Sam. 17:26).

N.   Jephthah asked not in a proper way, and the Holy One, blessed be he, responded to him not in a proper way.

O.   He asked not in a proper way, as it is said, "And Jephthah made a vow [to the Lord and said, 'If you will give the Ammonites into my hand.] then whoever comes forth [from the doors of my house to meet me, when I return victorious from the Ammonites, shall be the Lord's, and I will offer him up for a burnt offering]'" (Judges 11:20-31).

P.   Said to him the Holy One, blessed be he, "If a camel or an ass or a dog should come forth from your house, would you then offer him up as a burnt offering before me?"

Q.   What did the Holy One, blessed be he, do to him? He responded to him not in a proper way and designated his daughter, as it is said, "Then Jephthah came to his home at Mizpah, and behold, his daughter came out to meet him [with timbrels and with dances; she was his only child; beside her he had neither son nor daughter]. And when he saw her, [he rent his clothes and said, 'Alas, my daughter'. you have brought me very low and you have become the cause of great trouble to me]'" (Judges 11:34-35).

2.   A.   Could not he not get the someone to release him from his vow? But Jephthah said, "I am a king, and I shall not go to Phineas," and Phineas said, "I am high priest, and I am not going to go to a common person."

B.   Between the one and the other, that poor girl perished.

C.   In a proverb people say, "Between the midwife and the woman in travail, the poor woman's baby will die."

D.   And both of them were guilty for her blood.

E.   From Phineas the Holy Spirit was taken away, as it is said, "Phineas, the son of Eleazar, was ruler over them; in times past the Lord with him" (1 Chr. 9:20). He had been with him in times past, but not now.

F.   Jephthah's limbs fell off of him limb by limb, and he was therefore buried in many places.

G.   That is in line with the following verse of Scripture: "And Jephthah died and was buried in the cities of Gilead" (Judges 12:7).

H.   It is not written, "in a city of Gilead," but rather, "in the cities of Gilead."

I.   This teaches that a limb would fall off from him here and was buried where it fell, and a limb would fall off of him in another place and was buried where it fell.

3. A.   R. Yohanan and R. Simeon b. Laqish:

    B.   R. Yohanan said, "He became liable for money for purchase of an offering to be offered on the altar [in her place]."

    C.   R. Simeon b. Laqish said, "He did not become liable for money [for the stated purpose]."

    D.   For we have learned (cf. M. Tem. 5:6), "If one made a statement [of substitution] concerning something which is suitable to be offered on the altar, let it be offered on the altar. If he spoke of something which is not suitable to be offered on the altar, let it not be offered on the altar, and not only so, but even the matter of the consecration of the value of said beast does not apply."

4. A.   Said R. Jacob bar Abina, "Whoever makes a vow and pays off his vow may be certain that his prayer has been heard.

    B.   "What is the Scriptural proof for that statement? 'Praise is due to you, O God, in Zion, and to you shall vows be performed' (Ps. 65:1).

    C.   "And what is written directly afterward? 'O you who hear prayer, to you shall all flesh come' (Ps. 65:2)."

5. A.   Said R. Aha, "Whoever takes a vow and pays off his vow acquires such merit that he will pay off his vow [in time to come] in Jerusalem.

    B.   "That is in line with the following verse of Scripture: 'I shall pay off my vows to the Lord' (Ps. 116:18).

    C.   "Where? 'In the courtyards of the house of the Lord, in the midst of Jerusalem, praise the Lord' (Ps. 116:18)."

    D.   "Praise the Lord for he is good, for his mercy is forever" (Ps. 106:1).

The hodgepodge of materials on vows and remission of vows brings us to yet another collection at No. 1. I assume that the reference in the preceding to the remission of vows accounts for the selection of this long account, complemented by No. 2, 3. Nos. 4-5 then complete the matter with which the Parashah began, carrying out one's vows, ending on the (now predictable) messianic note. The relevance of the shared materials to the program of Leviticus Rabbah is self-evident. What the authors have assembled is a miscellany.

iv. Units of Discourse Common to Leviticus Rabbah and Pesiqta deRab Kahana

Here we have a special problem, since a number of complete parashiyyot of Leviticus Rabbah occur also in Pesiqta deRab Kahana. It will suffice to present in its entirety only a single such parashah = pisqa, stipulating that the traits of the others are the same as the one before us. The shared parashiyyot are as follows:

Leviticus Rabbah	Pesiqta deRab Kahana
20	26
27	9
28	8
29	23
30	27

Braude and Kapstein (William G. Braude and Israel J. Kapstein, trans., Pesiqta deRab Kahana [Philadelphia, 1975: Jewish Publication Society of America], pp. xlix-1) provide a satisfactory discussion and bibliography on the matter of which composition borrowed from the other (cf. in particular p. 1, ns. 48-50). For reasons spelled out above, the issue for our purposes produces no consequences whatever.

To make perfectly clear to the reader how the two documents relate, I present one pisqa of Pesiqta deRab Kahana followed by the counterpart in Leviticus Rabbah. The reader will understand that differences in wording represent choices made by the translators, and at issue is whether or not the pisqa of the one and the parashah of the other are essentially uniform in contents and structure. While the answer is that they are, the reader is best served by a direct encounter with the actual texts, though a single example suffices. To show the correspondences, I insert in Braude and Kapstein the reference to Leviticus Rabbah Parashah 27, since Braude and Kapstein supply no reference-system whatsoever.

PISKA 9
"A bullock, or a sheep" (Lev. 22:27) [= XXVII:I.1.A.]

1.   "Thy righteousness is like the mighty mountains; Thy judgments are like the great deep; man and cattle Thou preservest, O Lord" (Ps. 36:7). R. Ishmael and R. Aqiba differed in their interpretations of the first part of this verse. R. Ishmael said: To the righteous who obey the Torah which was given on the mighty mountains, the Holy One accords love in such abundance that it towers up like His mighty mountains: hence "Thy righteousness is like the mighty mountains." But to the wicked, to those who do not obey the Torah which was given on the mighty mountains, the Holy One, searching out the very depths of their beings, accords the strictness of His judgment: hence "Thy judgments are like the great deep." R. Aqiba, on the other hand, interpreted the verse as follows: God accords His justice as strictly to the righteous as to the wicked. He is strict with the righteous, [searching out the very depths of their being] and holding them to account for the few wrongs they commit in this world, so that in the world-to-come He can even the balance with full reward for their righteousness, [a reward so abundant that it will tower up like His mighty mountains]; upon the wicked, however, He bestows ease in this world in an

abundance [as great as His mighty mountains], rewarding them thus for their
few good deeds in this world, so that in the world-to-come He can even the
balance with entire requital for their wickedness, [a requital as profound as
His great deeps] [XXII:1.1].

R. [Judah had a different idea of the verse's meaning, for he] maintained that
the verse in the Psalm likens the righteous to the loftiness of the abode where
they are to dwell and likens the wicked to the abyss where they are to dwell.
Thus, likening the righteous to the abiding place which is to be theirs,
Scripture says [of Israel returning from the exile's world of darkness], "I will
feed them in a green pasture, and upon the mountains of the lofty One of
Israel shall be their fold" (Ezek. 34:14). Then likening the wicked to the
abiding place which is to be theirs, another verse says, "Thus saith the Lord
God: In the day when [the wicked king] went down to the grave I caused to
mourn (heebalti), I covered him with the abyss" (Ezek. 31:15). However, as R.
Judah Berabbi noted, the "ketib" of "heebalti," "caused to mourn," is "hey-
balti," "caused to go down," [so that the latter part of the verse is to be read "I
had him go down even deeper, I used him to cover over the abyss]." A parable
to explain the verse's intent: A cover for a wine vessel is not made of silver,
nor of gold, nor of copper, nor of iron, nor of tin, nor of lead (see Num. 31:22):
it is made of clay, which is of the same material as the earthenware vessel
itself. So, too, the Holy One said: Gehenna is darkness, the abyss is darkness,
and the wicked are darkness. Let darkness come and cover darkness: "[The
wicked] cometh in [the darkness of] a thick fog, he departeth in darkness, his
body serves as a cover for the darkness [of the abyss]" (Eccles. 6:4) [XXVII:I.2].

R. Jonathan, citing R. Josiah, transposed the verse of the Psalm, reading it:
Thy righteousness -- that is, Thy mercy -- towers above Thy judgments as the
mountains of God tower above the great deep. As the mountains hold back the
deep so that it cannot come up and overwhelm the world, so the deeds of the
righteous hold back punishment so that it cannot come and overwhelm the
world.

Then [reading the verse without transposing its words, R. Jonathan, citing R.
Josiah, said] in further comment on "Thy righteousness is like the mighty
mountains" (Ps. 36:7): As the mountains are without end, so [if not in this
world, then surely] in the world-to-come, the bestowal of reward upon the
righteous will be without end; and in comment on "Thy judgments are like the
great deep" continued: As the deep is without end, so [if not in this world,
then surely] in the world-to-come, the infliction of punishment upon the
wicked will be without end [XXVII.I.3].

Another comment: "Thy righteousness is like the mighty mountains (ibid.)."
As the mountains are clearly visible, so the deeds of the righteous are clearly
visible: "Because they fear Thee, [their deeds are always visible], are always
done in the full light of day or in the radiance of the moon by night" (Ps.
72:5). But "[deeds which bring on] Thy judgments are like the great deep." As
the deep is hidden, so are the deeds of the wicked hidden: "Their works are in
the dark" (Isa. 29:15) [XXVII:I.5].

Another comment: "Thy righteousness is like the mighty mountains" (Ps.
36:7). As the mountains are sown and yield fruit, so the deeds of the righteous
yield fruit: "Say ye of the righteous, that is shall be well with them; for men
shall eat the fruit of their doings" (Isa. 3:10). "Thy judgments are like the
great deep" (Ps. 36:7): as the deep cannot be sown to yield fruit, so the deeds
of the wicked cannot produce fruit: "Woe unto the wicked! it shall be ill with
him; for the work of his hands" -- [note that the text does not speak of the
fruit of his deeds but of the work of his hands, which, as the verse concludes]
-- "shall be done to him" (Isa. 3:11) [XXVII:I.4].

Another comment on "Thy righteousness is like the mighty mountains" (Ps.
36:7). R. Judah bar R. Simon read the verse: Thy righteousness -- Thy mercy
-- is as lofty as Thy mountains, which Thou didst accord to Noah in the ark for
a landing place: "The ark rested upon the mountains of Ararat" (Gen. 8:4).
And the judgments which Thou didst pass upon Noah's generation, Thou didst
carry out with such thoroughness that they reached down to the great deep
[whose waters surged up from below to mingle with the waters that fell from
above]: "On the same day all the fountains of the great deep were broken up"
(Gen. 7:11). Nay more, when Thou didst remember Noah, Thou didst remember
not him alone -- no, but him and all who were with him in the ark, as it is
written "God remembered Noah, as well as every living thing," etc. (Gen. 8:1).
[The stress upon God's concern for every living thing besides Noah and his
family will be understood when you reflect that the men of our generation are
just as sinful as the men of Noah's generation were. For an example of the
sinfulness of the men of our generation, consider that] when R. Joshua ben
Levi went to Rome, he saw marble pillars there which had been carefully
covered with wrappings to keep them from cracking during the heat and from
freezing during the cold. By contrast he saw there a poor wretch who had no
more than a reed mat under him and a reed mat over him [to protect him from
the heat and cold]. In regard to the pillars R. Joshua cited the words "Thy
care is like the mighty mountains" (Ps. 36:7): where Thou dost allow care to
be given, Thou allowest men to give it like the rush of streams from the
mountains; and in regard to the poor wretch he cited the words "Thy judgments
are like the great deep" (ibid.): where Thou dost allow punishment to be

inflicted, Thou allowest men to inflict it upon others down to the uttermost depths [XXVII:I.6-7].

[Since men are still as wicked as they were in Noah's time, why then does God permit the world to continue to exist? Because, as two stories in connection with the verse "Man and cattle," etc. (ibid.) show, the continued existence of the world depends on humbler creatures -- women, for example -- than men: The first story tells us that] Alexander of Macedon paid a visit to a king at the end of the world beyond the Mountains of Darkness and eventually came to a principality called Kartigna, inhabited entirely by women. These came out to meet him and said: "If you make war against us and defeat us, your name will go forth in the world as of one who laid waste a province of women; while if we make war upon you and defeat you, your name will go forth in the world as of one whom women made war against and defeated, so that you will always be ashamed to face any king." When he left, he wrote upon the city gate: I, Alexander of Macedon, was a fool until I came to the principality of Kartigna and learned wisdom from women [XXVII:I.&A-C].

[The other story tells us that] Alexander also went to another principality called "Africa [Propria]." The people came out to meet him with golden apples, golden pomegranates, and golden bread. "[What is the meaning of this]'? he asked. "Do you eat gold bread in your country?" They replied: "Do you not have it in your own country that you must come to us for it?" He replied: "I have not come to see your wealth -- it is your customs I have come to observe." As Alexander and his questioners were thus engaged in discourse, two men came before the king for judgment. One said: I bought a ruin from this man and while digging in it found a treasure, and so I said to him "Take your treasure -- I bought a ruin -- a treasure I did not buy." The other said to the king: "Sire! For my part, when I sold that man the ruin, I sold him everything that was in it."

The king addressed one of them and asked him: "Have you a son?" He replied: "Yes." The king asked the other: "Have you a daughter?" He replied: "Yes." "Go, then," said the king, "wed one to the other, and let the two make use of the treasure." Thereupon Alexander showed his amazement. The king asked: "Why are you amazed? Have I not judged well?" Alexander replied: "Yes." The king asked: "If such a case had come up in your country, how would you have handled it?" Alexander replied: "We would have removed the head of the one and the head of the other, and the treasure would have gone to the royal treasury." The king asked Alexander: "Does the sun shine where you dwell?" Alexander replied, "Yes." "Does rain fall where you dwell?" Alexander said: "Yes." The king asked: "Perhaps there are small cattle in your country?" Alexander replied, "Yes." The king said: "May the breath of life in such a man as you be blasted out! It is for the sake of the small cattle that the sun shines where you dwell, that the rain falls where you dwell: on account of the small cattle you are preserved alive." Such is the meaning of "Man and cattle Thou preservest, O Lord" (Ps. 36:7) -- on account of the cattle Thou preservest man, O Lord [XXVII:I.&D-DD].

[In further comment the verse is read "Men who are like cattle Thou preservest, O Lord" (ibid.)]. Hence Israel said: Master of universes, though we be men inclined to sin, save us, [should we sin], from punishment as Thou dost spare cattle from punishment, for, in truth, [the innocence of our faith in Thee is like the innocence of cattle]: like them we are drawn after Thee, saying to Thee, "Draw me after Thee, [for in following Thee], I shall be satisfied" (Song 1:4). And because, like cattle, we let ourselves be drawn after Thee, whither [do we find ourselves drawn? Each one of us] to his own Garden of Eden, declares the School of Rabbi, for, the Psalm goes on to say, "They will be abundantly satisfied with the fatness of Thy house; and Thou permittest them to drink from the river of Thine Edens" (Ps. 36:9). The text does not say "Thine Eden" but "Thine Edens," indicating, as R. Eleazar bar R. Menahem pointed out, that each and every righteous man has his own Garden of Eden, [for both in God's judgments or in lack of them, he sees evidences of mercy]. As R. Isaac taught: [When examined in depth], God's judicial decree for mankind like His judicial decree for cattle [is prompted by mercy]. His decree for mankind: "In the eighth day the flesh of his foreskin shall be circumcised" (Lev. 12:3); His decree for cattle: "From the eighth day and thenceforth it may be accepted for an offering" (Lev. 22:27) [XXVII:I.9-10].

2.   R. Tanhuma began his discourse with the verse "Whosoever without being required to bestirs himself [to help provide instruction in Torah which] under the whole heaven was [first] Mine -- I will repay by not turning a deaf ear to his prayer for male children" (Job 41:3-4a). To start with, R. Tanhuma applied the verse to an unmarried man who lives in an outlying place [without schools] yet pays the fee for teachers of Scripture and teachers of Mishnah [elsewhere]. Of such a man, the Holy One says: It is for Me to pay him [when he marries] by not turning a deaf ear to his prayer for male children [XXVII:II.1].

[Then R. Tanhuma quoted] R. Jeremiah bar R. Eleazar [who read Job 41:3 as also asserting "Whosoever without being required to bestirs himself (to help provide instruction in Torah which) under the whole heaven was (first) Mine -- I will repay (by having a Voice proclaim) under the entire heaven that such a man has wrought as I have wrought." And R. Tanhuma went on to quote R. Jeremiah's comment on the verse]: Some day in the future a Divine Voice reverberating on the mountain tops will declare, Whosoever wrought with God [as the unmarried man wrought], let him come and receive the reward due him. Of this it is said "At the due season shall it be told to Jacob and to Israel: 'Who hath wrought with God'" (Num. 23:23): whosoever wrought with God, let him come and receive the reward due him [XXVII:IL2A-D].

In another comment the verse is read to mean that the holy spirit is asking "Who hath given Me anything beforehand that I should repay him?" (Job 41:3). Who sang out in praise of Me before I put breath into him? Who could circumcise in My name before I gave him a male child? Who, at My request, made fringes before I gave him a garment? Who, at My request, made a mezuzah before I gave him a house? Who, at My request, built a parapet before I gave him a roof? Who, at My request, built a sukkah before I gave him a courtyard? Who, at My request, set aside the corners of the crop before I gave him a field? Who, at My request, set aside heave offering for priests and tithes for Levites before I gave him a threshing floor? Who, at My request, set aside an offering before I gave him cattle? "When a bullock, or a sheep, or a goat is brought forth," etc. (Lev. 22:27) [XXVIL:IL2.E-F].

3.   [In further reference to the verse just above], R. Jacob bar Zabdi, citing R. Abbahu, began his discourse with the verse "Bringing the iniquity" -- the making of the golden calf -- "to remembrance against the House of Israel will not continue to be a source of reassurance [for heathen nations]" (Ezek. 29:16), and went on to quote the following: "Above Him stood the seraphim; each one had six wings," etc. (Isa. 6:2). "With two he did fly" (ibid.), singing out God's praise as he flew; "with two he covered his face" (ibid.), so as not to gaze upon the Presence; "and with two he covered his feet" (ibid.), that his feet should not be exposed to the Presence. Since "the sole of the [seraphim's] feet was like the sole of a calf's foot" (Ezek. 1:7), [the seraphim covered their feet] so that "Bringing the iniquity to remembrance against the House of Israel will not continue to be a source of reassurance [for heathen nations]" (Ezek. 29:16) [XXVII:IL1].

Elsewhere we are told in a Mishnah "All horns are proper for blowing except that of the cow" (RH 3:2). Because a cow is of the same breed as a calf, therefore the horn may not be used, in order that "Bringing the iniquity to remembrance against Israel will not continue to be a source of reassurance [for heathen nations]" (Ezek. 29:16) [XXVII:IIL2].

In still another place we are told: "If a woman approach unto any beast, and lie down thereto, thou shalt kill the woman and the beast" (Lev. 20:16). In such a case, the human being commits a sin, but what sin does the animal commit? None. However, because the animal is a stumbling block whereby a human being falls into sin, Scripture orders that the animal be stoned to death. Another reason for killing the animal is that if it were allowed to live, people seeing it pass through the streets [would be reminded of the sin] and would be tempted to say: "There's the one on account of whom So-and-so was stoned to death." The animal is therefore put to death in order that "Bringing an iniquity to remembrance against the House of Israel will not continue to be a source of satisfaction [for malicious people]" (Ezek. 29:16) [XXVII:III.3].

We are also told in a Baraita that a woman suspected of infidelity is not to drink from the cup of a woman who was also suspected of infidelity [and who, having drunk from the cup, died. The woman under suspicion is not to drink from the same cup] in order to keep people from saying "A woman like her, also suspected of infidelity, drank from this cup and died," and thus bringing up a reminder of the former guilty woman's iniquity: "Bringing iniquity to remembrance should not continue to be a source of satisfaction [for malicious people]" (Ezek. 29:16) [XXVII:III.3-4].

Consider finally another instance [of how Scripture avoids "Bringing iniquity to remembrance"]. In the verse "When a bullock, or a sheep, or a goat is brought forth" (Lev. 22:27), is it precise to speak of a bullock as "brought forth?" Is it not termed a "calf" when it is brought forth? However, because Scripture says in Exodus 32:8 "They have made them a molten calf," Leviticus in speaking of the young of animals to be used for offerings -- "when a bullock, or a sheep, or a goat is brought forth" (Lev. 22:27) -- chooses deliberately to use "bullock," not "calf," [so as to avoid "Bringing iniquity to remembrance"] [XXVII:III.5].

4. ["God brings to pass that men should revere Him" (Eccles. 3:14b). These words are to be understood in the light of the verse that follows them]: "That which hath been is now; and that which is to be hath already been" (Eccles. 3:15). R. Judah and R. Nehemiah differ in interpreting the verse. R. Judah said: If any one says to you, "Had Adam not sinned, can we believe that he would have lived -- endured -- till now?" say in reply "That which hath been is now," for Elijah, ever remembered on good occasions, who never sinned -- is he not alive, does he not endure even now? "And that which is to be hath already been." If a man says to you, "Can we believe that the Holy One is capable of bringing the dead back to life?" say in reply, "That which is to be hath already been." Has He not already, by the hand of Elijah, then by the hand of Elisha, then by the hand of Ezekiel brought back the dead?"

R. Nehemiah said: If a man says to you, "Can we believe that the earth was covered with waters upon waters?" say in reply, "That which hath been is now:" is not the Ocean, all of it, waters upon waters? "That which is to be hath already been." If a man says to you, "Can we believe that the Holy One will make the sea dry land?" say in reply, Has He not already done so by the hand of Moses? "The children of Israel walked upon dry land in the midst of the sea" (Exod. 14:29) [XXVII:IV.1].

R. Aha, citing R. Simeon bar Hilfa, said: All that the Holy One will do in the time-to-come, He has already anticipated and done in part by the hand of the righteous in this world. The Holy One says: I shall quicken the dead. He has already done so by the hand of Elijah, by the hand of Elisha, by the hand of Ezekiel. The Holy One says: I shall make the sea dry land. Has He not already done so by the hand of Moses? "The children of Israel walked upon dry land in the midst of the sea" (Exod. 14:29). The Holy One says: I will open the eyes of the blind. Has He not already done so -- "The Lord opened the eyes of the young man" (2 Kings 6:17)? The Holy One says: I shall remember barren women. Has He not already done so -- "The Lord remembered Sarah" (Gen. 21:1)? The Holy One says: "Kings shall be thy foster-fathers, and their queens thy nursing mothers; they shall bow down to thee with their face to the earth" (Isa. 49:23). Has He not already brought about these things? Was not Nebuchadnezzer a king, and to whom did he bow down? To Daniel, as Scripture says, "The king Nebuchadnezzer fell upon his face, and worshiped Daniel" (Dan. 2:46) [XXVII:IV.2].

[As between pursuers and the pursued, such as "a bullock, or a sheep, or a goat"], "God seeketh the pursued" (Eccles. 3:15). R. Huna said in the name of R. Joseph: The Holy One will demand the blood of the pursued from the hand of those who pursued them. When a righteous man pursues a righteous man, "God seeks the one pursued." When a wicked man pursues a wicked one, "God seeks the one pursued." When a wicked man pursues a righteous man, "God seeks the one pursued." Even if you were to turn the matter about and speak of a righteous man pursuing a wicked one, nonetheless "God seeks the one pursued." You can see for yourself that He does so in this world, for Abel was pursued by Cain. "And in His seeking the one pursued," "The Lord looked for Abel and his offering" (Gen. 4:4). Noah was pursued by his generation. Therefore, since "God seeks the one pursued," "Noah found grace in the eyes of the Lord" (Gen. 6:8). Abraham was pursued by Nimrod. Therefore, since "God seeks the one pursued," Scripture says, "Thou art the Lord, the God who didst choose Abram" (Neh. 9:7). Isaac was pursued by the Philistines. Therefore, since "God seeks the one pursued," the Philistines were forced to say, "We saw plainly that the Lord was with thee" (Gen. 26:28). Jacob was pursued by Esau. Therefore, since "God seeks the one pursued," "The Lord hath chosen Jacob unto Himself" (Ps. 135:4). Joseph was pursued by his brothers. Therefore, since "God seeks the one pursued," "The Lord was with Joseph, and made all that he did to prosper" (Gen. 39:2). Moses was pursued by Pharaoh. Therefore, since "God seeks the one pursued," "He said that He would destroy them, but for Moses His chosen" (Ps. 106:23). Israel are pursued by the nations of the earth. Therefore, since "God seeks the one pursued," "The Lord hath chosen thee to be His own treasure" (Deut. 14:2) [XXVII:V.1.A-I].

R. Judah bar R. Simon said in the name of R. Jose bar Nehorai: Since the bullock is pursued by the lion, the sheep by the wolf, the goat by the leopard, the Holy One said: Bring no offering before Me of those that pursue -- only of those that are pursued: "When a bullock, or a sheep, or a goat is brought forth," etc. (Lev. 22:27) [XXVII:V.1.J-K].

5.   [For an offering to Me, I have not wearied thee by asking for other than "a bullock, or a sheep, or a goat." Hence], "O My people, what have I done for thee? And wherein [by contrast] have I wearied thee? Testify [truthfully] concerning Me" (Micah 6:3) -- that is, according to R. Aha, Testify truthfully concerning Me and receive the reward [of vindication]. Do not testify against [Me], your Friend, and thus bring yourselves to scrutiny and account. Then, to prove that God finds ways of vindicating Israel, R. Aha, citing R. Samuel bar Nahman, continued: On the three occasions that the Holy One came to argue with Israel, the nations of the earth were glad. When the Holy One said: "Come now, and let us argue it out, saith the Lord" (Isa. 1:18), the nations of the earth rejoiced, saying, How can these people argue successfully against their Creator? He will now obliterate them from the world. But when the Holy One saw that the nations were glad, He turned His case against Israel into an expression of favor: "Though your sins be as scarlet, they shall be white as snow" (ibid.). Thereupon the nations of the earth were astonished, saying: Is God's statement of His case a proper reproach of Israel? He has come merely to be indulgent with His children. Then again when the Holy One said: "Hear, O ye mountains, the Lord's controversy," etc. (Micah 6:2), the nations of the earth rejoiced, saying: How can these people contend with their Creator? Now He will indeed obliterate them from the world. But when the Holy One saw that the nations of the earth were glad, He turned His case against Israel into [a reproachful reminder of His past] kindnesses to them: "O My people, what have I done for thee, and wherein [by contrast] have I wearied thee? Testify about Me," etc. "Remember now what Balak king of Moab devised," etc. (Micah 6:3, 5). Then again when God said: "The Lord hath also a controversy with Judah," etc. (Hos. 12:3), the nations of the earth were glad, saying: Now He is certain to obliterate them from the world. But when the Holy One saw that the nations of the earth were glad, He turned His case against Israel into a reminder of His having made light [of their past offenses

such as the offense committed by Jacob in his mother's womb]: "In the womb he took his brother by the heel," etc. (Micah 12:4) [XXVII:VI.1-2].

[That God is Israel's Friend is plain from] a parable of a woman who was about to bring charges against her son because he had kicked her when he was in her womb. When the woman saw the judge sitting in judgment and heard him sentencing people to death, she said: If I make known the misconduct of my son to the judge, he will forthwith sentence him also to death. What did she do? She waited until the judge had finished trying the cases before him. After he settled the cases before him, he asked her: What was the misconduct of your son against you? She replied: He kicked me when he was in my womb. He asked her: Has he done anything to you since? She replied: No. He said to her: Then there is no offense in what he did. The nations of the earth were astonished: Is God's judgment in the case of Israel an appropriate one? No! It is a "non sequitur"! He has come merely to be indulgent with His children [XXVII:VI.3].

With reference to God's saying to Israel, "Wherein have I wearied thee?" (Micah 6:3), R. Berechiah told the parable of a king who sent a proclamation of his to a province. What did all the people of the province do? When they received it, they rose to their feet, uncovered their heads, and read it with fear and reverence, with trepidation and awe. Like the king, the Holy One said to Israel: The reading of the Shema is My proclamation. With regard to it, however, I do not put you to any trouble. I do not tell you that you are to read it [in a formal way], standing on your feet and uncovering your heads [in submission to Me], but simply "When thou sittest in thy house, and when thou walkest by the way," etc. (Deut. 6:7) [XXVII:VI.4-5].

Another comment: "Wherein have I wearied thee?" (Micah 6:3). According to R. Judah bar R. Simon, the Holy One said: I have made available ten clean beasts as food for you -- three of these subject to your control, and seven not subject to your control. Subject to your control: "The ox, the sheep, and the goat" (Deut. 14:4); no subject to your control: "The hart, the gazelle, the roebuck, the wild goat, and the ibex," etc. (Deut. 14:5). I have not burdened you. I have not told you to chase over mountains or weary yourselves in fields to fetch Me an offering out of those that are not subject to your control -- only such as are subject to your control, such as are reared at your trough: "When a bullock, a sheep, or a goat is brought forth," etc. (Lev. 22:27) [XXVII:VI.6].

6.   [In further comment on the foregoing verse, Isaiah's words are cited]. "Behold (Hen), ye are meayin, and the making of you meafa" (Isa. 41:24):

behold, you are from nothing ("meayin"), from a foul fluid, and the making of you is no more than haphazard chance: the hundred cries that a woman gives voice to when she sits upon the birth-stool intimate that your chances of death are ninety-nine, your chance of life only one. Yet even when you are "an abomination, one takes you up" (ibid.). Even though the new-born child issues foul and soiled, covered with fluids and blood from the womb of its mother, it is taken up, and all caress it, all kiss it, particularly if it is a male child, [for it is no botched-up idol of wood or stone, but flesh-and-blood wondrously made] [XXVII:VII.1-3].

Another comment: "Hen ye are meayin" (Isa. 41:24). According to R. Berechiah, the word "Hen," [usually translated "behold"], is a Greek word "ena," meaning "one," so that God is saying in the verse "For Me you are the one, the only one of all the nations of the earth," the others in My sight being nothing ("meayin"). Of them Scripture says, "All the nations are as nothing ("ayin") before Him" (Isa. 40:17). The words "And your reward meafa" (Isa. 41:24) mean, according to R. Levi, that all the kindnesses and consolations which I, the Lord, extend to you are your reward for the one cry ("peiyyah") you voiced before Me at Sinai when you said: "All that the Lord hath spoken, we will do, and obey" (Exod. 24:7). "An abomination He takes up from among you" (Isa. 41:24) refers to that abomination of which it is written "They have made them a molten bullock" (Exod. 32:4). It is of that very abomination that I say, Bring an offering unto Me: "A bullock," etc. (Lev. 22:27). [That which was an abomination, I thus take up and hallow [XXVII:VII.4].

7.   "With their 'wickedness' they make glad the King, for even in their act of denial [such as the making of the calf they intended no more than the representation of one of God's heavenly] princes" (Hos. 7:3). Why did Scripture deem it necessary to set the bullock as first among all the offerings? R. Levi answered this question with a parable of a noble lady. An evil rumor had gone forth, linking her with one of the notables in the kingdom, but when the king investigated the reports, he found no substance in them. What did he do? He prepared a great feast and put the notable at the head of the guests at the table. All this for what reason? To make it known that the king had investigated the reports and found no substance in them. So, too, because the nations of the earth were taunting Israel, saying to them: "You made the calf," the Holy One investigated the reports and found no substance in them. Therefore, the bullock was put at the head of the list of offerings: "A bullock, a sheep, or a goat," etc. (Lev. 22:27) [XXVII:VIII.1].

8.   [Because of the Holy One's investigation], said R. Huna and R. Idi in the name of R. Samuel bar Nahman, the children of Israel were exonerated from

blame for that unspeakable deed. Had Israel made the calf, one would have expected them to say, "This is our God, O Israel." It was, however, the [insincere] proselytes who had come up from Egypt with them -- it was they who made the calf and mocked Israel, "This is thy God, O Israel" (Exod. 32:4). R. Judah bar R. Simon said: It is written "The ox knoweth his owner, and the ass his master's crib, but Israel doth not know" (Isa. 1:3). Did they not know their Master? Of course they did. But they came to take God for granted. Likewise, "My people is foolish, they know Me not" (Jer. 4:22). Did they not know who their Master was? Of course, they did. But they came to take Me for granted. Likewise, "She did not know that it was I that gave her the corn," etc. (Hos. 2:10). Did she not know that it was I? Of course, she did. But she came to take Me for granted [XXVII:VIII.2].

9.   [Why "A bullock, or a sheep, or a goat for offerings]? A bullock" (Lev. 22:27) through the merit of Abraham: "Abraham ran unto the her, and fetched a young bull" (Gen. 18:7). "A ram" -- a sheep, through the merit of Isaac: "Abraham... looked, and behold behind him a ram caught in the thicked by his horns," etc. (Gen. 22:13). "A goat," through the merit of Jacob: "Go now to the flock, and fetch me from thence two good kids of the goats" (Gen. 27:9). Why did Rebekah say "good?" Because she meant, explained R. Berechiah in the name of R. Helbo, they will be good for you, [O Jacob], and good for your children -- good for you since through them you will receive [your father's] blessings; and good for your children, for, because of the offering of he-goats, atonement will be made for your children on Atonement Day: "On this day shall atonement be made for you," etc. (Lev. 16:30) [XXVII:IX.1].

10.   In comment on the verse "It shall be seven days under the dam" (Lev. 22:27), R. Joshua of Siknin told, in the name of R. Levi, the parable of a king who entered a province and issued a decree, saying: "Let no visitors here attend upon me until they shall have first attended upon my queen." So, too, the Holy One said to Israel: My children, you shall not bring an offering unto Me until a Sabbath day, [the queen of days], shall have passed over it. And since it is required that the youngling be a period of seven days under its dam, a Sabbath must fall within this period, just as a Sabbath must intervene in the period before a circumcision can take place. As R. Isaac observed: The ordinance with regard to man and the ordinance with regard to beast are alike [in the time intervals they specify]. The ordinance with regard to man: "In the eighth day the flesh of his foreskin shall be circumcised" (Lev. 12:3); and the ordinance with regard to beast: "From the eighth day and thenceforth it may be accepted for an offering made by fire unto the Lord" (Lev. 22:27) [XXVII:IX.2].

11. "And whether it be cow or ewe, ye shall not kill it and its young both in one day" (Lev. 22:28). R. Berechiah said in the name of R. Levi: "The righteous regardeth the life of his beast" (Prov. 12:10), the righteous being the Holy One who wrote in His Torah "Thou shalt not take the dam with the young" (Deut. 22:6). [The wicked, however, kill mothers and their children on the same day, as is said] "But mothers also -- the wicked being cruel" (Prov. 12:10). Such a wicked one was Sennacherib, at whose orders "The mother was dashed in pieces with her children" (Hos. 10:14) [XXVII:XL1].

Another comment: "The righteous regardeth the life of his beast" (Prov. 12:10), the righteous being the Holy One who wrote in His Torah "Whether it be cow or ewe, ye shall not kill it and its young both in one day" (Lev. 22:28). "But the tender mercies of the wicked are cruel" (Prov. 12:10): such was the wicked Haman, at whose orders "Letters... were sent... to destroy, to slay, and to cause to perish all Jews, both young and old, little children and women, in one day" (Esther 3:13) [XXVII:XL2].

R. Levi said: Woe to the wicked who busy themselves with evil counsel against Israel, each one boasting "My counsel is better than your counsel." Esau said: Cain was a fool, for he slew his brother while his father was still alive. Did not Cain know that his father would be fruitful and multiply? I shall not act so unknowingly: "Let the days of mourning for my father be at hand, and then I will slay my brother Jacob" (Gen. 27:41). Pharaoh said: Esau was a fool in saying, Let the days of mourning for my father be at hand," etc. Did he not know that while his father was still alive, his brother [Jacob] would be fruitful and would multiply? I shall not act as unknowingly as Esau. Under the very birth-stools of Israelites' mothers, while the male infants are still tiny things, I shall strangle them. At once Pharaoh charged his people: ["Ye shall look upon the birth-stool: if it be a son, ye shall kill him," and then charged his people]: "Every son that is born ye shall cast into the river" (Exod. 1:16, 22). Haman said, Pharaoh was a fool when he charged his people: "Every son that is born ye shall cast into the river, and every daughter ye shall save alive" (ibid.). Did he not know that the daughters would marry, would be fruitful, and would multiply? I shall not act as unknowingly as Pharaoh. I shall "destroy, slay, and cause to perish all Jews, both young and old, little children and women" (Esther 3:13). R. Levi went on: At the time of the Messiah's coming Gog and Magog will likewise say: Fools were all the former who busied themselves with evil counsel against Israel. Did they not know that Israel have their Partisan in heaven? We shall not act as unknowingly as all the other enemies of Israel -- first, we will make war against their Partisan, and then we shall turn upon Israel. Hence it is said "The kings of the earth set themselves, and the rulers take counsel together against the Lord and against His anointed"

(Ps. 2:2). But the Holy One will say to Gog and Magog: Oh ye wicked, do you
set yourselves to make war against Me? As ye live, I Myself will wage war
against you. Accordingly, Scripture: "[At first,] the Lord will go forth merely
as a mighty man, a man of war, even as He stirs up envy [of Israel in Gog and
Magog], whilst, [like a mortal], He will go forth and fight against the nations,
even as He fought in the day of battle" [at the Red Sea] (Zech. 14:3)
[XXVII:XL3-4]

12.   "And when ye sacrifice a sacrifice of thanksgiving unto the Lord -- you
will continue to offer it [even in the time-to-come] when you have all that
delights you" (Lev. 22:29). R. Phinehas, R. Levi, and R. Johanan citing R.
Mehanem of Gallia said: In the time-to-come all offerings will cease, except
the thank offering which will never cease. All prayers will cease, except the
prayer of thanksgiving which will never cease. Hence it is written of the
time-to-come "The voice of joy and the voice of gladness, the voice of the
bridegroom and the voice of the bride, the voice of them that say: 'Give
thanks to the Lord of hosts, for He is good, for His mercy endureth for ever'"
(Jer. 33:11): these are prayers of thanksgiving; "and of them that bring
offerings of thanksgiving into the house of the Lord" (ibid.): these are thank
offerings. So, too, David said: "Thy vows are upon me, O God" (Ps. 56:13). He
did not go on to say, "I will render a thank offering" but "I will render thank
offerings unto Thee" (ibid.), a statement which intimates that both thanksgiving and thank offering will be rendered [in the time-to-come] [XXVII:XII.1].

XXVII:I

1.   A.   "When a bull or sheep [or goat is born, it shall remain seven days
            with its mother; and from the eighth day on it shall be acceptable
            as an offering by fire to the Lord]" (Lev. 22:27).

      B.   "Your righteousness is like the mountains of God, [your judgments
            are like the great deep; man and beast you save, O Lord]" (Ps. 36:6).

      C.   R. Ishmael and R. Aqiba:

      D.   R. Ishmael says, "With the righteous, who carry out the Torah,
            which was given 'from the mountains of God' the Holy One, blessed
            be he, does righteousness 'like the mountains of God.'

      E.   "But with the wicked, who do not carry out the Torah, which was
            given 'from the mountains of God,' the Holy One, blessed be he,
            seeks a strict accounting, unto 'the great deep.'

      F.   "That is in line with the following verse of Scripture: 'Your
            judgments are like the great deep' (Ps. 36:6)."

      G.   R. Aqiba says, "All the same are these and those: the Holy One,
            blessed be he, seeks a strict accounting with [all of] them in accord
            with strict justice.

H. "He seeks a strict accounting with the righteous, collecting from them the few bad deeds that they did in this world, in order to pay them an abundant reward in the world to come.

I. "And he affords prosperity to the wicked and gives them a full reward for the minor religious duties that they successfully accomplished in this world, in order to exact a full penalty from them in the world to come."

2. A. R. Meir says, "The righteous are comparable to their abode [like the mountains of God] and the wicked are comparable to their dwelling [like the great deep].

B. "The righteous are comparable to their abode: 'I will feed them in a good pasture, and upon the high mountains of Israel will be their fold' (Ez. 34:14).

C. "The wicked are comparable to their abode: 'In the day when he went down to the netherworld, [I caused the deep to mourn and cover itself for him]' (Ez. 31:15)."

D. R. Judah b. Rabbi said, "'I caused to mourn (H'BLTY)' is written, 'I brought down (HWBLTY).'

E. "You should notice that they do not make a cover for a bowl of silver, gold, copper, iron, tin or lead [Num. 31:22] but only [for one] of clay, for it is a material of the same sort [as the bowl].

F. "So said the Holy One, blessed be he, 'Gehenna is dark, and the wicked are dark, and the deep is dark. Let the dark come and cover the dark in the dark,'

G. "as it is said, 'For [the wicked] comes in vanity and departs in darkness and his name is covered with darkness' (Qoh 6:4)."

3. A. R. Jonathan in the name of R. Josiah would rearrange the elements of this verse: "'Your righteousness over your judgments [prevails] like the mountains of God over the great deep.'

B. "Just as these mountains conquer the great deep, so that it may not rise up and flood the entire world, so the deeds of the righteous overcome punishment, keeping it from spreading over the world.

C. "Just as these mountains have no end, so the reward of the righteous in the world to come will know no end.

D. "'Your judgments are like the great deep' (Ps. 36:6):

E. "Just as there is no searching out the great deep, so there is no searching out the punishment that is coming upon the wicked in the age to come."

4. A. Another interpretation: "Your righteousness is like the mountains of God": Just as these mountains are sown and bring forth fruit, so the deeds of the righteous bring forth fruit.

B.   That is in line with the following verse of Scripture: "Tell the righteous that is shall be well with them, for they shall eat the fruit of their deeds" (Is. 3:10).

C.   "Your judgments are like the great deep": Just as the great deep is not sown and does not bring forth fruit, so the deeds of the wicked do not bear fruit.

D.   That is in line with the following verse of Scripture: "Woe to the wicked. It shall be ill with him, for what his hands have done shall be done to him" (Is. 3:11).

5.   A.   Another interpretation: "Your righteousness is like the mountains of God": Just as the mountains are [readily] visible, so the deeds of the righteous are [readily] visible.

B.   That is in line with the following verse of Scripture: "May they fear you in the sun" (Ps. 72:5).

C.   "Your judgments are like the great deep": Just as the deep is hidden [from view], so the deeds of the wicked are hidden [from view].

D.   That is in line with the following verse of Scripture: "Whose deeds are in the dark" (Is. 29:15).

6.   A.   Another interpretation: "Your righteousness is like the mountains of God":

B.   Said R. Judah b. R. Simon, "The act of righteousness which you did with Noah in the ark is 'like the mountains of God.'

C.   "That is in line with the following verse of Scripture: 'And the ark rested...on the mountains of Ararat' (Gen. 8:4).

D.   "'Your judgments are like the great deep': The judgments which you meted out to his generation you exacted from them even to the great deep.

E.   "That is in line with the following verse of Scripture: 'And on that day the springs of the great deep broke open' (Gen. 7:11).

F.   "And not only so, but, when you remembered him, it was not him alone that you remembered, but him and everyone that was with him in the ark.

G.   "That is in line with the following verse of Scripture: 'And God remembered Noah and all the living creatures' (Gen. 8:1)."

7.   A.   Another interpretation: "Your righteousness is like the mountains of God":

B.   R. Joshua b. Hananiah went to Rome. There he saw marble pillars covered with tapestries, so that in the hot weather they should not crack from expansion and in the cold weather they should not crack from contraction..

C.   When he went out, he met a poor man, with a mat of reeds underneath him and a mat of reeds on top of him.

D.   Concerning the marble pillars he recited the following verse of Scripture: "Your righteousness is like the mountains of God."

E.   He said, "Where you give, you give lavishly."

F.   Concerning the poor man he recited this verse: "Your judgments are like the great deep."

G.   "Where you smite, you pay close attention to every little detail."

8.   A.   A tale: Alexander of Macedonia went to the king of Kasia, beyond the mountains of darkness. He came to a certain town, called Cartagena, and it was populated entirely by women.

B.   They came out before him and said to him, "If you make war on us and conquer us, word will go out about you in the world that you destroyed a town of women. But if we do battle with you and conquer you, word will go forth about you in the world that you made war on women and they beat you. And you'll never be able to hold up your head again among kings."

C.   At that moment he turned his face away and left. After he went away, he wrote on the door of the gate of the city, saying, "I, Alexander the Macedonia, a king, was a fool until I came to the town called Cartagena, and I learned wisdom from women."

D.   He came to another town, and it was called Africa. They came out and greeted him with golden apples, golden pomegranates, and golden bread.

E.   He said, "Is this what you eat in your country?"

F.   They said to him, "And is it not this way in your country, that you have come here?"

G.   He said to them, "It is not your wealth that I have come to see, but it is your justice that I have come to see."

H.   While they were standing there, two men came before the king for justice.

I.   This one kept himself far from thievery, and so did that. One of them said, "I bought a carob tree from this man. I dug it open and found a jewel in it. I said to him, 'Take your jewel. I bought a carob. A jewel I didn't buy.'"

J.   The other said, "When I sold the carob to that man, I sold him the carob tree and everything that is in it."

K.   The king called one of them and said to him, "Do you have a male child?"

L.   He said to him, "Yes."

M.   The king called the other and said to him, "Do you have a daughter?"

N.   He said to him, "Yes."

O.   Then the king said to them, "Let this one marry that one, and let the two of them enjoy the jewel."

P.   Alexander of Macedonia began to express surprise.

Q.   He said to him, "Why are you surprised? Did I not give a good judgment."

R.   He said to him, "Yes, you did."

S.   He said to him, "If this case had come to court in your country, how would you have judged it?"

T.   He said to him, "We should have cut off the head of this party and cut off the head of that party, and the jewel would have passed into the possession of the crown."

U.   He said to him, "Does rain fall on you?"

V.   He said to him, "Yes."

W.   "And does the sun rise for you?"

X.   He said to him, "Yes."

Y.   He said to him, "Are there small cattle in your country?"

Z.   He said to him, "Yes."

AA. "Woe to you! It is on account of the merit of the small cattle that you are saved."

BB. That is in line with the following verse of Scripture: "Man and beast you save, O Lord" (Ps. 36:7).

CC. "Man on account of the merit of the beast do you save, O Lord."

DD. "Man because of beast you save O Lord."

9. A.   So did the Israelites say before the Holy One, blessed be he: "Lord of the world, we are mere men. Save us like a beast, for we are drawn after you."

B.   That is in line with the following verse of Scripture: "Draw me, we will run after you" (Song of Songs 1:4).

C.   "And whither are we drawn after you? To the Garden of Eden."

D.   For it is written, "They feast on the abundance of your house, and you give them drink from the river of your delights" (Ps. 36:9).

E.   Said R. Eleazar b. R. Menahem, "'Your delight' is not written here, but rather, 'Your delights.' On the basis of that fact we may conclude that every righteous person has an Eden unto himself."

10. A.   Said R. Isaac, "Judgment is stated with regard to man, and judgment is stated with regard to beast.

B.   "The judgment stated with regard to a man: 'And on the eighth day, he shall be circumcised' (Lev. 12:3).

C.   "And the judgment stated with regard to the beast: 'When a bull or sheep or goat is born, it shall remain seven days [with its mother]; and from the eighth day on, it shall be acceptable as an offering by fire to the Lord' (Lev. 22:26)."

The intersecting verse is worked out in reference to the righteous, compared to the mountains of God, and the wicked -- those subject to judgment -- compared to the great deep. This general approach links Nos. 1-7. Once people read the verse in this way, the range of conclusions they propose is fairly standard. There are a few secondary developments, but in the main a single pattern is followed, e.g., at Nos. 3-6. The only connection I can see between the Alexander-fables and the intersecting verse is the reference to the "mountains of darkness." No. 9 is added because of the conclusion of No. 8. No. 10, however, is entirely germane to our base-verse. But it is tacked on, since the connection to the preceding is tenuous. It too relies on Ps. 36:7. But it has no relationship to the earlier reading of the verse.

XXVII:II

1. A.   "Who has given me anything beforehand, that I should repay him? [Whatever is under the whole heaven is mine]" (Job 41:11 [Heb. 41:3]).

   B.   R. Tanhuma interpreted the verse to speak of a bachelor who was living in a town, and who gave wages for scribes and Mishnah-teachers: "Said the Holy One, blessed be he, 'It is my responsibility to pay him back for his goodness and to give him a male child.'

   C.   "That is in line with the following verse of Scripture: '[He who is kind to the poor lends to the Lord], and he will repay him for his deed' (Prov. 19:17)."

2. A.   Said R. Jeremiah b. Eleazar, "An echo is going to proclaim on the tops of the mountains, saying," 'Whoever has worked with God' -- whoever has worked with God shall come and collect his reward.'

   B.   "'That is in line with the following verse of Scripture: 'In time it will be said to Jacob and to Israel, 'What has God worked' (Num. 23:23).

   C.   "Now let him come and collect his reward."

   D.   "And the Holy Spirit says, 'Who has given me anything beforehand? I shall repay him' (Job. 41:11).

   E.   "Who praised me before I gave him a soul, who was circumcised in my name before I gave him a male child, who made a parapet for me before I gave him a roof, who made a mezuzah for me before I gave him a house, who made a sukkah for me before I gave him a place [for it], who made a lulab for me before I gave him money, who made show-fringes for me before I gave him a cloak, who separated peah for me before I gave him a field, who separated heave-offering for me and tithe before I gave him a harvest, who separated dough-offering for me before I gave him dough, who separated an offering for me before I gave him a beast!

   F.   "When a bull or a sheep or a goat [is born]" (Lev. 22:26).

One who does his religious duties before he is obligated to do so is praised, in line with the cited verse of Job. That is the point of No. 1, and it is made still more explicit at No. 2. But one can do religious duties only if through God's grace he gets the opportunity: "Whatever is under the whole heaven is mine," so 2:E. The intersecting verse recovers the base-verse because the latter speaks of when a bull or sheep is born -- that is, by God's grace. Only then can one make an offering (Margulies).

XXVII:III

1.　A.　R. Jacob b. R. Zabedi in the name of R. Abbahu opened [discourse by citing the following verse:] "'And it shall never again be the reliance of the house of Israel, recalling their iniquity, [when they turn to them for aid. Then they will know that I am the Lord God}' (Ez. 29:16).

　　B.　"It is written, 'Above him stood the seraphim: [each had six wings, with two he covered his face, and with two he covered his feet, and with two he flew}' (Is. 6:2).

　　C.　"'With two he flew' -- singing praises.

　　D.　"'With two he covered his face' -- so as not to gaze upon the Presence of God.

　　E.　"'And with two he covered his feet' -- so as not to let them be seen by the face of the Presence of God.

　　F.　"For it is written, 'And the soles of their feet were like the sole of a calf's foot' (Ez. 1:6).

　　G.　"And it is written, 'They made for themselves a molten calf' (Ex. 32:8).

　　H.　"So [in covering their feet, they avoided calling to mind the molten calf,] in accord with the verse, 'And it shall never again be the reliance of the house of Israel, recalling their iniquity' (Ez. 29:16)."

2.　A.　There we have learned in the Mishnah [M. R.H. 3:2]: "All [horns] are suitable except for that of a cow."

　　B.　Why except for that of the cow? Because it is the horn of a calf.

　　C.　And it is written, "They made for themselves a molten calf" (Ex. 32:8).

　　D.　So [in not using the horn of a cow, they avoid calling to mind the molten calf, in accord with the verse] "And it shall never again be the reliance of the house of Israel, recalling their iniquity" (Ez. 29:16).

3.　A.　It has been taught: On what account does a wife accused of infidelity not drink from a cup used by another woman [the water that brings a curse}? So that people should not say, "Out of this cup another woman drank the water and died."

B.   This is in line with the verse of Scripture: "And it shall never again be the reliance of the house of Israel, recalling their iniquity" (Ez. 29:16).

4.   A.   There we have learned: "And you shall kill the woman and the beast [that lay with her]" (Lev. 20:16). If a human being has sinned, what sin did the beast commit?

B.   But since through that beast a disaster has come upon a human being, the Torah has said that it should be stoned.

C.   Another consideration: That a beast should not walk through the market and people should say, "That is the beast on account of which so-and-so was stoned to death."

D.   This is in line with the verse of Scripture: "And it shall never again be the reliance of the house of Israel, recalling their iniquity" (Ez. 29:16).

5.   A.   And so too here: "When a bull or a sheep or a goat is born" (Lev. 22:27).

B.   Now is it born as a bull and not as a calf? But because it is said, "They made for themselves a molten calf," therefore the Scripture refers to it as a bull and not as a calf: "A bull, a sheep, a goat."

Here is a classic example of the systematic exposition of an intersecting verse, leading, at the climax, to a new insight into the meaning of the base-verse. The same point is made again and again, so that, when we reach the base-verse, we readily grasp the pertinence of the intersecting verse. That diverse materials have been assembled is self-evident. What is striking is how they have been put together to make a single, entirely cogent point, five times over and fully spelled out.

XXVII:IV

1.   A.   "That which is already has been, [that which is to be already has been. God seeks that which is pursued]" (Qoh. 3:15).

B.   R. Judah and R. Nehemiah:

C.   R. Judah says, "If someone should say to you that had the first Adam not sinned and eaten from that tree, he would have lived and endured even to this very day, tell him, 'It already has been.' Elijah lives and endures forever.

D.   "'That which is to be already has been': If someone should tell to you, it is possible that the Holy One, blessed be he, in the future is going to resurrect the dead, say to him, 'It already has been.' He has already resurrected the dead through Elijah, Elisha, and Ezekiel in the valley of Dura."

E.   R. Nehemiah says, "If someone should say to you that it is possible that to begin with the world was entirely made up of water in water, say to him, 'It already has been,' for the ocean is full of diverse water.

F. "'That which is to be already has been:' If someone should say to you, the Holy One, blessed be he, is going to dry [the sea] up, say to him, 'It already has been.' 'And the children of Israel walked on dry land through the sea' (Ex. 15:19)."

2. A. R. Aha in the name of R. Simeon b. Halapta: "Whatever the Holy One, blessed be he, is destined to do in the age to come already has he shown to [humanity] in this world.

B. "That he is going to resurrect the dead: he has already resurrected the dead through Elijah, Elisha, and Ezekiel.

C. "That he is going to bring [people] through water on to dry land: 'When you pass through water, I am with you' (Is. 43:2). He has already brought Israel through [water] with Moses: 'And the children of Israel walked on dry land through the sea' (Ex. 15:19).

D. "'And through rivers they shall not overwhelm you' (Is. 43:2). This he has already accomplished through Joshua: 'On dry land the Israelites crossed the Jordan' (Josh. 4:22).

E. "'When you walk through fire you shall not be burned' (Is. 43:2). This he has already accomplished through Hananiah, Mishael and Azariah.

F. "'And the flame shall not consume you' (Is. 43:2). This he has already accomplished: '[The fire had not had any power over the bodies of those men...] no smell of fire had come upon them' (Dan. 3:27).

G. "That God will sweeten bitter water, he has already accomplished through Moses: 'The Lord showed him a tree, and he threw it into the water, and the water became sweet' (Ex. 15:25).

H. "That God will sweeten what is bitter through something bitter, he has already accomplished through Elisha: 'Then he went to the spring of water and threw salt into it and said, Thus says the Lord, I have made this water wholesome' (2 Kgs. 2:21).

I. "That God blesses what is little [and makes it much], he already has accomplished through Elijah and Elisha: 'For thus says the Lord, the God of Israel, The jar of meal shall not be spent, and the cruse of oil shall not fail, [until the day that the Lord sends rain upon the earth] (1 Kgs. 17:14).

J. "That God visits barren women, he has already accomplished through Sarah, Rebecca, Rachel, and Hannah.

K. "'The wolf and the lamb will pasture together,' (Is. 65:25), he has already accomplished through Hezekiah: 'The wolf shall dwell with the lamb' (Is. 11:6).

L.   "'And kings will be your tutor' (Is. 49:23) he has already accomplished through Daniel: 'Then the king Nebuchadnezzer fell upon
his face and worshipped Daniel' (Dan. 2:46).

The intersecting verse is thoroughly explained through Scriptural examples, all of
which make the point that whatever people believe will happen already has happened. The
rather extensive illustration of that proposition occupies the entire passage. Margulies'
text, which I have translated, greatly differs from the standard printed one, as he explains
ad loc. The base-verse is reached in the next passage.

XXVII:V

1.   A.   "God seeks what has been driven away" (Qoh. 3:15).
      B.   R. Huna in the name of R. Joseph said, "It is always the case that
            'God seeks what has been driven away' [favoring the victim].
      C.   "You find when a righteous man pursues a righteous man, 'God
            seeks what has been driven away.'
      D.   "'When a wicked man pursues a wicked man, 'God seeks what has
            been driven away.'
      E.   "All the more so when a wicked man pursues a righteous man, 'God
            seeks what has been driven away.'
      F.   "[The same principle applies] even when you come around to a case
            in which a righteous man pursues a wicked man, 'God seeks what
            has been driven away.'"

2.   A.   R. Yose b. R. Yudan in the name of R. Yose b. R. Nehorai says, "It
            is always the case that the Holy One, blessed be he, demands an
            accounting for the blood of those who have been pursued from the
            hand of the pursuer.
      B.   "Abel was pursued by Cain, and God sought [an accounting for] the
            pursued: 'And the Lord looked [favorably] upon Abel and his
            meal-offering' (Gen. 4:4).
      C.   "Noah was pursued by his generation, and God sought [an account-
            ing for] the pursued: 'You and all your household shall come into
            the ark' (Gen. 7:1). And it says, 'For this is like the days of Noah
            to me, as I swore [that the waters of Noah should no more go over
            the earth]' (Is. 54:9).
      D.   "Abraham was pursued by Nimrod, 'and God seeks what has been
            driven away:' 'You are the Lord, the God who chose Abram and
            brought him out of Ur' (Neh. 9:7).
      E.   "Isaac was pursued by Ishmael, 'and God seeks what has been driven
            away:' 'For through Isaac will seed be called for you' (Gen. 21:12).
      F.   "Jacob was pursued by Esau, 'and God seeks what has been driven
            away:' 'For the Lord has chosen Jacob, Israel for his prized
            possession' (Ps. 135:4).

G.   "Moses was pursued by Pharaoh, 'and God seeks what has been driven away:' 'Had not Moses His chosen stood in the breach before Him' (Ps. 106:23).

H.   "David was pursued by Saul, 'and God seeks what has been driven away:' 'And he chose David, his servant' (Ps. 78:70).

I.   "Israel was pursued by the nations, 'and God seeks what has been driven away:' 'And you has the Lord chosen to be a people to him' (Deut. 14:2).

J.   "And the rule applies also to the matter of offerings. A bull is pursued by a lion, a sheep is pursued by a wolf, a goat is pursued by a leopard.

K.   "Therefore the Holy One, blessed be he, has said, 'Do not make offerings before me from those animals that pursue, but from those that are pursued: 'When a bull, a sheep, or a goat is born' (Lev. 22:27)."

Now the intersecting verse leads right back to the base-verse and makes its point in a powerful way. God favors the persecuted over the persecuter, the pursued over the pursuer. This point is made in an abstract way at No. 1, and then through a review of the sacred history of Israel at No. 2. The intent of the whole is established at the outset, so we have a unitary composition. Still, 2.A-C speak of an accounting for blood, and 2.D-K resort to slightly different rhetoric.

XXVII:VI

1.   A.   "O my people, what have I done to you, in what have I wearied you? Testify against me" (Mic. 6:3).

     B.   Said R. Aha, "'Testify against me' and receive a reward, but 'Do not bear false witness' (Ex. 20:13) and face a settlement of accounts in the age to come.'"

2.   A.   Said R. Samuel b. R. Nahman, "On three occasions the Holy One, blessed be he, came to engage in argument with Israel, and the nations of the world rejoiced, saying, 'Can these ever [dare] engage in an argument with their creator? Now he will wipe them out of the world.'

     B.   "One was when he said to them, 'Come, and let us reason together, says the Lord' (Is. 1:18). When the Holy One, blessed be he, saw that the nations of the world were rejoicing, he turned the matter to [Israel's] advantage: 'If your sins are as scarlet, they shall be white as snow' (Is. 1:18).

     C.   "Then the nations of the world were astonished, and said, 'This is repentance, and this is rebuke? He has planned only to amuse himself with his children.'

D. "[A second time was] when he said to them, 'Hear, you mountains, the controversy of the Lord' (Mic. 6:2), the nations of the world rejoiced, saying, 'How can these ever [dare] engage in an argument with their creator? Now he will wipe them out of the world.'

E. "When the Holy One, blessed be he, saw that the nations of the world were rejoicing, he turned the matter to [Israel's] advantage: 'O my people, what have I done to you? In what have I wearied you? Testify against me' (Mic. 6:3). 'Remember what Balak king of Moab devised' (Mic. 6:5).

F. "Then the nations of the world were astonished, saying, 'This is repentence, and this is rebuke, one following the other?' He has planned only to amuse himself with his children.'

G. "[A third time was] when he said to them, 'The Lord has an indictment against Judah, and will punish Jacob according to his ways' (Hos. 12:2), the nations of the world rejoiced, saying, 'How can these ever [dare] engage in an argument with their creator? Now he will wipe them out of the world.'

H. "When the Holy One, blessed be he, saw that the nations of the world were rejoicing, he turned the matter to [Israel's] advantage. That is in line with the following verse of Scripture: 'In the womb he [Jacob = Israel] took his brother [Esau = other nations] by the heel [and in his manhood he strove with God. He strove with the angel and prevailed, he wept and sought his favor]' (Hos. 12:3-4)."

3. A. Said R. Yudan b. R. Simeon, "The matter may be compared to a widow who was complaining to a judge about her son. When she saw that the judge was in session and handing out sentences of punishment by fire, pitch, and lashes, she said, 'If I report the bad conduct of my son to that judge, he will kill him now.' She waited until he was finished. When he had finished, he said to her, 'Madam, this son of yours, how has he behaved badly toward you?'

B. "She said to him, 'My lord, when he was in my womb, he kicked me.'

C. "He said to her, 'Now has he done anything wrong to you?'

D. "She said to him, 'No.'

E. "He said to her, 'Go your way, there is nothing wrong in the matter [that you report].

F. "So, when the Holy One, blessed be he, saw that the nations of the world were rejoicing, he turned the matter to [Israel's] advantage:

G. "'In the womb he took his brother by the heel' (Mic. 12:3).

H. "Then the nations of the world were astonished, saying, 'This is repentence and this is rebuke, one following the other? He has planned only to amuse himself with his children.'"

4.   A.   "And how have I wearied you?" (Mic. 6:3).

     B.   Said R. Berekhiah, "The matter may be compared to the case of a king, who sent three messengers to a certain city, and the inhabitants of the city stood up before them and paid them service in awe, trembling, fear, and trepidation.

     C.   "So the Holy One, blessed be he, said to Israel, 'I sent you three messengers, Moses, Aaron, and Miriam.

     D.   "'Now did they eat any of your food? Did they drink any of your drink? Did they impose upon you in any way? Is it not through their merit that you are maintained?

     E.   "'The mana was through the merit of Moses, the well through the merit of Miriam, and the clouds of glory through the merit of Aaron.'"

5.   A.   Said R. Isaac, "The matter may be compared to the case of a king who sent his proclamation to a city. What did the inhabitants of the city do? They stood up and bared their heads and read the proclamation in awe, trembling, fear, and trepidation.

     B.   "So the Holy One, blessed be he, said to Israel, 'As to the proclamation of the Shema and the proclamation of mine [the Torah] [that I sent you], I did not impose on you by telling you to read [the Shema] either standing on your feet or having bared your heads, but only [at your convenience:] 'When you sit in your house and when you walk by the way' (Deut. 6:7)."

6.   A.   Said R. Judah b. R. Simon, "Said the Holy One, blessed be he, 'I handed ten beasts to you, three in your domain, and seven not in your domain.

     B.   "'The three in your domain: "the ox, sheep, and the goat" (Deut. 14:4).

     C.   "'The seven not in your domain: "the hart, gazelle, roebuck, wild goat, pygarg, antelope, and mountain sheep!" (Deut. 14:5).

     D.   "'I did not trouble you, and I did not tell you to go up into the mountains and to tire yourselves in the fields to bring me an offering of those beasts that are not within your domain.

     E.   "'I asked only for those that are in your domain, the ones that grow at your crib: "Ox, sheep or goat" (Lev. 22:27).'"

The systematic exposition of the intersecting verse, Mic. 6:3, establishes a basic point, that God really does not trouble Israel, which leads us to the intersecting verse as climactic evidence of that point. God does not demand that the Israelites go to a great deal of trouble to find for the sacrifices animals not readily at hand. But before we reach that simple point, we work through a somewhat more complicated message. Whenever God begins a process of inquiry against Israel, the reaction of the nations of the world is such as to warn God off and to make him turn the process into an affirmation of God's love for Israel. This point comes in a number of versions, all of them following a single pattern of rhetoric and argument. There is a secondary motif, that, as Micah says, God does not impose inconvenience on Israel.

XXVII:VII

1. A. R. Levi opened [discourse by citing the following verse of Scripture:] "'Behold you are nothing, and your work is nought; [an abomination is he who chooses you]' (Is. 41:24).

    B. "'Nothing' -- from nill, from a foul secretion.

    C. "'Nought' ($M'P^C$) -- From the hundred ($M'H$) outcries (P^CYWT) that a woman cries out when she is sitting on the birth-stool, ninety nine are for death, and one for life."

2. A. It has been taught: She bears three names, "the revived," "the pledged," and "the broken."

    B. "The revived," because she died and was brought back to life.

    C. "The pledged," because she had been pledged to death, in line with the following verse of Scripture: "If you take your neighbor's garment as a pledge."

    D. "The broken," because she was broken unto death.

3. A. "An abomination is he who chooses you" (Is. 41:24).

    B. Even though the infant emerges from his mother's belly filthy and soiled, covered with secretions and blood, everybody caresses and kisses him.

4. A. Another interpretation: "Behold, you are nothing" (Is. 41:24):

    B. Said R. Berekhiah, "The word 'behold' (HN) is Greek, 'hina,' meaning one.

    C. "Said the Holy One, blessed be he, 'I have only one nation among the nations of the world.'"

    D. "Nothing:" This refers to those about which it is written, "The nations are nothing before Him" (Is. 40:17).

    E. "And your work is nought" (Is. 41:24):

    F. Said R. Levi, "All the good and comforting works that the Holy One, blessed be he, is going to do for Israel are only on account of a single exclamation (P^CYYH) which you made before Me at Sinai, when you said, 'Everything that the Lord has said we shall do and we shall hear' (Ex. 24:7)."

    G. "An abomination is he who chooses you" (Is. 41:24):

    H. That abomination concerning which it is written, "They made for themselves a molten calf" (Ex. 22:8), is the same abomination [that] they shall bring to me as an offering:

    I. "Bull or sheep or goat" (Lev. 22:27).

The intersecting verse, Is. 41:24, bears two distinct interpretations. In the first --
Nos. 1-3 -- the verse is made to refer to the condition of the new-born child. In the
second, No. 4, it refers to Israel, its redemption and God's forgiveness of Israel's sin with
the golden calf. The stress then is on the sacrificial system as a mode of overcoming and
expiating the idolatry of the people in the wilderness. The issue of the golden calf,
already familiar, evidently strikes the exegetes as important in explaining the verse at
hand. We shall see further instances of the same concern.

XXVII:VIII

1. A. "By their wickedness they make the king glad, [and the princes by
their adultery]' (Hos. 7:3).

   B. Now why was the bull recognized as the first of all of the offerings
['"Bull, sheep, goat" (Lev. 22:27)]?

   C. Said R. Levi, "The matter may be compared to the case of a
high-born lady who got a bad name on account of [alleged adultery
with] one of the lords of the state.

   D. "The king looked into the matter and found nothing. What did the
king do? He made a banquet and sat the [accused] man at the head
of the guests.

   E. "Why so? To show that the king had looked into the matter and
found nothing.

   F. "So the nations of the world taunt Israel and say to them, 'You
made the golden calf!'

   G. "The Holy One, blessed be he, looked into the matter and found
nothing. Accordingly, the bull was made the first among all the
offerings: 'Bull, sheep, goat' (Lev. 22:27)."

2. A. R. Huna, R. Idi in the name of R. Samuel b. R. Nahman: "The
[true] Israelites were saved from that act. For if the Israelites had
themselves made the calf, they ought to have said, 'These are our
gods, O Israel.' It was the proselytes who came up with Israel from
Egypt [who made the calf]: 'And also a mixed multitude came up
with them' (Ex. 12:38).

   B. "They are the ones who made the calf. They taunted them, saying
to them, 'These are your gods, O Israel' (Ex. 32:8)."

3. A. Said R. Judah b. R. Simon, "It is written, 'An ox knows its owner,
and an ass its master's crib, but Israel does not know' (Is. 1:3).

   B. "Did they really not know? Rather, they trampled under heel
[God's commandments]. [They did not pay adequate attention and
sinned by inadvertence (Margulies).]'

   C. Along these same lines: "For my people is foolish. Me they have
not known'" (Jer. 4:22). Did they not know? Rather, they trampled
under heel.

D.   Along these same lines: "And she did not know that it was I who
     gave her the grain, wine, and oil" (Hos. 2:8). Did she not know?
     Rather, she trampled under heel.

No. 1 carries forward the familiar line of thought that the sin of the calf had long
since been found to be null. The intersecting text provokes 1.C. No. 2 then explains why:
the true Israelites did not commit the sin at all. I am puzzled by No. 3; I do not see its
relevance to the passage at hand, nor does it relate to what follows. Margulies proposes
that it carries forward the view that the prophets exaggerated Israel's guilt, but in fact
Israel was not deliberately sinning at all. It is not that they were worse than the beasts,
but rather that they paid no attention and so sinned through inadvertence. This seems to
me plausible.

XXVII:IX

1. A.   "A bull, a sheep, or a goat" (Lev. 22:27):
    B.   "A bull" on account of the merit of Abraham, as it is said: "And
         Abraham ran to the herd and took a calf" (Gen. 18:7).
    C.   "A sheep" on account of the merit of Isaac, as it is written, "And
         he looked, and behold, a ram caught by its horns" (Gen. 22:13).
    D.   "A goat" on account of the merit of Jacob, as it is written in his
         regard, "Now go to the flock and get me two good kidgoats" (Gen.
         27:9).
2. A.   What is the meaning of "good"?
    B.   R. Berekhiah in the name of R. Helbo: "Good for you, good for
         your children.
    C.   "Good for you, for on their account you will receive indications of
         blessing.
    D.   "Good for your children, for on their account you will have
         atonement on the Day of Atonement: 'For on this day atonement
         will be made for you' (Lev. 16:30), [including the atonement of the
         sacrifice of the goat (Lev. 16:9)]."

The exegesis of the verse is clear as specified. The several beasts now are related
to the patriarchs, a fairly standard approach to the amplification of Scripture. The
secondary development of Gen. 27:9 presents no problems.

XXVII:X

1. A.   "[When a bull or sheep or goat is born,] it shall remain seven days
         with its mother; [from the eighth day on it shall be acceptable as
         an offering by fire to the Lord]" (Lev. 22:27).
    B.   Why for seven days?

C. So that the beast may be inspected, for if the dam should have gored it, or if some disqualifying blemish should turn up on it, lo, it will be invalid and not be suitable for an offering.

D. For we have learned [M. Nid. 5:1]: "That which goes forth from the side [delivered by Caesarean section] -- they do not sit out the days of uncleanness and the days of cleanness [Lev. 12:1ff.] on its account, and they are not liable on its account for an offering.

E. "R. Simeon says, 'Lo, this is like one that is born [naturally] [so that the rules of Lev. 12:1ff. do apply]."

3. A. Another interpretation: "It shall remain seven days with its mother" (Lev. 22:27).

B. Why for seven days?

C. R. Joshua of Sikhnin in the name of R. Levi said, "The matter may be compared to the case of a king who came into a town and made decrees, saying, 'None of the residents who are here will see me before they first see my lady.'

D. "Said the Holy One, blessed be he, 'You will not make an offering before me until a Sabbath shall have passed over [the animal that is to be offered], for seven days cannot pass without a Sabbath, and [for the same reason] the rite of circumcision [takes place on the eighth day] so that it cannot take place without the advent of a Sabbath.

E. "'And from the eighth day on it shall be acceptable [as an offering by fire to the Lord]' (Lev. 22:27)."

3. A. Said R. Isaac, "A rule is written with regard to a man, and the same rule is written with regard to a beast:

B. "The rule with regard to a man: 'And on the eighth day the flesh of his foreskin will be circumcised' (Lev. 12:3).

C. "The same rule with regard to a beast: 'And from the eighth day on, it shall be acceptable' (Lev. 22:27)."

The connection of 1.D-E to 1.A-C is not at all clear. The interpretation given by 1.A-C presents no surprises. No. 2 introduces the matter of the Sabbath, which any reference to eight days should provoke. No. 3 is familiar from X:I.

XXVII:XI

1. A. "And whether the mother is a cow or a ewe, [you shall not kill both her and her young in one day]' (Lev. 22:28).

B. R. Berekhiah in the name of R. Levi: "It is written, 'A righteous man has regard for the life of his beast, but the mercy of the wicked is cruel' (Prov. 12:10).

C.   "'A righteous man has regard' refers to the Holy One, blessed be
      he, in whose Torah it is written, 'You will not take the dam with
      the young' (Deut. 22:6).

D.   "'But the mercy of the wicked is cruel' refers to Sennacherib, the
      wicked one, concerning him it is written, 'The mother was dashed
      into pieces with her children' (Hos. 10:14)."

2. A.   Another interpretation: "A righteous man has regard for the life of
      his beast" refers to the Holy One, blessed be he, in whose Torah it
      is written, 'And whether the mother is a cow or a ewe, you shall
      not kill both her and her young in one day' (Lev. 22:28).

B.   "But the mercy of the wicked is cruel" refers to the wicked Haman,
      concerning whom it is written, "To destroy, to slay, to obliterate
      all Jews" (Est. 3:13).

3. A.   Said R. Levi, "Woe for the wicked, who make conspiracies against
      Israel, each one saying, 'My plan is better than your plan.'

B.   "Esau said, 'Cain was a fool, since he killed his brother while his
      father was yet alive. He did not know that his father would
      continue to be fruitful and multiply. That is not how I am going to
      do things. Rather: 'The days of mourning for my father are
      approaching; [only upon his death] will I kill my brother Jacob'
      (Gen. 27:41).

C.   "Pharaoh said, 'Esau was a fool. For he said, "The days of
      mourning for my father are approaching." But he did not know that
      his brother would continue to be fruitful and multiply in the
      lifetime of his father. That is not how I am going to do things. But
      while they are still little, under their mother's belly, I will strangle
      them. That is in line with the following verse of Scripture: 'Every
      son that is born you shall cast into the river' (Ex. 1:22).

D.   "Haman said, 'Pharaoh was a fool, for he said, 'Every son that is
      born...' He did not realize that the daughters would marry
      husbands and be fruitful and multiply with them. That is not how I
      am going to do things. Rather: 'To destroy, to slay, to obliterate
      all Jews' (Est. 3:13)."

E.   Said R. Levi, "So, too, Gog, in time to come, is going to say the
      same, 'The ancients were fools, for they made conspiracies against
      Israel and did not know that they have a patron in Heaven. That is
      not how I am going to do things. First I shall seek a confrontation
      with their patron, and afterward I shall seek a confrontation with
      them.' That is in line with the following verse of Scripture: 'The
      kings of the earth set themselves, and the rulers take counsel
      together, against the Lord and against his anointed' (Ps. 2:2).

F.   "Said to him the Holy One, blessed be he, 'Wicked man! Do you
      seek a confrontation with me? By your life, I shall make war with

you.' That is in line with the following verse of Scripture: 'The Lord will go forth as a mighty man' (Is. 42:13).

G.   "'And the Lord will go forth and fight against those nations' (Zech. 14:3).

H.   "And what is written there? 'The Lord will be king over all the earth' (Zech. 14:9)."

The exegeses of Lev. 22:27f, VIII-XI reach a climax and conclusion with an eschatological motif. The first two units treat Prov. 12:10 in an entirely appropriate way, tying it closely to the substance of the base-verse. But it is not a construction built on the basis of the intersecting verse. Nos. 1 and 2 make essentially the same point, one with Sennacherib, the other with Haman. Levi's systematic picture of Cain, Esau, and Haman, then is tacked on because of the prior allusion to Sennacherib and Haman. Nothing in No. 3 alludes to the base-verse. And yet the theme still resonates: the cruelties of the wicked, now the ever-increasing, but ever-more-futile, folly of the wicked who conspire against Israel. The cruelty of each is what joins No. 3 to Nos. 1-2. Nonetheless, it is difficult to deny that No. 3 was framed for its own purpose, prior to its serving to amplify the reference to Haman at No. 2.

XXVII:XII

1.   A.   "And when you sacrifice a thanksgiving sacrifice to the Lord" (Lev. 22:29).

       B.   R. Phineas and R. Levi and R. Yohanan in the name of R. Menahem of Gallia: "In time to come all offerings will come to an end, but the thanksgiving offering will not come to an end.

       C.   "All forms of prayer will come to an end, but the thanksgiving prayer will never come to an end.

       D.   "That is in line with that which is written, 'The voice of joy and the voice of gladness, the voice of the bridegroom and the voice of the bride, the voice of them that say, "Give thanks to the God of Hosts"' (Jer. 33:11). This refers to the thanksgiving prayer.

       E.   "'Who bring a thanksgiving offering to the house of the Lord' (Jer. 33:11). This refers to the thanksgiving offering.

       F.   "And so did David say, 'Your vows are incumbent upon me, O God I shall render thanksgivings to you' (Ps. 56:13).

       G.   "'I shall render thanksgiving to you' is not written here, but rather, 'I shall render thanksgivings [plural] to you' (Ps. 56:13). The reference [of the plural usage] then is to both the thanksgiving prayer and the thanksgiving offering."

The passage serves the next verse in sequence, Lev. 22:29. But it treats the theme, rather than the particular statement at hand, and serves equally well at IX:VII, above.

If we refer back to the discussion of types of units of discourse of Leviticus Rabbah and the order of types of units of discourse ordinarily followed (I, II, III, with miscellaneous items inserted for ascertainable reasons), we see an interesting fact. The types of units of discourse of Leviticus Rabbah Parashah 27 and the order of those types follow precisely the classification and pattern already established for Leviticus Rabbah overall. What that simple fact indicates is that where materials are shared by Leviticus Rabbah and Pesiqta deR. Kahana, the definitive literary patterns of Leviticus Rabbah -- types of units of discourse and their ordering -- govern. So whatever the role and use of the passage in Pesiqta deR. Kahana, the shared materials turn out to be entirely natural to Leviticus Rabbah and uniformly to accord with the characteristic patterns of that document. In the present, important case, therefore, the fact that materials occur in more than a single composition turns out to have no bearing upon the issue of whether one of the documents in which shared materials occur constitutes a composition or a scrapbook. Whatever the status or classification of Pesiqta deR. Kahana, what we see before us is typical of Leviticus Rabbah and particular to its sustained patterns of composing language and structures of organizing compositions. We deal with a text.

Part Three
COMPOSITION OR SCRAPBOOK?
TEXT OR MERE MISCELLANY?

Chapter Five

SHARED SOURCES, AUTONOMOUS COMPOSITION

i. Miscellanies or a Source: In Search of "Q" and the Synoptic Problem

Our analysis of the repertoire of materials shared between Leviticus Rabbah and other documents of its own day or succession addresses two simple questions, one cursorily, the other at length.

First, do all of the materials we have reviewed exhibit literary traits in common? Second, do the materials at hand conform to the literary preferences of Leviticus Rabbah?

The importance of the former of the two questions can be briefly explained. If the materials that occur in two or more compilations follow a single pattern of literary formulation and construction, then we may postulate that those materials derive from a cogent source and so constitute part of a larger, itself autonomous document. By such a postulate, that autonomous and distinct source will then have made its contribution here and there, to the Yerushalmi, to Leviticus Rabbah, to Genesis Rabbah, not to mention to Pesiqta deR. Kahana and even to the Bavli. Enjoying its own definition, organized around its own lines, exhibiting its own distinctive formal traits, one must call this otherwise unknown source by the German name for source, that is, Quelle, or merely RQ for rabbinische Quelle.

On the basis of the surveyed population, may such a source indeed be reconstructed? That is, out of a broad range of existing compilations and even compositions of rabbinic writings, are we able to collect and restore those bits and pieces of an antecedent rabbinic source (or set of sources) that have circulated on their own and also exhibit distinctive traits in common? And will these collected pieces then allow us to see part of that original source, the one from which they broke off? At stake in asking whether the materials common to two or more compilations and compilations is a considerable possibility.

A mere glance at the materials assembled in Chapters Three and Four suggests that the quest for the unknown rabbinic source leads nowhere. Why so? Because materials common to two or more documents turn out to be everything and its opposite: long and short; exegetical statements on verses of Scripture; autonomous statements of individual authorities; protracted stories, brief stories. In short, those shared materials may be anything at all. Among themselves they share no distinctive traits. That is to say, these same shared sources draw upon a broad variety of authorities' names or lack any identified authority. They focus upon a vast range of topics but coalesce around none in particular. They exhibit every sort of literary pattern. Some fit neatly into the literary structures of Leviticus Rabbah, which I have demonstrated to be subject to definition. Others exhibit traits or structures evidently characteristic of Genesis Rabbah (thus: similar to those of Leviticus Rabbah) on the one side, Yerushalmi's episodic sayings, on the second, the Pesiqta's protracted constructions (again: similar to those of Leviticus Rabbah), on the third. But still others share traits with none of the foregoing, on the fourth. And there are yet other sides too.

To avoid repeating the obvious through each of the appropriate criteria for definition of a single and uniform composition -- whether formal, topical, or even merely logical -- I state one simple fact. The shared sources share only one trait. It is that they appear in more than a single composition. We have therefore to dismiss the notion that sizable compositions, circulating from document to document, in fact originated in a single composition, one marked off by its definitive and distinctive traits.

That judgment pertains not only to sizable compositions, entire units of discourse or more, such as are shared between Leviticus Rabbah and Genesis Rabbah and Pesiqta deR. Kahana (Chapter Four). It applies also to brief sayings, such as pop up hither and yon, for example, in the Yerushalmi, Leviticus Rabbah and Genesis Rabbah (not to mention numerous other, still later compositions and compilations) (Chapter Three). Let me spell out what I mean. We note that there are two types of shared sources, long and brief. The long ones clearly conform to a variety of patterns. In no way do these long sayings suggest that they originate in a single, uniform, and now-lost, document. But what about the brief lemmas? These short sayings may make an appearance in a well-composed and sizable unit of discourse, e.g., a piece of a passage of Leviticus Rabbah but also in a quite different, and also well-composed and sizable unit of discourse, e.g., a piece of a passage in the Yerushalmi. In Chapter Three we noticed a few of these, and in Chapter Four, many more. Clearly, these brief lemmas did circulate broadly. No one can doubt that.

But if we draw together all of those lemmas that appear in two or more documents, do they exhibit distinctive traits in common? And if we compare all such sayings to equivalently brief lemmas that appear in only one document, do the latter exhibit traits of formulation and formation into larger compositions different from the former? These two questions govern. For we must establish dual criteria, one group of criteria to exclude, the other group of definitive traits to include. If then we attempt to include all the circulating brief sayings, those that appear in two or more compositions, by reference to shared and distinctive traits, and if we then propose to exclude all one-time brief sayings, the ones appearing in only one document, by reference to the absence of the shared and distinctive traits of the circulating sayings, we come up with nothing.

I lay down that judgment flatly and without proof. Why not? Because we should have to compose long lists of traits not distinctive to one set of sayings as against the other and demonstrate that said traits occur at random among either of the two sets of sayings. But a mere glance at the context of any brief saying shared among two or more documents provides adequate information. That is, brief sayings that occur in Leviticus Rabbah ordinarily share the traits of other sayings of Leviticus Rabbah and unique to that document, among which they occur, fore and aft. These same sayings, however, appear just as randomly and episodically in, e.g., Genesis Rabbah or the Yerushalmi. So the simple fact is that brief sayings, consisting of a line or two, rarely conform to those distinctive formal traits that allow us to distinguish in a given compilation or composition between one unit of discourse from another unit of discourse.

Only at a larger scale than the brief sayings, viewed one by one, do the processes of literary definition and differentiation begin to make sense in analyzing our documents. (As we shall see below, large-scale constructions prove miscellaneous too and rarely exhibit traits distinctive to Leviticus Rabbah.) Accordingly, brief sayings clearly serve numerous, that is, two or more, contexts. The reason brief sayings prove serviceable hither and yon is simple. By themselves they do not exhibit distinctive traits, so they present no formal problems to the compositors, or authors, of larger discussions. They are neutral, neuter whether viewed formally or construed substantively. Brief sayings constitute available building blocks, bricks all of a single dimension. Only in context, e.g., large examples of a single pattern of syntax or structure, do these brief sayings form discernible compositions.

Since that is the fact, we must wonder not at how many, but at how few, such shared brief sayings have come to our attention. Our original result, showing in a rough way that something in the range of 95% of the stichs of three _parashiyyot_ of Leviticus Rabbah appear to be particular to that composition, now returns to mind. Given the formal consistency and the absence of what seem to me to be highly patterned and distinctive formulary character of brief sayings (so often: X says, plus a standard or entirely commonplace and therefore random syntactic pattern), we should have expected a different result. We ought to have had sound reason to expect a far broader portion than we have found, a pattern in which a given composition is composed of sayings shared with two or more other compositions.

It would carry us far afield to speculate on the reason for the near-uniqueness of so much of the document at hand. But the issue in its proper context demands considerable reflection. A suitable answer cannot be merely that, in a given document, one set of subjects, rather than some other set of subjects, required one set of sayings, rather than some other. Or, to put it simply, no one can imagine that we can explain the near-uniqueness of the bulk of the contents of a given composition, in this case, Leviticus Rabbah, by reference to the near-uniqueness either of the overall topical program or of the concrete sentiments and values to be expressed. Such a thesis would contradict what, to the naked eye, constitutes the definitive trait of _all_ of the documents of the canon of Judaism. That is, that they are _canonical_. The document's authors therefore wish in many different ways to say some one thing.

If, then, we may return to the point at which we began, we may simply declare that shared sources do not derive from a single source, "Q." The shared materials, to be sure, ordinarily ignore the literary patterns of Leviticus Rabbah. But what is common on two or more documents turns out to be itself diverse and to exhibit random formal and formulary traits. On that basis we look in vain for "Q." How so? We search hopelessly for some large-scale and ubiquitous body of floating materials, fully formed, exhibiting characteristic literary traits, and entirely composed, available for use by any authorship for any given purpose. True, we may imagine that such a vast corpus of floating materials did circulate. But, lacking evidence as to its character, contents, viewpoint(s), and purpose(s), we can say nothing about it. Appeal to origin in such a shared an common "tradition" therefore tells us nothing that we did not know without the postulate that such a "tradition" circulated among the various rabbinic authorships. So if such a "Q" was there, we cannot define it or demonstrate what it contained and did not contain, how authors used or did not use it, why people would have reshaped one of its sayings for one set of purposes rather than for some other set of purposes. We cannot pursue any of those questions that make the postulate of "Q" suggestive and fructifying in other fields of inquiry into anonymous and collective authorships, parallel to the authorships at hand. So apart from the possibility of "Q," there is nothing at stake in the hypothesis of a floating tradition.

What must follow? It is that if we cannot show there was such a source common to two or more documents but can demonstrate only that random sayings circulated hither and yon, we also cannot invoke the perspective of analysis that demands systematic and synoptic reading of what otherwise constitute discrete documents. That is to say, we cannot link document to document as a common synoptic exercise and present the result as a shared position. We also cannot show how the authors of document X have used shared materials in a way distinctive from the way in which the authors of document Y have used those same shared materials. Why not? There is no fixed point, no shared source that permits comparison. And without a common point for comparison, information on what is like, and what is unlike, document X in document Y, lacks context, perspective, therefore also meaning. So, as I said, I see nothing at stake in the postulate of a shared source, short of the discovery of "Q," and a rabbinic source behind two or more documents. And as we shall now see in detail, we cannot show and so do not know that there was a "Q."

ii. Leviticus Rabbah in Particular

This discussion has carried us far from our specific purpose, which is to ask whether or not Leviticus Rabbah exhibits the traits of integrity, therefore autonomy. Lest we lose touch with the purpose for the assembly of the facts of Chapters Three and Four, we have now carefully to restate our purpose and so construct the analytical exercises that will lead us to the analytical exercises and conclusions of this study.

Let us begin with the restatement of the facts at hand.

1. Leviticus Rabbah conforms to distinctive literary patterns. There are three readily defined classifications to which we may assign approximately 70% of the units of discourse of which the document is composed. In the exposition of ideas of a complete parashah, moreover, discourse conforms to a fixed order, I, II, III. The other 30% of the document fall into the category of miscellany.

2. Leviticus Rabbah includes passages shared with other documents of its day. These are of two types, short and long.

What we wish to know, having described the simple literary traits of the document and investigated the passages of the document shared with other compositions or compilations, has to do only with Leviticus Rabbah. It is whether and to what extent Leviticus Rabbah exhibits integrity and so constitutes an autonomous and distinctive composition. It is, further, whether and to what extent Leviticus Rabbah constitutes a scrapbook, a collection of materials in no way formed into a single, formally disciplined, sustained and harmonious statement: a text.

iii. Differentiating among Shared Sources in the Setting of Leviticus Rabbah in Particular

We now ask whether the materials shared by Leviticus Rabbah with some other composition of the same age conform to the distinctive literary patterns of Leviticus Rabbah, on the one side, and organize materials in the same sequence of types of units of discourse as Leviticus Rabbah, on the other. What we shall see in detail is that nearly all units of tradition -- brief and long alike -- shared by Leviticus Rabbah with some other composition of composition or compilation prove miscellaneous. These shared miscellaneous materials attest to the integrity of Leviticus Rabbah. How so?

First, they point to the distinctiveness of the literary patterns of Leviticus Rabbah as well as to the uniqueness of the organization of types of units of discourse by the compositors of Leviticus Rabbah. So on the face of it the compositors of our document have given us a composition that conforms to a clearcut plan for both organization and expression of ideas.

Second, beyond the miscellaneous character of the shared materials is the simple fact of the slight and inconsequential place taken up by those shared materials in Leviticus Rabbah. What that means is that the compositors have made their document mainly of materials particular to their interests. They expressed their own literary and redactional preferences, only tangentially and randomly including bits and pieces of materials serviceable for purposes other than those of Leviticus Rabbah.

The upshot is simple. Leviticus Rabbah is no scrapbook, no random collection of this and that. It is an orderly, proportioned, well-considered composition. Leviticus Rabbah exhibits integrity. It enjoys autonomy. Why so? It is quite distinct from other collections or compositions of its age, even though it shares with them a shall and miscellaneous corpus of brief sayings and even protracted discussions. Let us now catalogue these shared materials in two exercises, first, brief, then, protracted, and, in both cases, among the four types of units of discourse we identified in Part Two.

We now classify the two varieties of shared materials -- brief, then protracted -- in accord with the four taxa yielded by the several units of discourse of Leviticus Rabbah: I. Base-verse/intersecting verse, II. Intersecting verse/base-verse, III. Exegesis of verse, IV. Miscellany. We deal only with the shared materials occurring in Genesis Rabbah and the Yerushalmi, covering those catalogued above in Chapters Three and Four.

1. The classification of brief sayings
I. Base-verse/intersecting verse
(Y. + Gen. R.)

None

2. The classification of brief sayings
II. Intersecting verse/base-verse
(Y. + Gen. R.)

None

3. The classification of brief sayings
III. Exegesis of a verse
(Y. + Gen. R.)

| III:III | 3 | Lev. 2:1,8 |

4. The classification of brief sayings
IV. Miscellanies
(Y. + Gen. R.)

VII:I	2N	Mishnah-citation
VII:V	1D-E	Yerushalmi-Tanna-saying
VII:VI	1D	Said x
XII:I	9C	X said
XII:II	2A	Said x
XII:IV	4A	X said
	3B	Mishnah-citation
XVIII:I	1C-H	Mishnah-citation + exegesis
XVIII:I	10A-B	X said ... he said to him
	12G	X + Y + saying
	12J	Mishnah-citation
III:II	1B	X, Y: + saying

1. The classification of protracted sayings
I. Base-verse/intersecting verse
(Y. + Gen. R.)

| V:I | 1-7 | Gen. 9:18/Job 34:29, Lev. 4:3/Job 34:29 |
| X:I | 1 | Gen. 18:25/Ps. 45:7-8, Lev. 8:1-3/Ps. 45:7 |

2. The classification of protracted sayings
II. Intersecting verse/base-verse
(Y. + Gen. R.)

None

3. The classification of protracted
III. Exegesis of a verse
(Y. + Gen. R.)

XVIII:I	4A-G	Qoh. 12:3 + phrase by phrase exegesis. N.B. Qoh. 12:3 is part of the intersecting-verse construction here.
XVIII:II	1C-F	Ps. 139:5. Proposition followed by proof-text.
XVIII:III	2H	Ex. 32:16 + read not. Proposition + proof-text.
IX:VI	1	X said, Y said + proof-texts on proposition.
XVI:VIII	2	Exegesis of Deut. 7:15.
XIX:V	6	Exegesis of Lev. 15:25.
XXXIII:V	1-2	Exegesis of z Chr. 13:17, etc.
XXXIV:XIV	1-5	Exegesis of Is. 58:7 + story.
XXXVII:I	1	Exegesis of Qoh. 5:5.
X:IX:3	8	Gen. 1:9 + exegetical observation.
XXXIV:IX	1-2	Deut. 28:13 + clarifications, + other verses clarified.
XXVI:I	2	Gen. 7:2, 11:4, etc., explained.

4. The classification of protracted sayings
IV. Miscellanies
(Y. + Gen. R.)

III:III	1B-C	Said x.
V:IV	2-4	Verse + extended stories.
V:VI	2	Said x + story.
IX:IX	1	Long story.
X:VI	1	Proposition + proof-texts (not exegetical).
X:VIII	1	As above.
XXII:X	1	As above.
XXII:IX	1	As above.
XXV:I	4	As above.
XXXII:VII	1-3	Thematic essay.
XXXVI:VI	1	Propositions + proof-texts.
XXXVII:III	1	Story.
IX:IX	3-4	X said + sayings + proof-text.
XVII:V	3	Proposition + proof-text.
XIX:II	6	As above.
XXIII:IX	3	As above.
XXV:VI	1-3	Argument a portion + proof-text + various propositions.
XXXVI:I	1	Proposition + proof-texts.
XXXVII:IV	1-5	Proper petitionary language + proof-texts.

iv. <u>Shared Sources and the Literary Structures of Leviticus Rabbah:</u> Genesis
<u>Rabbah and the Yerushalmi</u>

To state in a few sentences the results of the preceding classification, we note that
the shared sources, whether brief or protracted, fall into two categories, exegesis of a
cited verse of Scripture (III) and miscellanies (IV). As to the brief sayings shared between
Leviticus Rabbah and the two documents with which it most commonly intersects, Genesis
Rabbah and the Yerushalmi, only one falls into category III, and 12 into category IV.

So when we deal with brief sayings that float from one document to another, such
sayings, when they occur in Leviticus Rabbah, very rarely will conform to the literary
structures of Leviticus Rabbah. That is hardly a surprising result, since the literary
structures distinctive to Leviticus Rabbah and its classification of literature -- types I and
II -- are by definition protracted and exhaustively worked out.

But when we come to the classification of protracted sayings, we find the same
result. Now we have two entries in category I as against 13 in category III and 19 in
category IV. So once more we must conclude that what is shared among two or more
compilations of materials will not exhibit traits distinctive to Leviticus Rabbah (or to any
one of those other compilations either). What this means is very simple. When Leviticus
Rabbah shares materials with other documents, those shared materials will not ordinarily
take on or exhibit the literary traits definitive of Leviticus Rabbah.

The shared materials once more prove miscellaneous and casual. They are
miscellaneous in that they exhibit no traits both uniform and also particular to themselves. As I said at the outset, all that marks shared materials in common is the fact that
they occur in more than one compilation. By themselves, the shared materials common to
Leviticus Rabbah and Genesis Rabbah or the Yerushalmi exhibit no single formal pattern.
They express no distinctive viewpoint. They pursue no uniform program of inquiry. No
"Q" here.

v. <u>The Five Parashiyyot Shared with Pesiqta deR. Kahana</u>

When we come to materials shared between Leviticus Rabbah and Pesiqta deR.
Kahana, we deal with a quite different problem. Now, as we have seen, the shared
materials cover a sizable portion of both documents, 5 out of 37 <u>Parashiyyot</u> (13.5%) of
Leviticus Rabbah, 5 out of 28 <u>pisqaot</u> (17.9%) of Pesiqta deR. Kahana, according to the
count of Braude and Kapstein. We noted that the correspondences are word for word,
with minor exception, in the <u>parashah/pisqa</u> we examined in detail.

The question now before us is <u>not</u> whether or not the shared <u>parashiyyot</u> "belong" or
prove "particular to" Leviticus Rabbah as against their place, primary or secondary,
original or borrowed, in Pesiqta deR. Kahana. The sole issue is whether these enormous
constructions -- I repeat, entire <u>parashiyyot</u> -- exhibit traits characteristic of Leviticus
Rabbah. They certainly do. How do we know it? Because they conform to exactly those
literary structures I have shown to characterize Leviticus Rabbah. The order of the
types of units of discourse is the same -- I, II, III, with IV interspersed according to rules
we can discern -- as the order of types of units of discourse I have shown to characterize

the remainder of Leviticus Rabbah. That fact is self-evident in a review of the cited parashah.

It follows that where entire parashiyyot of Leviticus Rabbah are shared with some other composition, these parashiyyot prove integral to Leviticus Rabbah. Since they conform to the literary patterns and redactional program of the remainder of Leviticus Rabbah, they give ample evidence that Leviticus Rabbah, as a whole, is a document that exhibits integrity. Its definitive traits of literary composition -- form, pattern, redaction alike -- mark the document as autonomous at the very point at which the document intersects in a substantial and extensive way with some other document. As to the integrity or miscellaneous character of Pesiqta deR. Kahana, that is a question not relevant to the present inquiry.

vi. Miscellanies, Not a Shared Source

The original observation proves entirely valid. The materials shared by Leviticus Rabbah with other compositions of the same period or shortly afterward, Genesis Rabbah, the Yerushalmi, and Pesiqta deR. Kahana, exhibit in common only the trait that they occur in one or more documents of the age. They follow no uniform pattern or patterns. They reveal no cogent program of topics. They express no single viewpoint. The shared materials prove miscellaneous by every objective criterion of form and order we can devise. In no way can we demonstrate that two or more documents drew upon a single, prior composition. All we know is that two or more documents drew upon miscellaneous materials, circulating hither and yon, coming we know not whence, deriving from whatever circles or schools made up materials of the type at hand. That is to say, about the shared materials, miscellanies, we know nothing of consequence. There was no autonomous source, now represented only by the bits and pieces, uniform and cogent among themselves, scattered among the four documents with which we have dealt. Excluding the five parashiyyot shared by Leviticus Rabbah with Pesiqta deR. Kahana, the shared sources, whether long or short, prove random. Of them we cannot reconstruct a single cogent source, "Q." We may state flatly that the evidence at hand in no way suggests the existence of a rabbinic "Q." So synoptic sources represented by those at hand cannot ever be read synoptically; only odds and ends compare and intersect. And then there is little basis for comparison, because they are nearly identical. All we get out of the comparison is alternative wordings of a single text, the raw materials not for the history of ideas or groups but only for the apparatus of a critical text.

vii. Studying Synoptic Texts Synoptically

When two or more documents share the same saying or story, those documents at the points of their intersection simultaneously say the same thing and so may be regarded as synoptic. How so?

Synoptic texts are documents of a single canon that share in common sayings or stories. Studying such synoptic texts "synoptically" forces upon the character of the shared materials and upon the utilization, in two or more documents, of sayings or stories held in common. In the classic work, Tannaitic Parallels to the Gospels, Morton Smith first made the observation that the relationship existing between books comes under analysis in the comparison of what he calls "Tannaite Literature" and the Gospels:

> Every literature consisting of several books -- such as the Gospels or T[annaitic] L[iterature] -- makes possible the discussion of the relationship which exists between the books, and in the comparison of literatures it is possible to compare the relationship which exists between the books of one literature with the relationship which exists between the books of a second literature [Smith, p. 142].

Smith further observes that all four gospels are "very close to each other" and alleges that that is the case also in Tannaitic Literature:

> The striking fact is the large numbers of complete parallels to be found between its various books, especially between the Mishnah and Tosefta, Mekilta of R. Simon and Sifre on Deut., Sifre Zutta and Sifra, Mekilta and Sire on Numbers. But apart from these pairs, there are to be found many passages common to all the midrashim [Smith, p. 142].

In his enthusiasm for the proposition at hand Smith goes on even to allege:

> I cannot recall even a word by any Jewish scholar remarking ... that the problem of the relationship between Tosefta and the Mishnah is similar to the synoptic problem, and this in spite of the fact that they are so similar as to be practically inseparable, and that any theory begun from a study of the one literature should have immediate application in the study of the other [Smith, p. 143].

A curious footnote to Smith's framing of the matter derives from S.J.D. Cohen, who claims, "Synoptic texts must always be studied synoptically, even if one text is 'later' than another" [Cohen, p. 56]. (Precisely what Cohen means is not easy to determine, though in context his intent is to argue that one should never ["always"] study as an autonomous statement a document within a larger canon; all documents, he imagines, have always to be read in light of all other documents. We need not be detained by that silly proposition.)

   Let us turn to Smith's allegation that the relationships between certain rabbinic compositions are such that a theory begun in the study of the Gospels should have immediate application in the study of any document of the rabbinic canon of late antiquity. In order to do so, we rapidly review the premises of synoptic study of the gospels. These are, first, that the Gospels go over the same materials, e.g., sharing the same sayings and stories, and, second, that some of the Gospels drew upon an available source of such sayings and stories ("Q"). Smith himself goes further than the stated premises in claiming, in regard to all four Gospels:

As a matter of fact all of the four are very close to each other, and the more they are studied the more superficial their differences and the more important their similarities are seen to be [Smith, p. 142].

We may accordingly introduce a third premise in assessing the allegation of "parallels of parallelism" (in Smith's phrase). It is that given documents are "very close to each other," so differences among them are vastly outweighed by similarities.

Now the obvious strategy for examining the allegation at hand demands that we turn to compositions attributed to Tannaite authorship, since Smith makes explicit reference, in his catalogue, to those writings. But when Smith wrote, people took for granted that if a document's authors imputed sayings only to first and second century authorities ("Tannas"), then that document derived from, or formed part of, "Tannaitic Literature," of that period. In a formal sense, of course, that is so. But in a concrete historical sense it is unlikely. The reason is that documents assigned to Tannaite authorship now are known to have reached closure long after the second century. Since, in his treatment of the subject, Smith points toward Mishnah-Tosefta relationships, it is worth noting that the Tosefta has now been shown [Neusner, 1974] to stand as a secondary expansion and commentary to the Mishnah. So the Tosefta is not only not "Tannaitic" but probably fourth century [Herr]. The framers of the Tosefta, for instance, very often cite verbatim and then gloss or rework statements of the Mishnah. Much of the Tosefta is incomprehensible out of relationship to the Mishnah, but one can read Matthew without reading Mark.

Accordingly, it is easy to show that the problem of the relationship between Tosefta and the Mishnah is in no way similar to the Synoptic problem. Why not? For the synoptic Gospels to present us with a parallel to the actual relationship between the Mishnah and the Tosefta, Luke would have to be incomprehensible except in relationship (e.g., juxtaposition) to Mark, or Luke and Mark to "Q," just as vast tracts of the Tosefta prove incomprehensible except in juxtaposition to passages of the Mishnah. In point of fact the relationship between the Mishnah and the Tosefta bears no parallel of any consequence but one to the relationship between two Gospels or among all four of them.

That one exception is simple. It is the fact that, just as the Gospels share sayings and stories, the Mishnah and the Tosefta, among rabbinic compositions, share sayings and stories. But very often when the Tosefta shares materials with the Mishnah, the Tosefta cites those materials briefly and not completely, and then expands upon them. Where does an author of a Gospel cite another Gospel briefly, by way of allusion, and then expand upon what is clearly material quoted from another document? The answer is, no where. So the relationships in no way are parallel, even where materials are shared.

Let me state matters in somewhat more general terms. Just as two Gospels, e.g., Luke and Matthew, know sayings and stories unknown to one or more of the others, so two rabbinic writings, e.g., the two Talmuds (the one of the Land of Israel, ca. A.D. 400, the other of Babylonia, ca. A.D. 600) know sayings and stories unknown to other writings within the same canon. Stated in this way, the exception turns out to be trivial. Why so?

The relationship among two or more documents based upon the appearance, in all of them, of the same sayings or stories turns out to be altogether general. What do we know about those documents and the relationships among them because they share a given saying or story? In my judgment the answer is that we know they share a given saying or story. Beyond that fact everything remains as before. We do not grasp, solely out of the self-evident but trivial relationship of materials held in common, any further facts about the documents at hand, e.g., their common access to a prior source ("Q"), the viewpoint and contents of that prior source, the disposition of the authors of the several documents of what they chose to utilize out of that prior source, and the like.

That is to say, the discovery of parallel relationships between the books of one canon and those of another canon can produce consequential results only when results of two types emerge.

First, if the parallel relationships point to a common source, then the growth of the materials in the synoptic documents, out of the common source, will present important insight into the character of the documents at hand.

Second, if the parallel relationships permit description of the contents of the common source, then the pre-history of the documents, that is, the intellectual history of the authors, becomes accessible. In my view one of the great achievements of Gospels' scholarship is the discovery of "Q." Knowing only that the Gospels go over shared materials, without the recognition of "Q," we should not have that great edifice of learning comprised by Gospels' scholarship in the present century. All we should have is the Diatesseron. So "Q" is at the center. To state matters more generally, the critical issue is the nature and character of the shared materials. To this we turn in conclusion.

viii. A Composition, Not a Scrapbook

The ultimate purpose of asking whether Leviticus Rabbah constitutes an autonomous composition or a scrapbook, whether it exhibits the trait of integrity or the trait of miscellany, is to deal with the claim framed by Smith and others. They hold that rabbinic documents are "always" to be studied synoptically and not (as I claim) both in isolation from one another as well as in relationship to one another. So the heart of the matters is represented by the conception of "Q."

Let me review the arguments and facts adduced in this book as these relate to the issue of "Q," that is, the claim that rabbinic documents (here represented by Leviticus Rabbah) constitute components of an essentially synoptic system (or, in Judaic theological language, of a "tradition" or "one whole Torah").

What we have done is to ask whether on the basis of common materials we discover that "parallel of parallelism" to which Smith points. That is to say, do we really find the relationships which exist between the books of one canon (or some of those books) parallel to the relationships which exist between the books of the other canon? Can a theory begun in the study of the Gospels -- e.g., "studying synoptic texts synoptically" -- immediately apply to the study of two or more documents of the rabbinic canon of late antiquity? Specifically, do documents of the latter canon go over the same materials, and do the materials shared among the documents point toward a common source, upon which the several compositions at hand have drawn? Are the documents "very close" to one another? If these points prove to characterize two or more documents of the rabbinic cannon, then Smith's fundamental observation will prove sound and define further research.

The three questions at hand required that we focus, to begin with, on one document, only then to work our way to examine others with which it intersects. Why so?

1. We first of all established the extent to which a given document stands on its own, and the extent to which it shares materials -- phrases, sentences, paragraphs, whole units of discourse -- with some other. For the proportion, not only the character, of the materials shared among the Gospels defines the relationships among them, as Smith alleges at the very outset ("all the four are very close to each other"). We found that the proportion of shared materials in a given composition proved negligble. So, to begin with, any allegation of parallel relationships proves false.

2. A single document, moreover, supplied a logical place from which to go off in search of parallels in other and related documents. Why so? The canon of Judaism in late antiquity is sizable. Compiling lists of parallels among a vast variety of compositions thus far has yielded collections merely of variant readings [for example, Melamed, 1943, 1967, 1973]. So it seemed best to work from a well-defined point of reference and collect parallels relevant to that one point. So we required a base-document that intersects in substantial ways with more than a single composition.

The one document I chose for an appropriate probe of the results to e expected from studying synoptic texts synoptically is Leviticus Rabbah. The reason is simple. That document intersects with two others of the period in which it came to closure, Genesis Rabbah and the Yerushalmi (the Talmud of the Land of Israel). Conventional dates for the Yerushalmi, Genesis Rabbah, and Leviticus Rabbah, tend to come together around the end of the fourth century and the beginning of the fifth. These documents in time stand far closer to one another than do those in Smith's catalogue of "Tannaitic literature." They share materials of various kinds, all deriving from the same geographical area and (people generally suppose) the same schools. Accordingly, if we are going to uncover relationships to begin with relevant to comparison with the relationships among the Gospels, we do well to begin with that family of writings circumscribed by the same place and time repre-sented by the three documents at hand. Leviticus Rabbah intersects, moreover, with yet another, later document, Pesiqta deR. Kahana. Here we found the condition met that the documents be "very close," since Pesiqta deR. Kahana and Leviticus Rabbah share nearly verbatim no fewer than five complete and protracted compositions or chapters. Accordingly, we were able to frame questions about the character of the source of shared materials ("Q") not at random and on a small scale but in a systematic way and upon a large scale. And, it goes without saying, that curious claim that "synoptic texts must always be studied synoptically" has now come up to the light of day, for we can see precisely what it means to do exactly that. So we may now ask whether the results are such as to require always doing so.

3. The answer is that the intersecting materials among the documents (excluding Pesiqta deR. Kahana) took up too slight a portion of Leviticus Rabbah to sustain the allegation that the only way to study the allegedly-synoptic documents, Genesis Rabbah and Leviticus Rabbah, or the Yerushalmi and Leviticus Rabbah, was synoptically. To state the simple truth, if we were to study those documents "always" but also only synoptically, we should end up ignoring most of the materials in those documents.

4. Much that is shared, moreover, proved episodic and random. Little that is shared played a significant role in those components of a large-scale composition in Leviticus Rabbah.

So far as the data we have examined indicates, Smith is wrong to allege there is any sort of "parallel of parallelism." The opposite is the case. Cohen's contribution, of course, turns out a still more extreme error and makes one wonder whether we accurately understood what he wishes to claim. In any event for Genesis Rabbah, Leviticus Rabbah, and the Yerushalmi, there is no "Q." As to the shared compositions of Leviticus Rabbah and Pesiqta deR. Kahana, these prove integral to Leviticus Rabbah (whatever role they play in the other composition). The shared materials only reenforce the claim that the document is autonomous and exhibits a profound integrity of both literary pattern and redactional policy.